Ending Gender-Based Violence

Ending Gender-Based Violence

Justice and Community in South Africa

HANNAH E. BRITTON

UNIVERSITY OF ILLINOIS PRESS
Urbana, Chicago, and Springfield

The cover art is part of a series by Judith Mason memorializing the anti-apartheid activist Phila Portia Ndwandwe. Ndwandwe was abducted by Security Forces, who detained, tortured, and killed her. Ndwandwe was awarded the Order of Mendi for Bravery for "demonstrating bravery and valor and for sacrificing her life for her comrades in the cause for non-racial, non-sexist, and democratic South Africa." http://www.thepresidency.gov.za/national-orders/recipient/phila-portia-ndwandwe

© 2020 by Hannah E. Britton
All rights reserved
1 2 3 4 5 C P 5 4 3 2 1
♾ This book is printed on acid-free paper.

Library of Congress Cataloging-in-Publication Data

Names: Britton, Hannah Evelyn, author.
Title: Ending gender-based violence: justice and
  community in South Africa / Hannah E. Britton.
Description: Urbana: University of Illinois Press, 2020. |
  Includes bibliographical references and index. |
Identifiers: LCCN 2019046252 (print) | LCCN 2019046253
  (ebook) | ISBN 9780252043093 (cloth) | ISBN
  9780252084966 (paperback) | ISBN 9780252051975
  (ebook)
Subjects: LCSH: Women—Violence against—South
  Africa. | Community-based social services—South
  Africa. | Justice, Administration of—South Africa. |
  South Africa—Social conditions—21st century.
Classification: LCC HV6250.4.W65 B753 2020 (print) |
  LCC HV6250.4.W65 (ebook) | DDC 362.880820968—dc23
LC record available at https://lccn.loc.gov/2019046252
LC ebook record available at https://lccn.loc.gov/2019046253

I wish to dedicate this work to the service providers, community leaders, and survivors who choose each day to create change, to take a stand against oppression, and to take care of each other.

Your work is making a difference.

Contents

List of Abbreviations   ix

Preface   xi

Acknowledgments   xv

Introduction: "Democracy Stops at My Front Door"   1

Chapter One: Genealogy of Gender-Based Violence in South Africa   29

Chapter Two: Place   47

Chapter Three: People   74

Chapter Four: Police   98

Chapter Five: Points of Contact   125

Conclusion: Moving beyond Carceral Feminism   149

Methodological Appendix   159

Notes   163

References   169

Index   191

List of Abbreviations

ANC	African National Congress
ANCWL	African National Congress Women's League
CBO	community-based organization
CPF	Community Police Forums
DRC	Democratic Republic of Congo
EFF	Economic Freedom Fighters
FCS	Family Violence, Child Protection and Sexual Offences
HIV/AIDS	Human immunodeficiency virus / acquired immune deficiency syndrome
LGBT	lesbian, gay, bisexual, trans*
LGBTQ	lesbian, gay, bisexual, trans*, queer
NGM	National Gender Machinery
NGO	Nongovernmental organization
PEP	Postexposure prophylaxis
RDP	Reconstruction and Development Programme
SADC	Southern African Development Community
SAPS	South African Police Services
TCC	Thuthuzela Care Centres
WHO	World Health Organization

Preface

In 1996 I was working on my first book about women's political advancement in the newly democratic South Africa, *From Resistance to Governance: Women in the South African Parliament* (2005). This book grew out of years of antiracist and antiapartheid activism in South Africa and the United States. One day during my research I was asked by friends to join them in a meeting with some relatives. As it turns out, a young woman in the family had been badly beaten by her husband, again. The scene was painful; the woman had suffered severe battery; the meeting was tense. The husband's family was not defending him, but neither were they willing to intercede in what was a clear pattern of violent domestic abuse. I sat, saying nothing but lending the support my friends had asked for—to just be present and not to speak, to serve as a witness to the conversation. My friend was firm, strong, and unyielding in her demands. She insisted her brother and sister-in-law intervene. The husband's family said very little and agreed to nothing.

Following the exchange, I was filled with questions: *Why were we not going to the police?* I was told the police could not be trusted to do anything, and involving the police would only enrage the husband and his family, putting them all at greater risk. This was 1996, only two years after democratic elections. The police were just beginning to be retrained to be protectors of peace rather than violent enforcers of apartheid. In my friend's opinion, domestic violence had never been a concern of the police, and no one in the family trusted the police at that time.

What did you expect to happen? My friend hoped that the husband's family would admonish and control the husband. I was then given a very useful, cogent explanation of how issues of domestic violence had been dealt with under customary law: the husband's family bore the responsibility of keeping the husband "in line," especially once lobola, or bride-price, had been paid. I also recognized that my presence in the conversation was to demonstrate that this situation was no longer just a "family matter." My presence was meant to send a message that outsiders were aware of this abuse, specifically, the "girl from the US who comes to live here from time to time."

My friend explained that, previously, the men in the family would have handled this "swiftly" and effectively, most likely through pressure, threats of violence, or actual physical retribution. It was then I realized there were no men present in the meeting, not from our side or from their side. I was surprised that I had not noticed that. I often found myself comfortably ensconced in women-only spaces when I was with them, often in the kitchen, preparing food and caring for children. I wondered if the lack of men at this meeting had been by design. *Was it a woman's job to deal with this crisis, as family violence is a private issue?* No, she said, it was not. She told me no men were present because they were either long absent from the family or were "off drinking." She would have preferred the men to be present, accountable, and involved. She also had long ago stopped waiting for that to happen.

It was in this moment that I realized that the liminal space we seemed to occupy was created by tearing two worlds apart, first, a world where customary systems were used to address family conflict, and, second, a postapartheid world where the South African Constitution and local institutions were supposed to protect women's rights. At this moment, neither of these aspirational worlds was within reach.

In many ways, this book began that day, during that conversation, watching my friends unable to address a crisis either through the structures that they had relied on previously or through the fledgling promises of equal rights and government programs. I also started speaking with service providers at crisis centers around the country and began meeting activists in the anti-gender-based-violence movement. I continued this research after the publication of my first book, working to find answers to both the failures of implementation and the successes of community leadership to address gender-based violence. Perhaps there is no more salient benchmark of South Africa's democracy than its ability to address the full-scale assault on women. The record numbers of women in parliament, the eloquently crafted legislation, and national gender institutions are painfully inadequate when women continue to face violence on the streets, in their homes, and in the workplace.

I recognize the limitations of much of my earlier scholarship. Many of us have focused on getting women into office—the formula and electoral strategies of insider change, of state feminism. Capturing and preserving what the democratic transition was like for South African women as a group in parliament will stand as one of the most important achievements of my career. Yet, even in that moment, I realized that gender empowerment was as much about implementation as it was about representation.

Given the twenty years of democracy in South Africa and the protections and rights afforded women in the constitution, the continued widespread violence against women is a constant reminder of the challenges that still remain. As this project has taught me, tracing the story of implementation—or in most cases failed implementation—is much more complicated than understanding electoral strategies and political representation, but it is perhaps a truer measure of the extent of democratic transformation.

Acknowledgments

This work was made possible by the generous financial support of the US IIE Fulbright Program's Faculty Research Fellowship and through the support of several units at the University of Kansas, including the Institute of Policy & Social Research (IPSR); the College of Liberal Arts and Sciences; the Department of Political Science; the Department of Women, Gender, and Sexuality Studies; and the Office of Research's General Research Fund.

I want to thank my South African friends and family, who have supported me for decades: Portia, Holly, Mpho, Kgalaletso, and Nkosinathi Kekana; Rose, Robert, and Kgothatsu Manasoe; Mergedis and Hannah Nathan; Abu and Hermoine Solomons; Ivor, Karin, and Jason Jenkins; and Jana Venter. Ivor, Karin, and Portia—thank you for allowing me to share your lives for all these years. Words fail to express my gratitude. I am inspired every day by how you care for your families and your country.

I also wish to thank my former partners at Idasa, especially Yvette Geyer, Michelle Rueters, Paul Graham, and Ivor Jenkins. Thank you for your leadership and the service you have given and continue to give in the pursuit of democracy. Esther Nasikye Hephizibah, I value our research partnership and friendship while you interned at Idasa. Your work and thinking about these issues have been vital to me. Jenny Hoobler and Ryan Kilpatrick, you are now part of my South African family. I am so grateful for your work, friendship, and commitment to education, leadership, and justice.

There have been a remarkable number of unrelated medical challenges during this process. Stephanie Suber, Emily Minderman, and Heather Shire, in the last decade, you have never wavered in your support of me, my health, and this project. I also want to thank Morgan Miller, Britani Congleton, Tara Stecklein, and Jared Konie for their support and care. Emily Kofron, I owe you a special thanks. You have walked with me through this entire work, and

Acknowledgments

you have seen its impact on me and on the lives of those around me. Thank you for celebrating this work with me.

I want also to thank those who have taken time to read parts of my work, especially Corinne Schwarz, Tanner Willbanks, Mariah Crystal, Marcy Quiason, Laura Dean, and Elene Cloete. Taylor Price, thank you for being so willing to work through the ideas and themes of this book as a whole. Laura Zimney, thank you for your design of the figures in this book and your friendship. Thank you also to those who have helped me with questions, drafts, ideas, support, and laughter, including Frans Viljoen, Karen Stefiszyn, Tami Albin, Dave Tell, Adrianne Kunkle, Cecilia Menjívar, Gary Reich, Christina Bejarano, Sherrie Tucker, Alesha Doan, Betty Jo Ross, Jan Emerson, Linda Pickerel, Connie Leonard, Marta Caminero-Santangelo, Jason Olenberger, Juliana Carlson, Justin Preddie, Chris Brown, Burdett Loomis, Monica Biernat, Megha Ramaswamy, Emily Rauscher, Clarence Lang, Joane Nagel, Liz MacGonagle, Ayesha Hardison, Ann Schofield, Folabo Ajayi-Soyinka, Charlene Muehlenhard, Ann Cudd, Cécile Accilien, Barbara Barnett, Nick Syrett, Emily Ryan, Laura Zimney, Emily Sharp, Erika Kirkland, Mary Peace McRae, Robin Riley, Eve Mullen, Carla Corroto, Charmaine Courcelle, and Meghan Millea. A special thanks to IPSR: Steven Maynard Moody, Nancy Cayton Myers, Xan Wedel, Larry Hoyle, Travis Weller, Susan Mercer, Jena Gunter, Whitney Onasch, Carrie Caine, Kate Lorenz, Christie Holland, and Genna Hurd. Don Haider-Markel, you have always worked to get me the support I needed for my research, as well as the time to think, write, and heal. Dorothy Daley, thank you for, well, everything—being my sister friend, sounding board, research partner, fearless colleague, and a voice of reason. Thanks also to Sarah Freese, Peg Livingood, and Linda Watts, who have given my family so much support.

I wish to acknowledge the valuable space my family has given me to do this work. Thank you, Bob, for your remarkable patience as I try to juggle life, family, work, and writing with fairly inconsistent results. Thank you, Evelyn. You are our joy and light, and we both hope we can leave this world a better place for you. Thank you to Scott, Mona, and John Miller and to Audrey, Brennan, Troy, Marilyn, Travis, and Tristan Mott for trusting us to build this family with you and for your unconditional love for Evelyn. Thank you to Janet Bauman, who has been with us every step of the way. Thank you to Mary and Chet Tryanski, Sandra Britton, and my brother, Alan. Mom, you have always taken my work seriously and allowed me to take important risks. Thank you, Mpho, for keeping us sane, laughing, and focused on the important things. We also thank you for bringing Mariana into our lives. Mpho, we are so proud of you every single day.

Acknowledgments

Dawn Durante, I want to thank you for your belief in this project. It is monumentally better because of your close reading of the manuscript at each stage of the process and your input on the theoretical through lines in this book. It gives me great pleasure to again be working with UIP and to support the transformational work you publish. I also want to thank the remarkable suggestions and revisions made by the two anonymous reviewers and by Mary M. Hill, the outstanding copyeditor who painstakingly edited this book with precision, clarity, and care.

Finally, I want to thank all my students, who show me each day what this world can be. Your tireless passion, your drive for finding answers, and your courage in the face of adversity are models for us all.

Ending Gender-Based Violence

INTRODUCTION

"Democracy Stops at My Front Door"

August 2016. Then South African president Jacob Zuma addressed the nation about the recent municipal election results in a live broadcast from the Independent Electoral Commission in Pretoria. As he began to speak, four young women stood up and moved silently in front of the stage in view of the cameras and in front of the podium. Each woman held a small handwritten sign:

> I am 1 in 3 #
> 10 years later
> Khanga
> Remember Khwezi

After Zuma finished his speech, security came forward, pushing the women into and onto the stage, ripping the signs from their hands, and then aggressively removing them from the room—with Zuma appearing initially to laugh (Nicolson 2016).

This silent protest brought to the national stage the perennial issues of sexual assault, rape, and abuse in South Africa. Reminding the country of the Zuma rape trial a decade earlier, the women were also calling attention to the failures of the government to address the persistent, rampant levels of gender-based violence in the country. Zuma was acquitted of the rape charge in what became one of the most charged political flashpoints, dividing women's groups and exposing the massive ideological rift in the African National Congress (ANC) and the country at large (Hassim 2009). The 2005–6 rape trial and this recent silent protest also showcase the failures to achieve gender equality as outlined in the South African Constitution.

The trial, *S v. Zuma*, involved Fezekile Ntsukela Kuzwayo, an AIDS activist who became known as "Khwezi" during the trial to protect her identity, and then deputy president of the ruling ANC party Jacob Zuma (Tlhabi 2017).[1] Kuzwayo claimed that Zuma, a family friend, had raped her during an overnight visit to his Johannesburg home. Her father and Zuma spent ten years at Robben Island in prison during the apartheid struggle, and she viewed Zuma as an uncle figure. Zuma claimed the sex was consensual, indicating that she had worn a short kanga, a traditional wrap, which he saw as an invitation to intercourse. He claimed, again as evidence of consent, that she had spoken to him about intimate personal life details and said she was lonely (Hassim 2009). Zuma was also aware of her HIV-positive status, but he indicated that he did not use a condom. Instead, he stated that he showered in order to protect himself from contracting the disease (Evans and Wolmarans 2006).

The rape trial split the country, as ANC party loyalists, like the ANC Women's League (ANCWL), and traditionalists framed the trial as political slander designed to bring down their chosen leader, while countless other groups rallied in support of "Khwezi," seeing her as emblematic of other sexual assault victims who never receive justice. Zuma was acquitted because the courts questioned Kuzwayo's account of the attack, and the defense doggedly brought her past sexual history into the trial to undermine her credibility. The judge deemed the sex consensual, and Kuzwayo's life in South Africa became untenable. During the trial, Zuma supporters, many from the ANCWL, harassed Kuzwayo as she entered the courts, burned her picture, and threatened her physically (Gouws 2016; Hassim 2009; Tlhabi 2017). Following the trial, her home was burned, and she received death threats and constant harassment. She went into political exile in the Netherlands and died in October 2016, a few months after the silent protest.

Simamkele Dlakavu, one of the young women who protested Zuma in August 2016, said she and her friends were deploying a "black feminist protest strategy—of silence" to symbolically break the silence around rape in the country (Nicolson 2016). They organized the protest spontaneously when they heard that Zuma would be speaking that night, apparently even borrowing the paper and pens from the event venue to make their small signs after they arrived. After the protest, several ANC women in top government positions condemned the protesters and claimed this was a publicity stunt by an opposition party.

* * *

On February 14, 2013, Olympic and Paralympics track star Oscar Pistorius admitted to shooting and killing his girlfriend, model and actress Reeva Steenkamp. He claimed that he thought he was shooting an intruder in the bathroom near his bedroom. He shot the closed door four times to protect himself and Steenkamp, who he allegedly thought was in bed, not the bathroom. Judge Thokozile Masipa initially found Pistorius guilty of culpable homicide and sentenced him to five years in prison. He was transferred to house arrest after only one year into his sentence.[2]

On appeal, the Bloemfontein Supreme Court, a five-judge panel, found that Pistorius had used unprovoked excessive force, regardless of who he thought was in the bathroom, which constituted murder. Justice Eric Leach began his statement explaining the court's judgment: "This case involves a human tragedy of Shakespearean proportions: a young man overcomes huge physical disabilities to reach Olympian heights as an athlete; in doing so he becomes an international celebrity; he meets a young woman of great natural beauty and a successful model; romance blossoms; and then, ironically on Valentine's Day, all is destroyed when he takes her life" (*International Business Times* 2015). The judgment continued to say that the lower court had misinterpreted the legal principles, stating that Pistorius's guilt was not linked to whether or not he knew he was shooting Steenkamp; rather, he knew and believed a person was behind the door. The court then referred the case back to the trial court to pronounce a new sentence that fit the conviction of murder. At the sentencing hearing in July 2016, Judge Masipa sentenced Pistorius to six years in jail, far short of the fifteen-year minimum sentence for murder.

Much public condemnation has been heaped on Judge Masipa both for her initial finding that Pistorius had not committed murder and for her decision to only sentence him to six years when her initial decision of culpable homicide was overturned. Perhaps most notably, Judge Masipa argued that this was not a "gender crime," as she believed the state did not prove that Pistorius knew it was Steenkamp in the bathroom. Judge Masipa also described their relationship up to that point as normal—even though Steenkamp's text messages discussed her fear of Pistorius and stated that she had felt attacked by him in previous conflicts (Freeman 2014). Many women's NGOs and the ANCWL viewed this finding in particular to be deeply troubling. As Pumza Fihlani (2016) of the BBC reported, "For them, Ms Steenkamp had become the face of abused women around the world. In their eyes, she was in an abusive relationship with a seemingly untouchable man and had paid with her life for the love she had for him."

* * *

Jacob Zuma, Oscar Pistorius. While each case is unique in the public eye, they both demonstrate the unevenness—if not outright injustice—of carceral approaches to gender-based violence in South Africa. The legal system can often be the arbiter of justice and a key institution reversing inequality. Yet as these high-profile cases demonstrate, the courts and the people who occupy the justice system also reflect their larger social and political context, a society still marked by deep inequalities, including racial and gender inequality (Moreland 2014).[3] While many hope that legislation and judicial decisions can point society toward a new direction, their implementation and adjudication are still products embedded within the social world, and they often reproduce or entrench these inequalities (Menjívar and Walsh 2016; M. Hunter 2010).

While much of the research on gender-based-violence policy looks at the adoption of national laws, this book takes a decidedly different turn. It shifts the focus upstream to identify some of the main accelerants of gender-based violence, to understand how gender-based violence is part of larger structural inequalities, and to delineate what is working and what is failing in terms of implementation and community response. In doing so, this research moves the unit of analysis to the community level, examining how local actors in nine demographically diverse communities respond to gender-based violence in a landscape still deeply marked by the apartheid legacies of racial inequality, economic oppression, and gender discrimination. It is also a story about peeling back the layers of why gender-based violence continues in South Africa almost unchecked and about understanding how place and space matter in the overall effectiveness of national policies.

The narratives in this book reveal that gender-based violence is nested within a complex, decades-old web of inequality, violence, racism, and sexism. Each of the communities in this book continues to be shaped by the legacies that were also at the very foundation of apartheid. This book contains the voices of service providers, community leaders, and government officials who work with those affected by gender-based violence on a daily basis.

In my interviews and conversations with community leaders, gender activists, and service providers, I identified four *p*'s that affect efforts to end gender-based violence: *place, people, police,* and *points of contact*. The first two factors operate at the most local level. Communities are affected by their unique political geography of *place*, a community's distance from or proximity to services, as well as individuals' identification with the community itself and their lived, daily experiences of social oppression. Second, communities that have been actively addressing gender-based violence have relied on strong issue advocates, specifically, *people* who are leaders within organizations, religious communities, and government. These leaders often challenge social norms and break with patriarchal practices to embrace a framework of human rights and gender equality. Place and people signify how important it is that policies, interventions, and funding involve the conditions of local contexts.

The third and fourth factors represent the interaction local communities have with nationally coordinated institutions. The communities that considered themselves successful also had the engagement of the *police* as partners. This is a particularly chilling finding, as there continues to be widespread condemnation for the inaction of the police on gender-based violence. Finally, communities needed some package of state mechanisms through which survivors could engage the state. These *points of contact* include victim services units in police stations, sexual-violence services in medical centers, shelter services, and counseling services.

The service providers I interviewed also strongly argued that issues like gender-based violence must be approached intersectionally, with an understanding of the institutional and structural violence operating in the larger society (Alcalde, Basu, and Burrill 2015; Bueno-Hansen 2015; Gass et al. 2011; Menjívar 2011; Alcalde 2010). Any attempt to look at gender-based violence in a vacuum or as a single issue ignores the legacies of apartheid that continue to entrench larger social structures of racism, physical violence, and sexism. Apartheid's most lasting imprint may be the normalization of violence across so many sectors—in the home, in educational settings, within medical interactions, and within the state and liberation movements. This can be physical violence, but it can also be *structural violence* (Galtung 1969)—the violence of neglect, poverty, inhumane living conditions, inadequate health care, and hunger. In South Africa, these inequalities are often mapped onto racial groups, class categories, and geographical spaces because of these colonial and apartheid era policies of racial segregation.

The current neoliberal shift—which continues to limit funding to social services, community projects, and the support of civic leadership—perpetuates this structural violence (Bumiller 2008). It will harm not only efforts to end gender-based violence but also efforts to create democratic, just, and sustainable communities. It is this structural violence that often coexists with and may be the by-product of neoliberal policies that undermines efforts to end violence and inequality by promoting the downsizing of government services and initiatives that could promote structural change.

South African Exceptionalism: Living in the Shadow of Apartheid

Journalists and scholars often emphasize South Africa's exceptionalism. They are not always suggesting exceptionalism in positive terms, though in reference to South Africa's economic position and financial structures that has often been the case. South Africa is also seen as exceptional because of its other differences—most importantly, perhaps, because it is a country that fought against white minority rule to gain political liberation only in 1994. While most African countries achieved independence from European control between 1950 and 1980, a handful of countries continued to be in the clutches of a white minority that prospered economically, politically, and educationally while the black majority was forced to serve the elites as their own lives and productive potential withered away. First as part of British colonial rule and then followed by apartheid, the white minority population flourished in South Africa through the physical, legislative, and psychological suppression of the black majority. While racial segregation was imposed in various regions of the country earlier, South Africa formally adopted apartheid nationally in 1948, codifying the "apart-ness" or separation of the population along racial and ethnic lines. A series of laws followed in subsequent years, resulting in a society that was deeply segregated by race in terms of living spaces, educational opportunities, medical care, and public amenities. Even personal relationships were governed by the apartheid state through legislation limiting intimate partnerships and marriage to heterosexual relationships confined within racial categories. Despite claims of a sacred private sphere, the South African state has a very long history of policing the household and sexuality.

A full examination of apartheid history is beyond the scope of this text, but what follows is a discussion of how the apartheid system codified racial segregation economically and spatially and of how the system simultaneously reified gender hierarchies, often through violent means. The role of gender politics during apartheid and the democratic transition has been a site of extended scholarship, highlighting the vital role of women as activists, political leaders, and members of mass protests (Goetz 1998; Seidman 1999; Meintjes 2003; Gouws 2004; Britton 2005; Hassim 2006; Britton and Fish 2009; Walker 2013).

Under apartheid, people were registered at birth by their race, with the minority white population at the top of the social hierarchy, followed by Indians, then coloureds, and then blacks. "Coloured" is a specific racial category created by the apartheid government to include individuals of mixed race. In this book, I will use the term and South African spelling "coloured" when referencing this population, as it is a specific historical reference that still carries significant social and political meaning today. During apartheid, many activists rallied against the term "coloured" and chose to refer to themselves as black in alliance with the liberation struggle and the oppressed black majority. Many felt that attempts to celebrate their differences during apartheid would have played into the government's goals to divide the population. The apartheid state regularly tried to co-opt the coloured population with limited political and economic rights. Since the end of apartheid, many intellectual leaders and activists in the coloured community have chosen to reclaim and reappropriate the term. In so doing, they are able to examine the important social, political, and artistic achievements of the community and to understand their unique cultural position in postapartheid society.

There were more fine-grained categories within the apartheid racial classification system. Black South Africans became further categorized by ethnicity and subsequently geographically divided, with many relocated to ethnic "homelands." Homelands were a creation of South African politicians and scholars to legitimize the forced removal of the black majority and their confinement in small pockets of underdeveloped rural areas. This policy was reinforced by a curtailment of the black population's freedom of movement. Only those black South Africans with employment passes could enter the urban areas, and the homelands became pockets of overpopulation. Without proper access to enough land and water to be self-sufficient and without access to urban employment, these homelands became wastelands for many.

At the same time, the white population needed a cheap labor force within urban areas to mine South Africa's immense resources, to work in the rapidly growing industrial and construction sectors, and to be domestic laborers in white homes—cleaning, cooking, gardening, caring for children and the elderly. The apartheid state brought black South Africans, mostly men, from the homelands into the urban areas to do this labor, separating families for up to eleven months a year. The townships were created to provide housing for the black labor. Townships were located outside the white urban areas, requiring black South Africans to travel at some cost and distance each day to service the white economy and home life. Informal settlements formed around townships soon after as families attempted to reunite or as more people migrated into the cities to look for work. These settlements, or shanty towns, were considered illegal by the apartheid government. The informal settlements were frequently destroyed and the occupants arrested or forcibly relocated back to the homelands.

Apartheid policies exacerbated structural inequalities among the population through the violence of forced displacement, forced labor, and forced overcrowding. The apartheid state also used gender-based violence to police bodies, to destabilize communities, and to demoralize the resistance movement. The South African government deployed the military, police, and security forces to violently suppress the population through assassinations, arrests and false imprisonments, disappearances, state terror, torture, and sexual assault. These state-sponsored forces used gender-based violence intentionally as a tool to stifle public protests, as a weapon to enforce racial segregation, and as a strategy to undermine the antiapartheid resistance struggle located both in South Africa and throughout southern Africa (Britton and Shook 2014; Moffett 2009; Britton 2006; Krog 2001; Shikola 1998).

The South African liberation struggle was international in scope. The domestic struggle used legal challenges, mass action, consumer boycotts, and sabotage to push for liberation. The international movement pushed for economic sanctions, political censure, cultural isolation, and athletic boycotts. Women were invaluable—although often overlooked—in these movements, providing the backbone of implementing consumer boycotts, receiving military training abroad, and initiating mass action long before their male counterparts (Hassim 2006; Britton 2005; Wells 1993). Western and European powers were decades late in recognizing the illegitimacy of the apartheid state, which occurred only after the assassination of political leaders, the imprisonment of struggle activists, the murder of political protesters, and the curtailment of most civil liberties.

South Africa's hard-fought transition to democracy involved a protracted negotiation to draft a constitution based on the values of racial, ethnic, and gender equality. The South African Constitution grants all persons the rights to gender equality, personal security, and freedom from violence. Most importantly and progressively, the constitution delineates that persons should be free from violence coming from either public or private sources, which would cover all forms of gender-based violence, including sexual assault, rape, domestic violence, child abuse, and intimate-partner violence (South African Constitution 1996).

During the transition, South Africa also became part of the international movement for state feminism. State feminism is an applied strategy of trying to create government institutions/agencies for advancing women's issues, as well as targeting political offices to increase the representation of women in elected positions often through quotas, active recruitment of women candidates, or other affirmative action measures (Stetson and Mazur 1995; Beckwith 2000; Baldez 2001; Revillard and Bereni 2016). State feminism is also a theoretical approach, using insider strategies for feminist change and creating the political space necessary for sustained engagement with policy makers, budgets, legislation, and program implementation (Friedman 2000; Chappell 2002; Britton and Fish 2009; Revillard and Bereni 2016). The recent push toward feminist engagement with the state is an interesting and unanticipated event, given the often-contentious relationship between feminist movements and state institutions (Walsh 2008; Friedman 2000; Chappell 2002; Tremblay 2008). This scholarship suggests that feminists and gender advocates are developing ways to utilize state power and resources to improve the quality of women's lives. It also implies that insider strategies are both normatively valuable and pragmatically effective (Stetson and Mazur 1995; Staudt 1998; Beckwith 2000; Baldez 2001; Kulawik 2009).

Gender activists and women leaders in Africa have engaged their states to improve the quality of life for women, as well as to alter current discriminatory social practices, often with uneven success (Tamale 1999; Seidman 1999; Goetz and Hassim 2003; Bauer and Britton 2006; Hassim 2006; Fallon 2008; Shaw 2015). This engagement includes the creation of women's policy agencies, regional bodies, national ministries, government departments, and legislative committees. Women leaders in Africa have also successfully advocated for increased representation of women in national office. Several African countries moved from the very bottom to the very top of the list in terms of women's political representation in national legislatures, South Africa being the first among them to do so, followed soon by Rwanda, which has topped the list for over a decade (Britton 2005; Bauer and Britton 2006; Bauer 2008; Tripp and Kang 2008; Tremblay 2008). Such state-society collaborations have the potential to yield progressive legislative changes, but there are also problems when a "movement takes office" (Klandermans, Roefs, and Olivier 1998) and protest strategies are traded in for governance feminism (Halley 2006). This shift is not just a change in tactics from protesting to legislating. It also has the potential to alter ideological positions as outsiders become insiders who align themselves with state power and as feminists have to navigate these new roles and obligations (as seen in South Africa in Britton and Fish 2009; Mama 2004; Hassim 2004; Salo 2005).

Many instances of state feminism and attempts to alter state institutions, including those in southern Africa, have failed to address the very real material conditions that are fostering a climate of violence (Gouws 2016; Shaw 2015). These national-level policies, agencies, and programs often operate at levels well above where most individuals exist and are out of step with the violence individuals experience in their private relationships, homes, and local communities. Helen Moffett (2009) captured this disjuncture between public rights and private discrimination best in her conversation with former ANC MP Pregs Govender. Govender told Moffett about when she was serving as the chair of the Joint Standing Committee on the Improvement of Quality of Life and Status of Women. A male MP at that time praised Govender's work but then asserted that in his daily life "democracy stops at my front door" (172).

This powerful quote has been used widely in the anti-gender-based-violence sector in South Africa. It is strikingly, although coincidentally, similar to a slogan used by the Chilean NGO Safe Space, which organized around the idea of "Democracy in the Home and in the Country" (Parson 2010). By directly linking the public and private spheres, Safe Space worked toward broad embodiments of democracy within both national and familial authoritarian structures (Parson 2010). This NGO worked to address the context of violence against women, including structural violence, government authoritarianism, and violence in kinships and intimate relationships. To realize democracy at its fullest would mean that it is manifested within the state and the community and in the home. Given the history of colonialization and apartheid in South Africa or the context of authoritarianism in Chile (Parson 2010, 2013), any efforts toward a rights-based democracy would also need to address larger systems of structural violence, economic injustice, and gender and racial inequality.

State Feminism's Complicity with Carceral Feminism

State feminism in South Africa is increasingly aligned with carceral approaches to social problems, in which violence and abuse are treated as legal issues that require arrests, prosecutions, punishment of perpetrators, and protection of survivors (Gouws 2016).[4] Carceral approaches tend to focus on *individual* cases rather than *structural* factors that can normalize violence (Bernstein 2010; Bumiller 2008). Carceral feminism focuses on criminalizing and incarcerating perpetrators, often at the expense of other feminist agendas that focus on economic injustice, racial discrimination, and gender inequality. Feminist movements to address these structural barriers and inequalities are sidelined in order to focus on the criminalization of sexual assault, rape, and domestic violence (Gouws 2016; Gottschalk 2006, 2015). The carceral feminist fixation on criminalization and prosecutions aligns, consciously or unconsciously, with neoliberal strategies that shift attention away from the state's failure to enact economic justice and racial equality. The result is often that carceral feminist strategies contribute to mass incarceration (Gottschalk 2006, 2015), and these efforts have not been race neutral (Alexander 2012).

Carceral feminism is not the ultimate consequence of state feminism. However, by embracing state feminism, gender advocates may become more deeply aligned with the state and subsequently co-opted by state practices. Increasingly, these practices are driven by neoliberal ideologies. In South Africa, feminists who were part of the liberation struggle and who moved into the halls of parliament have often found that their political prowess has given way to appeasing the party leaders who keep the women in power and embracing traditional gender scripts that essentialize women as mothers or victims (Gouws 2016; Britton and Fish 2009; Britton 2006; Seidman 1999).

The potential of South African democracy has been undermined in part by the neoliberal turn in economic policies and development strategies.

Specifically, carceral approaches to feminist concerns are advantageous for government leaders because they can address activist pressures of gender equity while further entrenching individual-level solutions that are easier to implement, though they sometimes lack meaningful long-term outcomes. These government officials often prefer carceral approaches to social problems because they can retreat into strategies and benchmarks they know best: arrests, prosecutions, and sentencing. These approaches also tend to look at gender-based violence in isolation from the larger national or community-wide contexts, including the structural violence (Galtung 1969) of neoliberalism and its resultant inequalities.

Carceral feminism has limitations in almost every context. By focusing on prosecution above prevention, carceral approaches are reactive and emphasize action after violence has occurred. Costs and resources go into trials and imprisonment rather than structural changes that could address economic, gender, and racial inequality. These costs seem to be compounded exponentially in resource-poor environments. Limited resources move to investigations and arrests, and there are inadequate services for survivors who face limited safe shelter, counseling, and long-term social and economic support.

While the push toward the prosecution of perpetrators is reasonable, there is an equally troubling risk that feminists and feminist causes will be used by the state to legitimize a prosecutorial approach to justice (Gouws 2016). As Ken Corvo and Pamela Johnson argue, "Given . . . the recent trend towards the recriminalization of 'deviance,' . . . one might suspect that a degree of cooption of the feminist model to serve law and order purposes has occurred, in effect allowing the vilification of domestic violence perpetrators to take hold as officially sanctioned policy" (2003, 265). Carceral approaches to gender-based violence also fail to address the upstream structural factors that drive and accelerate violence. Feminists and policy makers need to look at violence within its larger social context, as well as the complexity of factors that could prevent survivors from reporting violence, especially if they perceive law enforcement and the legal system to be racist and/or sexist (Corvo and Johnson 2003). Globally, survivors often have to overcome barriers to reporting, such as fear of shame, corruption, and ineffectiveness of institutions (see, e.g., Menjívar and Walsh [2016] in Guatemala; McCleary-Sills et al. [2015] in Tanzania; Medie [2013] in Liberia; Parson [2010, 2013] in Chile; Alcalde [2011] in Peru; and Hautzinger [2007] and Nelson [1996] in Brazil).

Shifting the focus of social problems to upstream solutions and prevention measures may seem an obvious solution, but it has been slow to take hold in the gender-based-violence sector. Gender-based violence is often dismissed or normalized, and discussions of prevention are often aborted before they take hold. This challenge is compounded in South Africa by the legacy of apartheid inequality and its contemporary manifestations in new patterns of migration, economic inequality, and social unrest—all of which complicate the ability to identify prevention strategies.

Prevention efforts are hard to measure, quantify, and evaluate. This challenge is even more pronounced in societies that have experienced conflict and war. I spoke with a member of the justice system, a black South African woman who was working on multisector tools to assist survivors of sexual assault, about ways of responding to gender-based violence. She asserted that prevention was complicated by the history of South African conflict: "When you come from a history like ours . . . I mean, postconflict countries struggle with prevention because these are attitudinal things. I mean, you need to change. And changing people's attitudes takes a long time."[5] She suggested two important signposts for this project as a whole. First, she described the very difficult challenge of using the state to alter patterns of behavior and norms of gender. Such social changes in attitudes toward violence, gender, and inequality are essential in the efforts to prevent violence, yet these often-intractable attitudes can become reified during times of social transformation. She noted how difficult it is to measure such a change, because there are no empirical baselines from the previous regime. It is one thing for the state to measure rates of reporting, arrests, and prosecutions. It is another thing altogether to measure attitudes about violence, gender, and inequality and how they may be driving gender-based violence.

The second challenge she mentioned is addressing gender-based violence in a postconflict society. Research shows that gender-based violence may spike at the end of a conflict as the push for normalcy becomes linked to a return to "traditional" roles and ways of life that are, often mythically, associated with women's domestic and political subjugation (Lundgren and Adams 2014; Bhana, de Lange, and Mitchell 2009; Seedat et al. 2009; Britton 2006; Moffett 2009). Even in societies like South Africa with a postconflict reconciliation and justice process (see also Bueno-Hansen [2015] in Peru), a state's ability to foster transformation of the hierarchies of race and gender has been limited. As I will explore in the coming chapters, rape and sexual assault continue in South Africa today for a variety of reasons, including the patterns of gender-based violence from the apartheid era. While assault was previously used to disrupt the liberation movement, today it has been deployed to hinder women's advancement in the social, economic, and political world.

What is important for the purposes of this book is to consider how these patterns of gender-based violence, including rape, sexual assault, and sexual harassment, have continued into postconflict South Africa. Even in the best of circumstances, it can be hard to convince governments to shift their attention—and spending—from carceral solutions to prevention strategies. It is always challenging to argue for broad shifts in social norms, as well as attitudinal change in individual thinking and behavior (Parson 2010, 2013). This is complicated even further in South Africa's postapartheid context.

Gender-Based Violence in South Africa

Gender-based violence is a large and purposefully inclusive term that can encompass intimate-partner violence (economic, physical, psychological), child abuse, rape, sexual assault, sexual coercion, forced marriage, human trafficking (labor, sex, and organ trafficking), violence directed at persons because of their sexual identity, commercial sexual exploitation, forced prostitution, sexual initiation, female genital cutting, gender-based violence during wartime and conflict, genocidal rape, female infanticide—the list is almost endless (Watts and Zimmerman 2002). For the purposes of this book, I was open to examining all cases that my participants identified as gender-based violence. My interviews with service providers ultimately centered on the cases they saw most frequently, including intimate-partner violence, rape, sexual assault, and child abuse. While there have been several high-profile cases of violence and abuse in the lesbian, gay, bisexual, and transgender (LGBT) communities, service providers only occasionally mentioned that violence. Research on the violence against and resistance by the LGBT community in South Africa has been extensively documented elsewhere (Currier 2012), and I anticipate much more research needs to be done to understand and document this oppression.

Gender-based violence is about power in many ways—gender, racial, social, economic, and political power. Power often becomes so enshrined in institutions, practices, and oppressive hierarchies that it is no longer seen, recognized, or challenged (Britton and Shook 2014; Parson 2010, 2013; Montoya and Agustín 2013; Alcalde 2011; Britton 2006; Latour 2005, 45, 67; Foucault 1977). This can happen over time, but power hierarchies may also be driven and reinscribed by other fast-moving forces, such as war, conflict, colonization, economic restructuring, and nation building. In the face of these forces, political and economic leaders may invoke culture or tradition to legitimize new layers of oppression and violence.

While these processes become read as traditions perpetuated by predestined and invisible forces (Latour 2005; Montoya and Agustín 2013), most of these norms are in fact the result of conscious decisions and strategic moves made by those working to stay in power. As such, these norms and traditions are in fact mutable, and it is possible to make conscious decisions to alter their course and power. It is here, within this possibility for change, that activists and policy advocates find space for survivors, communities, and leaders to resist violence and oppression by disrupting social norms. Finding those spaces and making violence and power visible are the heart of this book.

Gender-based violence in South Africa is a key example of political forces that have attempted to normalize multiple interlocking systems of oppression and structural violence. Gender-based violence is not *cultural* or part of tradition (Narayan 1997; Green 1999; Merry 2006; Scully 2010; Menjívar 2011; Montoya and Agustín 2013; Britton and Shook 2014). There is nothing *African* about the violence. This is not *tribal* violence. People of all races, classes, and ethnic groups experience high levels of gender-based violence. In this respect, the voices in this book become part of a more universal narrative of resisting gender-based violence everywhere.

Yet *culture* continues to be raised as an explanation for gender-based violence in South Africa. It is called upon in a monolithic way, as if culture is something unchanging with ageless historical roots. But as research has shown globally (Narayan 1997; Merry 2006; Montoya and Agustín 2013; Misri 2014) and certainly in Africa (Green 1999; Burrill, Roberts, and Thornberry 2010; Scully 2010; Britton and Shook 2014), culture can be created, packaged, and deployed in particularly insidious ways, justifying racial segregation, gender discrimination, and abhorrent physical and structural violence. During apartheid, scholars were dispatched to find evidence of cultural differences among ethnic groups; government leaders then based almost a century of segregationist legislation on those constructed histories. The culture that was reified, celebrated, and violently enforced was not real or static—it was used again and again in distorted ways to legitimize the violence of colonial policies, racial segregation, gender oppression, and apartheid laws.

While gender-based violence is not cultural, *context* does matter. Violence of any kind may be driven, shaped, and framed by particular contextual factors, and gender-based violence is no exception (Parson 2010, 2013; Menjívar 2011; Burrill, Roberts, and Thornberry 2010; Scully 2010; Merry 2006). As Deepti Misri states, "'Violence' must be understood not merely as a phenomenal event that occurs out of time and place but also as a historically and socially specific process that moves in the realm of discourse and helps construct it" (2014, 9). Gender-based violence, then, is not isolated from wider institutions of socially sanctioned violence, state violence, or structural inequality and must be approached with an intersectional lens (Gouws 2016; Bueno-Hansen 2015; Gass et al. 2011; Menjívar 2011; Crenshaw 1997, 2012; Alcalde 2010, 2011). Gender-based violence is nested within this context of historical and contemporary violence and rooted in deep structural inequalities that are mapped onto race and class in pronounced ways (Burrill, Roberts, and Thornberry 2010). To think of gender-based violence in a vacuum "hides the complex ways victims understand and manage the consequences of what they live through" (Bueno-Hansen 2015, 9). Research demonstrates that the impact of gender-based violence will differ across races, social classes, and geographies, particularly in terms of access to services, health care, and material resources needed to exit abusive situations and to survive inequality in general, requiring intersectional understandings of violence and its possible solutions (Gouws 2016; Bueno-Hansen 2015; Crenshaw 1997, 2012; Worden 2000; Burman, Smailes, and Chantler 2004; Sokoloff and Dupont 2005; Alcalde 2010, 2011; Menjívar 2011; Wies and Haldane 2011; Montoya and Agustín 2013). This is certainly the case in South Africa.

The South African context of civil conflict, state-fostered racism, social and economic inequality, forced labor, and forced migration created moments and processes through which violence became reinforced as normal, routine, and even unremarkable. This includes the physical, psychological, and institutional violence within which gender-based violence becomes incorporated and seen as commonplace (Jewkes 2002; Seedat et al. 2009; P. Andrews 1999, 2007; Gass et al. 2011; Goldscheid 2011). The pathways of physical and structural violence in South Africa were not limited to the apartheid period; electoral democracy did not erase these configurations of inequality. As Pascha Bueno-Hansen asserts, the violence is not predetermined or linear, and understanding "power relations through a community-based analysis presses beyond the limits of linear temporality to contextualize sexual violence relationally across different historical moments" (2015, 110). Today, we see contemporary manifestations of apartheid inequality and a renewed push toward a carceral state.

Apartheid was undeniably horrific, and democracy was a hard-fought achievement. Yet some patterns of injustice have only deepened in the last twenty years during democracy. Incarceration has very clearly *increased* since apartheid. In 1995 there were 118,205 persons in prison. In 2014, two decades after the first democratic elections, there were 158,648 persons in prison, which is down from the peak of 187,640 in 2004, a decade after the first democratic elections (Institute for Criminal Policy Research 2016).[6] The push toward minimum sentencing, which has contributed to the United States' levels of mass incarceration, has also increased in South Africa (Kilgore 2016).

Income inequality has persisted in South Africa and has worsened since the end of apartheid (Leibbrandt et al. 2010; Saniei-Pour 2015; *BBC News* 2015). More importantly, the *wealth* inequality is one of the highest globally and is significantly worse than income inequality in South Africa. Wealth inequality is the measure of assets, property, and holdings, as well as debt. Income is an important measure of inequality, but wealth is often considered to be even more important, since it can produce income and profits on its own, separate from income. For instance, the top 10 percent of the population in South Africa earns 55–60 percent of the income but holds up to 95 percent of the wealth, which is much harder to account for or address (Orthofer 2016b). The "middle class" is composed of the next 35 percent of the population, earning 30–35 percent of the income but only holding 5–10 percent of the wealth in the country. The bottom 50 percent of the population, who "earn about 10% of all income," have "no measurable wealth" (Orthofer 2016a). These legacies are deep, and the job creation and progressive taxation policies since the end of apartheid have not gone far enough to transform this system.

At the same time, gender-based violence also has not abated. Globally, an estimated 30 percent of women who have been in partnerships have experienced physical or sexual intimate-partner violence (Heise, Ellsberg, and Gottemoeller 2002; Devries et al. 2013; World Health Organization 2013). Prevalence varies widely across regions, and within Africa there are significant differences. Central Africa reports that an average of 65.64 percent of ever-partnered women have experienced violence within relationships, the highest rate in the world. Southern Africa reports a rate of 29.67 percent, the lowest on the continent and in line with the majority of other global regions (Devries et al. 2013). Yet we see some differences in the severity, because intimate-partner violence in South Africa is often lethal (Seedat et al. 2009). In general, scholars have found that South African society is widely tolerant of gender-based violence, as long as it is not "severe," and the society generally sees it as normal, unremarkable, and at times even legitimate (Jewkes, Levin, and Penn-Kekana 2002; Goldscheid 2011).

The statistics on gender-based violence in South Africa are troubling at best. Each day, 144 women report rape to the police, yet there are many more—including men, women, and transgender individuals—who do not report the assaults because of the stigma they may face and because of a lack of confidence in the criminal justice system (Jewkes and Abrahams 2002; Vetten et al. 2010). Early estimates showed that only one out of every nine rapes were reported to the police (Jewkes and Abrahams 2002), and the Medical Research Council now estimates that in some areas only one in twenty-five women report rape (in Gauteng), indicating that potentially thirty-six hundred women are raped each day in South Africa out of the total population of fifty million (Nicholson and Jones 2013). Approximately sixty-four thousand sexual assaults are reported each year, and of these only about 10 percent lead to convictions (Polgreen 2013).

Thirty percent of men self-report perpetuating intimate-partner violence (Hatcher et al. 2014). K. L. Dunkle and colleagues (2006) found that 28–32 percent of South African men in rural Eastern Cape self-reported that they had engaged in intimate-partner violence. Rachel Jewkes and colleagues (2009, 2011) report that one out of every four men in an Eastern Cape / KwaZulu-Natal survey admitted to having raped someone. Of those, 50 percent admitted to committing rape more than once. Three out of four of the admitted rapists stated they had first raped someone while they were teenagers (Jewkes et al. 2009, 2011). In Gauteng the numbers were worse: in a Medical Research Council survey, 37 percent of men admitted to raping someone, and 7 percent admitted to gang rape (Faul 2013). A similar study in KwaZulu-Natal and the Eastern Cape found that 27.9 percent of men had raped someone, some had done so with accomplices in a gang rape, most of them admitted to having raped more than once, and many of them first raped someone while they were a teenager. Additionally, 3 percent had raped a man, and just over 5 percent had raped a child (Jewkes et al. 2010, 2011). Thirty-three percent had no remorse or guilt, and only one in five men who admitted they had raped someone was ever arrested (Jewkes et al. 2010).[7]

No matter which study or figure is used, the message is clear: sexual violence is shockingly widespread in South Africa. As troubling as these figures are, they align with most cross-national studies of gender-based violence and intimate-partner violence globally. Thirty percent of women internationally face intimate-partner violence (Devries et al. 2013; World Health Organization 2013), and rates of violence perpetrated by men are also in line with global findings (Barker et al. 2011; Fulu et al. 2013). In many ways, South Africa mirrors global gender-based-violence patterns.

Policy Approaches to Gender-Based Violence

Ensuring far-reaching protections in the constitution was a vital step forward in the quest to address epidemic levels of gender-based violence in the country. As Penelope Andrews asserted, "One could plausibly argue that violence against women in its many forms is clearly a violation of women's dignity, and that the state's failure to take steps to prevent violence is in contravention of the Constitution" (2001, 701). These protections were only a first step in the top-down approach to addressing women's inequality in the public and private spheres, as well as women's right to safety and security in their own homes. Several additions were needed to ensure these rights were extended into policy and programs. The South African government has continued to promulgate this rights-based framework in postapartheid legislation.

South Africa has enacted several key pieces of anti-gender-based-violence legislation, including the Domestic Violence Act No. 116 of 1998 and the Criminal Law (Sexual Offences and Related Matters) Amendment Act No. 32 of 2007. I argue that these rights and policies matter because the timing, content, and shape of policies can give survivors and activists the solid legal footing they need to combat gender-based violence. Without these policies, very little progress could be made comprehensively. Yet the policies ultimately represent a necessary but not sufficient condition for ending gender-based violence.

The Domestic Violence Act No. 116 of 1998 was one of the first pieces of legislation dealing with gender-based violence passed by the new South African government after the democratic transition. The ANC had promised to enact stronger domestic violence legislation within its first term as the ruling party in parliament (C. Hunter 2006). The act was the result of the significant multiparty collaboration of women within and outside of parliament and was due in large part to the work of the then Joint Monitoring Committee on the Improvement of the Quality of Life and Status of Women and its chair, MP Pregs Govender, to fast-track the legislation through parliament's first term (Hassim 2003; Meintjes 2003; Britton 2005). For the purposes of brevity, this law will not be discussed in detail here, but please see Lisa Vetten's work (2014) for a thorough discussion of the legislation and the subsequent backsliding of commitments and diminishing substance of the law since the passage of the legislation.

South Africa's Criminal Law (Sexual Offences and Related Matters) Amendment Act No. 32 of 2007 is one of the most comprehensive laws in the region. The law specifically mentions how freedom from violence, including gender-based violence, is a right that was enshrined in the South African Constitution: "AND WHEREAS the Bill of Rights in the Constitution of the Republic of South Africa, 1996, enshrines the right of all people in the Republic of South Africa, including the right to equality, the right to privacy, the right to dignity, the right to freedom and security of the person, which incorporates the right to be free from all forms of violence from either public or private sources, and the rights of children and other vulnerable persons to have their best interests considered to be of paramount importance" (preamble, 3). The legislation draws great strength from this linkage to the constitution. The language of the constitution ensures the right to security, the right to dignity, and the freedom from both public and private sources of violence, thereby covering all forms of rape and sexual exploitation, even within the confines of the household (P. Andrews 2002).

Despite international notoriety about South Africa's rate of gender-based violence and despite the rhetorical commitment on the part of the ANC to address it, the path to passing the act was a hard-fought battle, and the success of the bill can be attributed to the tenacity of South African women's organizations and antiviolence coalitions (Vetten and Watson 2009). The Shukumisa Campaign formed to pressure for comprehensive legislation to address gender-based violence (Gouws 2016). Starting in 2004 as the National Working Group on Sexual Offences, the working group grew into an alliance of forty organizations (Gouws 2016). Member organizations made dozens of submissions to parliament, conducted a national bus tour for advocacy around the issue and the stalled legislation, protested outside of parliament, and maintained pressure on parliament until the bill was finally passed (Vetten and Watson 2009). The Shukumisa Campaign's efforts were essential in the eventual passage of the law, and the campaign continues to serve as a monitoring force of the implementation of the law and other government programs to address gender-based violence (Gouws 2016).

Cross-national research finds that the most important factor in whether or not countries pass gender-based-violence legislation is the existence of a strong women's movement, which appears to be even more important than having a high number of women in national office or the leadership of a progressive party (Htun and Weldon 2012; Weldon and Htun 2013). As Amanda Gouws's (2016) research shows, this is also the case in South Africa. Despite the large number of women in the national parliament and the leadership of the supposedly progressive ANC ruling party, gender-based-violence legislation stalled for years. It was only through the continued pressure by antiviolence and women's organizations and their strategic collaboration with key MPs that the bill was passed (Gouws 2016; Vetten and Watson 2009).

After years of negotiation and lobbying following its initial proposal in 2003, the 2007 law strengthens protections for children and the mentally disabled, improves evidence collection and handling, and fosters higher quality transitional arrangements for survivors. It greatly expands definitions of sexual violation and replaces the long-outdated, narrow definition of rape with a detailed definition covering all forms of sexual offenses, including sexual penetration without consent, regardless of gender or type of penetration.[8] The law also covers prohibitions on child pornography, trafficking, exploitation, and prostitution, as well as the cultivation and grooming of children for prostitution, trafficking, and pornography (Criminal Law [Sexual Offences and Related Matters] Amendment Act No. 32 of 2007, chap. 3). The legislation also defines and includes compelled sexual assault, compelled rape, and compelled self-sexual assault (chap. 2). Each of these protections is also affirmed and delineated for mentally disabled persons (chap. 4).

Much like the Namibian Combating of Rape Act No. 8 of 2000, the South African legislation puts an emphasis on coercion, which places the burden on the accused perpetrator, rather than consent, which often places the burden of evidence on the survivor (Britton and Shook 2014). Forms of coercion include the use of force and intimidation and the threat of harm against the survivor, other persons, or property (Criminal Law [Sexual Offences and Related Matters] Amendment Act No. 32 of 2007, chaps. 1, 3). Additionally, the legislation outlines circumstances within which survivors might not have been able to resist because of force, fraud, or coercion or because the survivor was asleep, unconscious, in an altered state of consciousness, mentally disabled, or under the age of twelve (chap. 1). While this shift to coercion is an important step forward from the previous legislation, it still demonstrates the limitations of prosecutions based in "the binary of consent/coercion," which focuses on an individual-level crime rather than on how the violence "is embedded in a dense matrix of historic power relations that fall beyond the scope of adjudication" (Bueno-Hansen 2015, 110). As the cases of former President Zuma and Oscar Pistorius demonstrate, the justice system is not designed to distill the complexities of structural violence and may not be the appropriate institution to understand how individual experiences of violence are embedded in the context of larger state violence (Bueno-Hansen 2015, 127–28).

The law promotes prosecutor-guided investigations and closer collaboration between the South African Police Services (SAPS) and other service providers and prosecutors. This is important because the law focuses not only on prosecution but also on protection of victims. It includes a comprehensive approach for national interagency collaboration, the framework for a program of action, and, hopefully, a foundation for future work on prevention. The act also discusses in extensive detail the creation and implementation of a national registry for sex offenders.

Gender activists pressured for this legislation in large part because it gives them a policy framework through which to secure convictions and ensure the swift implementation of justice. South Africa was remarkably slow in passing the sexual offenses legislation, yet the legislation did benefit from lawmakers learning about the limitations of other national policies.[9] The South African policy went beyond any other piece of legislation in the region at the time of its passing. It is not merely limited to the prosecution and punishment of perpetrators; instead, it has clear benchmarks for protecting survivors and improving service delivery at various stages of recovery, victim services, and the criminal justice process.

The South African law includes provisions for the protection and rehabilitation of survivors of gender-based violence, including the ability to compel HIV/AIDS testing of the accused perpetrators and HIV/AIDS treatment (including postexposure prophylaxis [PEP] treatment and medical and psychological counseling) for survivors. The successful treatment of survivors with PEP depends on pressing charges against the accused perpetrator and/or reporting the assault to medical authorities within seventy-two hours to receive the PEP treatment within the window of efficacy. Survivors may also request HIV testing of the accused perpetrators within ninety days, but this is dependent upon pressing charges and cooperation with law enforcement. Detailed instructions in the act cover issues of privacy for both the accused and the survivor.[10] These provisions are very similar to those in other legislation across the region, and the South African legislation demonstrates one of the most detailed descriptions of when and how compelled testing could occur.

Just as the constitution recognizes the intersectionality of oppression (P. Andrews 2007, 22), the sexual offenses legislation recognizes the complexity of social conditions that have normalized gender-based violence. The act makes several references to being sensitive to and attempting to change the "social context" of sexual offenses: "The prevalence of the commission of sexual offences in our society is primarily a social phenomenon, which is reflective of deep-seated, systemic dysfunctionality in our society, and that legal mechanism to address this social phenomenon are limited and are reactive in nature, but nonetheless necessary" (Criminal Law [Sexual Offences and Related Matters] Amendment Act No. 32 of 2007, preamble). Throughout the legislation, there is language cautioning against the secondary victimization of survivors and their families, which also demonstrates an awareness of antiviolence work and engagement with the organizations and advocates in this field.

In a departure from other anti-gender-based-violence legislation in the region, the act does not delineate the sentencing guidelines and fines for each offense. Thus, while there is still a significant emphasis on the role of police and courts in the investigation and prosecution of the offenses, the text of the legislation stresses the roles, responsibilities, and guiding values (such as preventing secondary trauma) of law enforcement rather than merely focusing on prison terms for the perpetrators. This gives a much more holistic approach for law enforcement to follow, one that stresses accountability, survivor-centered approaches, training, and education.

As a whole, the legislation reflects a broad sense of the context of gender-based violence in South Africa and the need to understand the legacy of apartheid and the patterns of discrimination and abuse that continue today. It also demonstrates the need for a comprehensive and coordinated approach to survivor protection, justice, and assistance by criticizing failure of the bureaucracy, courts, police, and medical professionals in the past. The legislation sets the foundation for a rights-based approach to combating gender-based violence in both its public and its private manifestations.

The Community-Based Approach

This project focuses on the community as a unit of analysis for understanding how gender-based violence manifests itself, how it is addressed, and how it is understood. This community-level approach is intended to resist the ideas of gender-based violence in isolation from other forms of structural violence and of violence as a private, individual problem (Bueno-Hasen 2015). This community-level approach is predicated on an intersectional understanding of complex social problems. Gender-based violence is located within a framework of racial, geographic, class-based, and gender inequalities (Gouws 2016; Merry 2006). By looking at gender-based violence through the eyes of community leaders and service providers, it is possible to see how individual-level violence and harm intersect with and are part of larger social, economic, ethnic, and place-based structures (Adelman 2017).

So much gender-based violence occurs in what is traditionally considered the private sphere, which policy makers sometimes argue is outside of their mandate. Yet in South Africa, as in other parts of the world, this division between the private and the public is arbitrary and not reflective of people's lived realities of space and place and their understandings of home (Meth 2003; Bassadien and Hochfeld 2005; Burrill, Roberts, and Thornberry 2010). As mentioned earlier, the South African state also has a long history of policing the private sphere and intimate relationships.

Feminist geographers in particular interrogate the impact of public/private spaces and the meanings of home in relation to gender-based violence and "domestic" violence (Meth 2003). In places like South African townships and informal settlements, "women are highly vulnerable to actual violence, including sexual, both in the home and in public spaces," where crime and sexual violence are constantly "crossing private-public boundaries" (Meth

2017, 410). This is true even on simply a practical level. Given the proximity of people's houses in townships and informal settlements, the number of people living in hostels, the number of people who have no permanent shelter, the number of people living in a family, and the closeness of communities, most abuse does not occur "privately." It is often heard, witnessed, and known by people inside and outside the immediate family. Even violence occurring outside the home in public spaces may be witnessed and allowed to continue. Using models of intervention based on the idea that silenced survivors need to come forward may be unhelpful in this and other similar contexts (Bassadien and Hochfeld 2005). Larger issues of changing norms, beliefs, and discourses that normalize violence are at the heart of prevention and understanding larger structural and historical inequalities (Bueno-Hansen 2015; Merry 2006; Burrill, Roberts, and Thornberry 2010).

My approach in this project is to expand the focus of understanding gender-based violence as a private harm or as an individual-level crime to understand the broader networks of power that shape, affect, and may prevent the violence. While gender-based violence is unquestionably a physical, emotional, and material reality for individual survivors, it is also part of a larger system of inequality shaped by historical legacies, economic systems, gender inequality, and racial injustice (Gouws 2016). By looking at the community level in this project, my intention is to understand gender-based violence as part of the wider social context. As Bueno-Hansen argues, the "community-based analysis aligns with a decolonial analytical approach to highlight patters of domination rooted in coloniality and heteropatriarchy" (2011, 110). Attempts to examine gender-based violence myopically or in isolation from the larger social context do not take into account the full lived experiences of survivors or the configurations of inequality that constrain them.

Service Providers

Service providers have a crucial vantage point from which to see the complexity of social problems and to have a systems-wide understanding of how survivors engage with services (Wies and Haldane 2011; Guy, Newman, and Mastracci 2008). Their voices need to be central to discussions of policies and programs to address gender-based violence because their perspectives are critical to understanding why violence continues and why current policies are falling flat in their communities (Wies and Haldane 2011).

The service providers I interviewed in South Africa include the police, prosecutors, medical professionals, social workers, counselors, religious leaders, and members of community organizations. I selected the participants following an organizational scan of the network of community services and organizations in each of my selected communities, which I outline in the methodological appendix. I began with the selection of communities as the central unit of analysis, then mapped the network of organizations and community services within each community, and finally contacted each organization to set up interviews with members and leaders in the organization. As my research progressed, I was also directed to individual issue advocates within these communities to include, and I would then analyze how those organizations fit into my network mapping. While I conducted research in a range of communities, the majority of this book focuses on nine communities, listed below with pseudonyms:

> Arbeidstad: a middle- and working-class community that is predominately white with a combination of residential and industrial areas
> Bokang: an informal settlement located next to established black township and urban areas
> Difate: a long-standing and established urban black township
> Huisdorp: an urban community located in the center of a major city dominated by commercial activities; the vast majority of daily occupants come into the city for work, while the residential population was primarily black South Africans and African immigrants living in apartment buildings
> Lookodi: a newly formed urban black community created after the end of apartheid through a government Reconstruction and Development Programme (RDP) initiative to improve formalized housing for a mix of residents coming from many areas
> Mabitso: a rural black community
> Nokuthula: a rural black community
> Olive Vlei: a wealthy white area located on the suburban ring of a major city
> Roedorp: a long-standing and established formerly "coloured" urban township

These communities represent a broad spectrum of communities in contemporary South Africa.[11]

The service providers I interviewed operate in the highly charged sector of gender-based-violence prevention and intervention, a sector that is replete with emotions, trauma, physical injuries, and long-term psychological costs for the survivors and the service providers themselves (Alcalde 2011; Wies and Haldane 2011). In their work, service providers and community activists need to be able to manage and harness their emotional labor effectively rather than merely suppress it in order to conduct rigorous investigations, provide immediate care for survivors, assist their clients in navigating the aftermath of gender-based violence in all its forms and manifestations, and sustain themselves emotionally and physically so that they can continue to provide effective services, medical care, and legal support (Mastracci, Guy, and Newman 2012). These issues of emotional labor and secondary trauma often are in tension with a masculine institutional culture and how leaders are trying to ensure space to work through this trauma.

The subsequent chapters will reveal that service providers, street-level workers, and community leaders have a range of responses to larger social inequalities, including gender inequality and racial biases.[12] Some of these street-level workers, community activists, and religious leaders work actively to disrupt racial and gender oppression. Others demonstrate how service providers may actually reinscribe regressive notions of gender, class, and race through their actions, which is a global pattern (Menjívar and Walsh 2016; Parson 2010, 2013; Alcalde 2011). Therefore, the narratives in this book do not romanticize service providers and community leaders as noble and pure champions of social transformation. Neither do the narratives implicate all leaders as failures of social change. The collective voices in this book show that their role is more complex, more nuanced. In this way, the voices in this project demonstrate that service providers and community leaders have agency in not only how they choose to implement public policy and initiate social change but also how they may choose to uphold structures of inequality, especially those structures that legitimize their power.

The following chapters contain the voices of street-level workers who challenge existing ideas of gender violence, create new community networks to end sexual assault, and find more humane and transformative ways to work with survivors. Chapter 1 sketches a genealogy of gender-based violence in South Africa through the narratives of the service providers, community leaders, and issue advocates I interviewed. Their narratives offer a direct challenge to the idea that some force, often mislabeled as culture (Latour 2005), drives gender-based violence in the country. In contrast, service providers developed nuanced, detailed, and at times even granular explanations of how power is shaped and crafted by norms, practices, and institutions (Foucault 1977; Crowley 2009). Rather than attributing gender-based violence to a singular cause, they insisted that this violence is situated within a history of violence and inequality. They see multiple accelerants of gender-based violence linked to the legacy of apartheid, contemporary patterns of inequality, and context-specific factors. Reading these patterns against the backdrop of the international scholarship on gender-based violence, I identified four key groupings of accelerants: substance abuse, environmental factors, poverty / economic inequality, and factors specific to the South African context. While the first three categories are found globally, there are still aspects of each that revealed the persistence of inequality, racism, and sexism at the heart of apartheid government. The final category of factors I identified from the narratives was rooted in South Africa's shifting social roles in the postapartheid era, xenophobia of the last decade, and continued legacy of apartheid and violence. I argue that it is unproductive to look at gender-based violence in isolation. It is supported by other structures of violence: racism, xenophobia, homophobia, and sexism. Gender-based violence is also steeped in the structural violence of poverty, drug abuse, food insecurity, inhumane living conditions, and lack of basic services, which is exacerbated by neoliberal economics (Cabezas, Reese, and Waller 2007).

The book then moves into a discussion of the four factors that are important in the efforts to challenge gender-based violence. The first two, place and people, are locally grounded and demonstrate the importance of understanding the community context and individual issue advocates. Chapter 2 examines the impact of place and space on this struggle. The legacy of apartheid continues almost unabated today spatially, visibly, and materially. Since communities are at the heart of intervention strategies, I explored the strength and existence of community networks across the nine research sites in the study. This project spanned urban and rural areas; white, coloured, and black populations; formal and informal settlements; and long-standing communities and newly formed townships. I was particularly interested in understanding characteristics that affect community responses to sexual violence. Chapter 2 identifies (1) the key institutions and actors in each community, (2) the availability and proximity of services for survivors, and (3) the level of engagement in gender-based violence. While gender-based violence is not limited by race, space, or place, chapter 2 shows that place affects *how* the violence manifests itself. While there are some universal characteristics of power and violence, the context of violence matters, the history of a place matters, and the strength of a community matters, especially as communities design intervention programs. Service providers believed that gender-based violence is woven into the context and history of their communities. The resources and structures that continue to carve out social inequalities continue to be deeply enmeshed with the inequalities of place.

Chapter 3 examines the role of people—individual issue advocates, community organizers, religious leaders, and traditional leaders—in the effort to stop gender-based violence. As the previous chapters argue, communities that are better able to address gender-based violence also have strong, developed, empowered networks in place to deal with a range of local issues. This chapter again asserts that national institutions and national policy alone are not sufficient for social change. Cultivating people and community organizers, especially at the local level, appears to be a crucial step in the implementation process and in producing actual change. Cultivating a new group of bureaucratic actors within these networks is important, but it is not without its strategic risks, given the often-regressive frameworks and ideologies within which these actors operate.

I examine the next two factors, police and points of contact, in the broader national institutions that have been designed to prevent gender-based violence, to deliver services to survivors, and to arrest and prosecute perpetrators. Service providers talked at length about the importance of the police in efforts to build sustainable communities and to end gender-based violence. Police involvement came in many forms—through victim support centers, community police forums, individual detectives, and station commanders working to address violence. The importance of the police is a problematic finding at best, given the widespread corruption and ineffectiveness of the South African police. While police involvement does not seem sufficient to address gender-based violence, it does appear to be necessary for the punishment of perpetrators, the protection of survivors, and the prevention of abuse and assault. In chapter 4 I examine police stations across a range of communities to uncover what officers identify as their key resource gaps, as well as the challenges they face trying to prevent violence that often occurs within the home or intimate-partner relationships. The chapter also examines the emotional labor the police perform in this sector and the high levels of burnout and secondary trauma police officers experience.

Chapter 5 examines the points of contact where survivors interact with the national government at the community level. These points of contact serve as outposts where survivors can receive assistance, protection, and a range of other services. Many of these points of contact have been developed in conjunction with the national policy framework, and they often take on the strengths and weaknesses of the communities they serve. The points of contact I examine in this chapter include the sexual offenses courts; trauma centers and victim support rooms in police stations; the Family Violence, Child Protection and Sexual Offences (FCS) units in the South African Police Services; and the multisector Thuthuzela Care Centres (TCCs). These points of contact serve as institutions of intervention working toward violence prevention through the creation of sustainable, healthy communities. Yet they all are operating within a carceral framework, often directly under the auspices of the National Prosecuting Authority (NPA). As such, their services and missions lean toward prosecutorial solutions, which are a reactive approach rather than a preventative method.

In the conclusion, I return to the argument that the main strategies of the anti-gender-violence campaigns have centered on legal responses and prosecutorial approaches advocated by carceral feminism. While prosecutions and protection of survivors are necessary, they are incomplete strategies. The service providers, community leaders, and religious leaders in this study instead argue that simply raising awareness and jailing perpetrators will not solve this problem. Instead, they argue that gender-based violence is nested within many other interlocking forces of violence, racism, sexism, and inequality. Understanding gender-based violence from this intersectional framework is essential for creating stronger communities that are sustainable and focused on ending all forms of violence, including gender-based violence. This preventative approach will require upstream solutions that challenge violence and address inequality before exploitation occurs.

* * *

The legislative framework established by the South African government has created an enabling policy environment for service providers to initiate social change. But the legislation alone is not sufficient. Simply writing progressive laws does not ensure that gender-based violence will be taken seriously by government actors (P. Andrews 2007; Goldscheid 2011; Gould 2013; Medie 2013). Similarly, prosecutorial approaches rarely address how the state continues to use structural violence to enforce gender, racial, and economic inequality (Bueno-Hansen 2015). In order for policy change to be effective, it must go hand in hand with social transformation.

As my interviews with service providers reveal, the continued incidences of gender-based violence haunt South African policy makers because the violence is a stark reminder of how the liberation struggle's goals of a "nonracial" and "nonsexist" society have not been met. While the roots of today's inequalities are linked to the legacies of apartheid, the openness and transparency of the new democracy mean that many of these preexisting inequalities—and the violence used to enforce them—are becoming more visible (Moffett 2009; P. Andrews 2007). There is an inescapable contradiction between, on the one hand, South Africa's rights-based political system and, on the other hand, the continued violence of inequality. The cornerstones of democracy—free speech, free press, and free expression—create space for society to address these inequalities and these sites of continued violence and oppression. They also then necessitate an interrogation of women's electoral success and institutional gains with the failure to address gender-based violence and inequality in all its forms.

CHAPTER ONE

Genealogy of Gender-Based Violence in South Africa

As South Africa grapples with the reality of gender-based violence in all its forms, service providers and street-level workers struggle to make sense of the violence and search for its root causes. Here I examine the discussions I had with street-level workers, religious leaders, and members of community-based organizations about the causes or, more precisely, the accelerants of gender-based violence in South Africa. Power—including forms of economic, racial, and gender inequality—is at the center of their understandings of sexual assault. But how power manifests itself in the South African context is particularly instructive and essential for designing effective intervention programs. Their understandings and articulations of power were genealogical in nature (Foucault 1977; Latour 2005), demonstrating a nuanced understanding of how institutions, norms, and structures can both overtly and discreetly transmit that power.

Service providers argued that gender-based violence does not occur in a vacuum and needs a multisectoral approach. This intersectional understanding of power and violence complicates policy solutions presented by carceral feminism. Carceral approaches to gender-based violence reinforce the idea that violence is primarily an individual-level problem requiring the prosecution of perpetrators and the protection of survivors. The patterns and narratives in my interviews reveal, by contrast, that gender-based violence operates within larger structures of inequality and violence. The focus on individual survivors or perpetrators also ignores the structural factors that may drive the behavior: "Poor program outcomes are seen as the fault of the clients, not as the result of flaws in program theory or implementation" (Corvo and Johnson 2003, 272). Addressing gender-based violence requires an understanding of the lived reality of most South Africans, which is one of widespread poverty and generalized violence (Goldscheid 2011).

CHAPTER ONE

Table 1.1. Accelerants of gender-based violence

Accelerants of gender-based violence	Manifestations
Substance abuse	Alcohol Drugs
Environmental factors	History of family violence Gang activity
Poverty and inequality	Lack of basic services Inhumane living conditions Poverty Food insecurity Unemployment Cost of living increases Illiteracy
South African context	Shifting social roles Xenophobia Festive season

Here I shift my focus to the street-level view of medical personnel, local leaders, service providers, and community activists. Each of the people I interviewed had some direct interaction with gender-based-violence prevention programs, prosecution efforts, or survivor services. They also all had strong, informed opinions about what was accelerating or fostering gender-based violence (see table 1.1).

Substance abuse and a history of family violence were by far the most common explanations for the forces moving gender-based violence forward. These were not the only factors mentioned, and many of the accelerants these people identified are particularly embedded in the South African context. Many street-level workers believe that structural violence, poverty, and inequality generally foster gender-based violence and crime. They were not arguing that poverty causes violence, as sexual assault and intimate-partner violence happen across economic classes. However, the particular forms of poverty in South Africa are heavily influenced by apartheid segregation and inequality. Service providers and community leaders also discussed what they saw as the legacies of apartheid, including inequality, xenophobia, sexism, and migration patterns. One particularly interesting theme was how the shifting gender roles in South Africa challenged existing power hierarchies. Many believed that gender-based violence was being used to put women and LGBTQ persons "back in their place." They witnessed the violent enforcement of these power inequalities on people's bodies and psyches. These structural and context-specific manifestations are particularly important for understanding how violence may present—or justify—itself in other democratizing, postconflict, or racially segregated societies (Parson 2010, 2013; Adelman 2017; Alcalde 2011; Menjívar 2011), which I explore in the next section.

As the narratives demonstrate, service providers argue that gender-based violence must be understood within this broader framework of inequality and violence, which continues unabated in contemporary South Africa. Their discussions echo the World Health Organization's (WHO) ecological framework for understanding violence and violence prevention (Center for Disease Control 2018; World Health Organization 2016).[1] The WHO model is based in global research that shows that "no single factor can explain why some people or groups are at a higher risk of interpersonal violence, while others are more protected from it" (World Health Organization 2016). The model is particularly useful for situating individuals within a larger social and institutional context (Rasool 2016; Michau et al. 2014; Burrill, Roberts, and Thornberry 2010). Four levels of factors influence violence and its prevention: individual-level factors, relationship-level factors, community-level factors, and societal-level factors, such as socioeconomic policies and inequalities, social changes, conflict and war, norms of gender relations and racial hierarchies, norms of acceptability of violence, and accessibility of weapons. Prevention and intervention efforts must be intersectional and target this nested range across individual, interpersonal, institutional, and societal factors (Jewkes, Flood, and Lang 2015; Heise 2011).

Service Providers' Understandings of Gender-Based Violence

Here, I present some key examples of the forces that accelerate gender-based violence. The fluidity of the social-ecological model was consistently articulated in my interviews with service providers, community leaders, and street-level workers, all of whom talked about the multiple accelerants of gender-based violence in their communities. They also were very thoughtful about how the particular national context—postapartheid South Africa—continued to influence the scale, scope, and manifestations of violence.

Substance Abuse

Many street-level workers linked gender-based violence and substance abuse, either alcohol or drug usage and addiction. Some providers also linked substance abuse to other conditions such as poverty, unemployment, and inhumane living conditions, recognizing the complexity of layers of oppression. Most service providers believed that substance abuse served as an impetus for gender abuse, even pushing otherwise nonviolent people into violence. All stated that alcohol and drugs serve, at the very least, as disinhibitors to violent behavior.[2] Other service providers thought alcohol actually *caused* gender-based violence. One local government official, a man elected to local government in the coloured township of Roedorp, felt that stronger laws to reduce access to alcohol, combined with counseling services for survivors and perpetrators, could work together to address gender-based violence: "So alcohol is the evil in the community. I don't believe people will go around beating their wives or children if they are not under the influence. You do get the exception where a man is just that kind of person. But if we were to climb down on alcohol and the use of it and responsible use of alcohol, I think it could go a long way to curbing domestic violence in the community." This belief that alcohol was a cause of violence, almost a justification of violence, was not an isolated sentiment. This elected official was not calling for a ban on alcohol but rather stated that the government and the South African Police Services (SAPS) should monitor its access and promote responsible use. Abusing alcohol, he believed, can impair someone's judgment and decision-making abilities, thus setting the stage for interpersonal violence.

Street-level workers presented similar sentiments toward drug usage and abuse. In a group interview in the black township of Bokang, which also included an informal settlement, one black South African man who was a longtime officer in the SAPS saw a direct linkage between drugs and violence: "Within our community, especially our youth, you find there is a high rate of what do you call it, substance abuse, alcohol, multiple drugs, nyaope, which leads to most of our assault cases." Nyaope was discussed repeatedly in interviews, especially with police and members of community organizations. Nyaope is a highly addictive, often cheap, and poorly produced drug. It is a mixture of a range of illegal substances—marijuana, cocaine, and heroin—as well as unexpected components like rat poison, cleaning products, chlorine, vinegar, and even antiretrovirals used to treat HIV/AIDS. Nyaope has different names across the country, including "sugars" and "pinch." The withdrawal symptoms from this highly addictive drug are similar to those of heroin: extreme pain, nausea, cramping, aggression, agitation, and severe mood changes. The most successful programs to end addiction involve significant costs for medical supervision and medicine.

Nyaope is fueling a wide range of crimes, and the service survivors I spoke with feel that it is undermining the fabric of society, often targeting very young users. Another black South African man who was an officer with the SAPS in the Bokang station explained his observations on nyaope: "There are drugs. There are drugs called nyaope. These small boys are using it, and they end up breaking into houses for that. . . . Those that are delivering drugs in our township, if you can catch them, there will be no more drugs in our area." Nyaope is considered a cheap drug, often just two dollars (US) per dose (Hornak 2015). For the chronically unemployed and impoverished populations in the townships, nyaope addictions have fed crime, violence, carjackings, and theft. Given the inconsistency in production, one cannot predict how people will behave while on the drug, though it is most often associated with sedation. But many service providers felt that users exhibited agitation, paranoia, aggression, and violence, often within relationships, when "coming down" from the effects of nyaope.

I spoke with an older social worker who identified as a coloured woman and who was employed in a community organization addressing alcohol and drugs in Roedorp, a coloured township. In her estimation, the community had managed to overcome a history of gang violence, but she was concerned that the new drug was actually increasing crime, specifically within families: "Mothers are complaining. Mothers are crying every day. They [children] steal the microwaves, they steal the phones, and go and sell it for drugs. Husbands are taking from their wives. . . . [The police] have stopped a bit of crime, but it is only the drugs. The other types of crime—it is very quiet now." As street-level workers explained, the layers of stress and abuse triggered by these drugs may also be linked to stress and abuse within relationships.

The patterns identified by the service providers in this study echo the findings of scholars looking at the intersection of alcohol abuse, substance abuse, and intimate-partner violence or gender-based violence across the world (Jewkes, Flood, and Lang 2015; Lundgren and Adams 2014; Devries et al. 2013; Graham et al. 2011; Heise 2011; Gil-Gonzalez et al. 2006; Testa, Quigley, and Leonard 2003; Jewkes 2002). There are also contradictory studies in which domestic violence survivors say that their abusive partners became kinder and more loving, not more violent, when intoxicated (Alcalde [2010] in Peru).

The intersection has also been thoroughly examined in the South African context (Watt et al. 2015; Hatcher et al. 2014; Thaler 2012; Gass et al. 2011; Dunkle et al. 2006; Abrahams et al. 2006). In two South African provinces, Rachel Jewkes and colleagues (2010) found a particularly strong linkage between alcohol use and gang rape, with over half of participants discussing the role of alcohol in gang rapes. Mohamed Seedat and colleagues stated that "many" women killed by their partners had "high blood alcohol concentrations" when they were killed, and "most" of their male partners who murdered them were "similarly intoxicated" (2009, 1012). Kai Thaler's research in Cape Town found racial differences associated with the impact of alcohol usage and norms accepting intimate-partner violence: "Coloured men and women who binge drink are more likely to be accepting of violence than their more sober counterparts," and they were also more likely than the black population surveyed in the same study (2012, 16).

Scholars are not arguing that alcohol causes gender-based violence or that it excuses gender-based violence, but many do assert that its use is associated with increased risk of violence (Graham et al. 2011; Gelles and Cavanaugh 1993), either as perpetrators or as survivors. There are multiple explanations for this risk, including impaired thinking, lowered inhibitions, increased risk taking, and playing into "cultural scripts" about the effects of alcohol on behavior (Heise 2011). The street-level service providers in this study consistently reported similar experiences in which violence and rape often co-occurred with substance abuse.

Environmental Factors

Service providers across all sectors saw linkages between a history of family violence and gender-based violence later in life, either as an abuser or as a victim. While not everyone who comes from an abusive household will become an abuser, many of the cases the service providers and community leaders had seen involved a prior history of abuse. Scholars have also drawn correlations between suffering or witnessing domestic violence in childhood with higher levels of intimate-partner violence rates as adults, either as perpetrators or as victims (Heise 2011), though those findings are not consistent across studies. This pattern has also been observed in South African studies (Thaler 2012; Gass et al. 2011; Seedat et al. 2009; Jewkes, Levin, and Penn-Kekana 2002). Given the widespread instances of child abuse in South Africa, the linkages to future abuse are alarming. Seedat and colleagues estimate that 39 percent of girls "report having undergone some form of sexual violence . . . before they were 18 years old," and 35–45 percent of children have also observed the violent abuse of their mother during childhood (2009, 1013). Experiencing or witnessing intimate-partner violence during childhood may teach children that violence is normal and negatively affect their confidence and their sense of self, which in turn may hinder them from exiting a violent relationship in the future (Bensley, Van Eenwyk, and Simmons 2003; Jewkes, Levin, and Penn-Kekana 2002).

Service providers and police also found that gangs were fostering violence within their organizations. While the most serious crimes involved older youth and young adults, gang culture was being pushed to younger students, as a black, middle-aged SAPS officer who was part of a group interview in the Bokang station, which served a black township and informal settlement, stated: "Another contributing factor is also gangsterism. We had a situation in this sector where primary school kids, what do you call it, taking batons and knives to school. It is like they are grooming themselves." Certain areas, like the formerly coloured township of Roedorp and older sections of the formerly black township Difate, were more concerned about gang activity, particularly the level of violent assaults. One young social worker, a black South African woman, at a Thuthuzela Care Center explained that the rapes that she had encountered from Roedorp were markedly more gruesome than those from other areas, she believes because the rapes were gang related. Jewkes and colleagues (2010) also found similarly high patterns of rape within the coloured population, higher than in all other South African ethnic groups. The authors posited that this difference might be related to the higher levels of gang activity in those communities and particular forms of masculinity and socialization that appear based in violence and control (Abrahams et al. 2009; Luyt and Foster 2001).

Poverty and Inequality

A consistent theme in the interviews was the impact of poverty and inequality on violence of all kinds. While poverty may not lead to violence, inequality does lead to social stress and instability. Poverty has also been associated with higher risks of severe intimate-partner violence (Lundgren and Adams [2014] in Uganda; Jewkes 2002), but the evidence is inconsistent (Jewkes, Levin, and Penn-Kekana 2002). South Africa stands out as a country marked by vast inequality and violence. Alan Wood (2006) examined the correlation between inequality and violence across sixty-three countries, and South Africa topped the list for both income inequality and homicides. South Africa continues to have one of the highest levels of income inequality internationally (World Bank 2016), a pattern that is still racially linked despite incremental changes in the postapartheid economy.

The larger context of violence, inequality, and poverty creates interlocking webs of structural violence that are hard to disentangle from their role in interpersonal violence (Menjívar 2011). Kelley Moult (2005) found that many instances of domestic violence are sparked by conflicts over money and maintenance. When combined with a national context of normalized violence, where violence becomes a first response to conflict, this inequality may be incendiary. The larger issue is not whether poverty leads to gender-based violence but rather the impact of the widespread poverty on the ability to address the structural factors of gender-based violence.

Street-level workers from every sector talked about poverty in a number of different ways, including inadequate housing, illiteracy, unemployment, hunger, and cost of living. A SAPS officer, a black South African man in the Bokang station, stated, "You see, in the township like this, the problem is poverty. Poverty is the main, main, main problem. That is the thing that is generating crime in our area. People are not working, not having nice houses, staying in a tin house, things like that." Others described the informal settlements as inhumane, overcrowded areas with dehumanizing living conditions lacking sewage, electricity, and privacy. The overcrowding of families within small houses in townships and the proximity of families and neighbors in informal settlements also means that there is no real demarcation of a private sphere. In fact, because of the way most communities are organized, most abuse is not private: it occurs in the presence of others inside the home or is witnessed and heard by others (Meth 2017; Bassadien and Hochfeld 2005). Interventions that presuppose a separation of private and public spheres may be therefore inappropriate in the South African context. Service providers also commented on the lack of authority and social networks in many of their areas, as many in the settlements were domestic or international migrants new to the area.

Another station commander, an older white Afrikaner man working in a black township, argued against this correlation between poverty and violence. He thought this line of thinking implied that poor people were inherently bad or criminal: "Because sometimes from our side [white South Africa], they will say poverty is causing crime. And I can't agree with that. The people with the highest level of integrity are poor people. . . . In my whole career, I remember once we arrested a person for house breaking and only food was taken. The other property was there, like radios, TV [were] there, but just the food. So that person was hungry." While he spoke of this idea as a theory circulating in the white population, I also heard the same sentiment from black police officers. While the service providers did not believe poor people lacked integrity, they believed high levels of unemployment also drove the lack of hope, restlessness, and scarcity of dignity. During the third and fourth quarters of 2011, when I conducted the bulk of the interviews, South Africa had unemployment rates of 25 percent and 23.9 percent, respectively (Statistics South Africa 2012). This trend has only worsened nationally. In the first quarter of 2016, unemployment reached 26.7 percent. When expanded to include workers who are no longer looking for work, unemployment rates reached 36.3 percent. The statistics are more troubling when looking at youth under the age of twenty-four, who face an unemployment rate of 52.9 percent (Statistics South Africa 2016). Given that this group comprises 47 percent of the population (Holodny 2016), a very large portion of the population are unemployed and vocally protesting, as witnessed in the Fees Must Fall educational equity campaigns in 2015 and 2016. Education can be a pathway out of poverty and a prerequisite for employment, but accessing quality education in many areas is either too expensive for most families or woefully inadequate, if affordable. Only 15 percent of students who begin a university or technical college degree graduate (Brown 2015). A generation of people are facing high debt, few job prospects, high unemployment rates, and poverty. Again, to demonstrate the persistent racial inequality, the unemployment rate for whites is 7.2 percent; Indians, 12.5 percent; coloureds, 23.6 percent; and blacks, 30.1 percent (Statistics South Africa 2016).

Unemployment undermines basic human survival in this context. A SAPS officer, a black South African man working in a black township, concurred, "We have economic challenges where people do not have food on the table. . . . They will end up selling their bodies, and that contributes to domestic violence." A young black South African man working as a social worker in a children's home in a periurban township described the cycle of violence coming from unemployment: "In most cases, it is economic, and then it leads to emotional disturbance within the family, do you know that? . . . Because, the woman, you required a husband to provide food. And the husband is not doing that. . . . And that small amount he is getting, he is going to drink it because of maybe the stress." As I heard in many other interviews, the participants talked about how interconnected accelerants of hunger, poverty, emotional stress, and substance abuse may lead to violence and deepening vulnerability.

Even in more affluent areas, the pressures of keeping up with a middle-class lifestyle create tensions in the home. In a predominately Muslim Indian community, a woman counselor in a Muslim women's association stated, "One more thing I would like to bring forward is the increasing financial situation. It creates a huge battle. It is something you cannot discount." A Muslim theologian, a South African man of Indian descent, in the same interview expanded on this idea: "You see, the thing is that what has happened with increased financial demands on the home is people are loving very affluent lifestyles. And the cost of living has gone up, and the salaries haven't increased or the earnings haven't increased proportional to the cost of living.... Now there comes tensions, you know, in the home." The quest for symbols of economic wealth or an affluent lifestyle may create great tensions in a household, becoming more pronounced when there is a stagnating economy and the costs of living continue to increase.

These poignant articulations of poverty may seem to be taking the discussion of gender-based violence off course. Yet in all my interviews, these material conditions were seen both as accelerants of gender-based violence and as important as a form of violence in and of themselves. Much like Sharon Abramowitz and Mary Moran (2012) found in Liberia, my interviews revealed that in a broader, structural understanding of violence, economic support and poverty are forms of gender-based violence. Poverty is also one of the main reasons that survivors withdraw their charges of domestic violence. Dee Smythe and Lillian Artz (2005) link the withdrawal of cases to the fear women have of losing their source of economic support. Combined with a dependence on male breadwinners, this leaves many women fearful for their survival and their children's futures (Alcalde 2011; Goldscheid 2011; Menjívar 2011; Smythe and Artz 2005; Moult 2005; Parenzee, Artz, and Moult 2001). This dependence is worsened by other economic barriers to accessing formal justice mechanisms, such as transportation costs, time away from work, and lost wages (Moult 2005). Addressing domestic violence without addressing these larger systemic issues is proving challenging, if not impossible.

South African Context

Sexual Entitlement and "Gender Jealousy"

When notions of sexual entitlement and conservative gender ideologies are thrown against the massive political changes in contemporary South Africa, the result has been fractious and felt upon the bodies of women. While there are many possible motivations for rapists, South African researchers have a growing body of rigorous empirical data on why men rape centering on sexual entitlement. In a randomized study by Jewkes and colleagues in KwaZulu-Natal and the Eastern Cape, of the 27.6 percent of men who admitted raping someone, most of them stated they did so "out of a sense of sexual entitlement" (2010, 27).[3] This idea is often linked to ideas of men's ownership of women or superiority to women (Bassadien and Hochfeld 2005). The occurrence and perpetuation of intimate-partner violence and gender-based violence are globally pervasive and connected to conservative gender hierarchies (Lundgren and Adams 2014; Hatcher et al. 2013; Barker et al. 2011; Jewkes and Morrell 2010; Watts and Zimmerman 2002).

Women's rights have often conflicted with existing ideas of family structure and gender power throughout society (Dworkin et al. 2012; Goldscheid 2011; Andrews 2002, 2007; Burrill, Roberts, and Thornberry 2010; Merry 2006). In response, scholars and activists have speculated about efforts to further entrench male dominance in the face of women's political and social advancement. As I describe below, service providers in this study often pinpointed these shifting gender norms as a cause for gender-based violence, especially for intimate-partner violence. Violence is strategically and intentionally used to block women from politics, economic opportunities, and educational opportunities. Some argue that a crisis of masculinity is resurfacing in South Africa (Jewkes, Levin, and Penn-Kekana 2002), dangerously coinciding with a postapartheid context that normalizes violence. Men then use violence to discipline women back into their sanctioned roles (see Hermkens [2008] for a similar pattern in Papua New Guinea). Individual gender transgressions by women could collide with larger social transformations, amplifying the violence of male responses.

The regulation and containment of women's roles does not depend exclusively on men (Alcalde 2011; Uthman, Lawoko, and Moradi 2009). A middle-aged social worker, a white South African woman who managed a counseling center based near an informal settlement, talked about the complex ways in which gender roles support and maintain the normalcy of violence and women blaming:

> One of the interns opened my eyes when I arrive here, and she said to me, "I don't understand why you get so excited if you heard that a child witnessed a stabbing. We witness it all the time." So it is a violence-driven community. . . . I am having trouble to verbalize what I have in my mind. . . . There is a cultural perspective that a woman has a certain role to fulfill. And I think often domestic violence is tolerated, even if it is a correct word—exacerbated, worsened—by the cultural perspective that a woman should be or fulfill certain roles or whatever. So if a woman is more like myself, a little more academically minded or outside-minded, and she is not so focused on her home, she might even, the family might even condone violence there, and the community. So as long as you fit the cultural expectations, I think you are fine in the community. Then the community can—will and can—support you. But I think where there is violence, people will take sides . . . and usually against the woman, because she is not respectful. . . . And lack of support structures, and a woman comes in and complains about her husband raping her. And she gets told that it is her responsibility. That is not rape. We have it here, "That is not rape. You are married to him—it is your responsibility."

CHAPTER ONE

According to this social worker, she must work at cross-purposes to assist survivors who are being blamed for their own victimization because they are challenging tradition and culture. In some cases, both women and men perpetuate these social norms. Nearly two-thirds of women in South Africa believe that spousal abuse is sometimes acceptable (Aizenman 2015), and over 50 percent of men believe it is acceptable to beat their wives (No Ceilings 2016). The dissonance this provider recognized came when someone challenged or stepped outside prevailing gender norms.

There is also a theory, circulating more widely now, that the public/political advances of women in South Africa have led to a backlash in the home and in interpersonal relationships. There have been significant ruptures in women's political agency since the end of apartheid as women secure leadership roles across government. There is substantial literature now linking postconflict violence to the shifting gender roles during and after conflicts (Britton and Shook 2014; Lundgren and Adams 2014; Scanlon 2008; Samuelson 2007; Utas 2005; Krog 2001; Meintjes, Pillay, and Turshen 2001; Moser and Clark 2001; Turshen 2000; Green 1999; Turshen and Twagiramariya 1998; Shikola 1998) and how these shifting roles frequently result in increases in or justification for gender-based violence and a violent backlash against women (Lundgren and Adams 2014; Bhana, de Lange, and Mitchell 2009). While many have discussed these patterns in academic scholarship (Seedat et al. 2009; Britton 2006; Moffett 2009), I was surprised to hear it so often from service providers. They came from a range of racial and economic backgrounds and received very little professional training in gender-based violence causes or prevention. Many would not describe themselves as feminists. One older black man serving as an officer in the Bokang station stated it in these terms:

> Society is changing in terms of gender. Before the man was the breadwinner. The man earned a salary. The woman, her place was traditionally, and within the man's mind, in the kitchen. Now you find because of gender empowerment, females are in more powerful positions. Females earn more money than the husbands. . . . The man basically in terms of our traditional . . . "I am the man. I am the one who is wearing the pants. I am the protector. Now my wife is earning the money. I can't compete with her now." Because in terms of being a female, she is empowered, because women are empowered. So I think that gender . . . confusion where if you tell a wife, "Shut up," she says, "Eh! I am earning more than you. Get out." So that also leads to that. Gender jealousy. I don't know how you call it.

The idea of *gender jealousy* cuts across communities. In interviews with members of a Muslim women's association, I asked them to discuss causes of gender-based violence. They initially covered the aforementioned issues of substance abuse and income inequality but then discussed the tension that comes from reversing gender roles. One Muslim counselor and South African Indian woman said, "Then we also have something which you should have heard of. It is called role reversal. And these days we have a female counterpart being overly educated, firstly, and a lot of times the male would be humiliated the wife earns X amount and I earn just that. Sometimes you find she goes out to work, and he stays at home." They talked about these ruptures in status, employment, education, and gender roles as a source of domestic stress and discord.

This discussion of gender jealousy is similar to the tensions described in postwar Liberia by Abramowitz and Moran, who found that changes in legal systems—and the decision to deal with gender-based violence in the courts system, medical sector, or social services sector rather than in the community or within families—have "created tremendous uncertainties for both men and women about the meanings of kinship, marriage, and property rights, as well as the conditions of social and governmental control" (2012, 133). They also emphasized that this confusion of legal and social changes created "serious fears for many men" (133) in terms of their roles in marriage, property rights, and the household. As I found in South Africa, these changes can create an incommensurable tension between an understanding of the larger, rights-based constitutional framework and the more local, familial understanding of social roles and norms.

Xenophobia

South Africa has had multiple waves of xenophobic violence, including most recently in 2019. While dozens of murders and other instances of anti-immigrant violence occurred in the first few years of democracy, South Africa received international attention when widespread xenophobic riots and violence broke out across the country in 2008. Xenophobia in South Africa is particularly troubling, given that many of the attacks were on migrants from African countries such as Mozambique and Zimbabwe that hosted the antiapartheid struggle when the movement was forced underground and resistance fighters were exiled. These former host countries now face their own economic uncertainty, and many people from them have migrated to South Africa looking for better opportunities. The high rates of inequality, unemployment, and poverty in South Africa, combined with the racist antiforeigner rhetoric, have proven to be a powerful elixir of xenophobic violence.

A growing literature examines the interlocking causes of xenophobic violence in South Africa, how it compares to xenophobia elsewhere, and if the term is even useful in this context (Langa and Kiguwa 2016; Saleh 2015; Hickel 2014; Hassim, Kupe, and Worby 2008; Mngxitama 2008; Landau, Ramjathan-Keogh, and Singh 2005). These ideas include unpacking how notions of race and ethnicity, migration, and economic insecurity interact with particular forms of masculinity, gender, and nationalism (Langa and Kiguwa 2016; Hickel 2014; Amisi et al. 2011; Mngxitama 2008; Landua, Ramjathan-Keogh, and Singh 2005). Typical anti-immigrant rhetoric is that African or Indian foreigners are taking up space in the already flooded and depressed economic market (evidence of which is disputed by Landua, Ramjathan-Keogh, and Singh 2005) and buying women's attention and affection, reinforcing ideas that women are property that can be acquired (Langa and Kiguwa 2016). Some scholars understand xenophobic violence as a structural response to the economic constraints of neoliberalism and the continued hardships of inequality, housing shortages, and unemployment faced by most black South Africans (Amisi et al. 2011). Others think such ideas are too simplistic to explain the range and nature of the violence, which has context-specific manifestations like arson (Saleh 2015) that may also be linked to local forms of witchcraft used to reclaim and cleanse areas from outsiders and their harmful influence (Hickel 2014). While a full discussion of South African xenophobia is beyond the scope of this project, most agree it cannot be delinked from the particular forms and understandings of masculinity, race, and ethnicity cultivated in a postapartheid state to support a political and economic system based on inequality, material consumption, economic wealth, and individualism (Langa and Kiguwa 2016; Amisi et al. 2011). In this way, xenophobic violence becomes entwined with other forms of structural, physical, and psychological violence.

I heard many of the themes above within my own interviews—either people recounting the antiforeigner rhetoric against African or Indian immigrants (importantly, never against white immigrants) or people who embraced and offered up the rhetoric as explanatory for the violence. One black man working as a SAPS officer spoke about this climate of violence fueled by what he called xenophobia: "It is not long that we are free from apartheid.... Only one race was given services, so the government has a lot to do, and it is doing a lot. Now, here come another group of people.... There were stories in the newspapers where foreigners are getting houses which rightfully belong to South Africans, RDP houses. So those are some of the things which lead to broader violence and intolerance."[4] He links the anger caused by the economic oppression and political disenfranchisement of apartheid to the contemporary wave of xenophobia. While xenophobia seems to be an international phenomenon, he attributes the violence his community experienced to an explosive mix of government corruption and mismanagement combined with the memories of apartheid inequality. This same anti-immigration rhetoric was widely available on talk radio shows and in everyday conversations. Many believed that migrants were flocking to South Africa, overwhelming the economy without reinvesting locally, and taking government resources.

During my interviews, I noticed when xenophobia was linked to rape and sexual assault, which I had not seen widely developed in the literature. Some scholars linked xenophobia to gender issues, in particular, how women were property taken by foreigners. There is broad scholarship on rape as a weapon of war and genocide but less scholarship on the linkages between xenophobia and sexual assault. One SAPS officer, a black South African man in a township, made the link directly to the rape of migrants: "That is, they can come here from another country and have a successful life. 'Why can't we have a successful life?' So they are targeted. It could be another form of xenophobia, but they want to get the benefit of using xenophobia as an excuse for rape." Similarly, when I discussed xenophobic violence in another interview, a community leader in the same township talked about the vulnerability that migrant women face. She stated that if migrant women report the violence, they may inadvertently trigger their own deportation.

A young social worker, a black South African woman based in a medical/legal care center in a black township, talked about this silent violence of xenophobic rape, which goes almost entirely unreported. She was concerned that when people migrate to South Africa, they do so because they were victimized economically or politically in their own countries and are now in South Africa without family or community support structures. She assisted one survivor from Zimbabwe who was poor, had migrated to find a better education and a job, and was living by herself. The woman was raped, and the social worker related that she thought the woman was targeted because she was Zimbabwean. The survivor decided it was too difficult to take the case forward and decided to move back to Zimbabwe.

Xenophobia and xenophobic violence are not unique to South Africa. This South African case may provide a cautionary tale: when xenophobic rhetoric is building in a country, response and prevention efforts need to include a focus on gender and gender-based violence. While other forms of xenophobic violence may be more visible in media coverage, gender-based violence is a silent weapon because survivors do not come forward due to the fear of deportation and the stigma of sexual assault. These discussions also underscore the main theme of this book: looking at gender-based violence in isolation will not lead to effective prevention strategies, successful prosecutions, or long-term care for survivors. Instead, understanding how gender-based violence is part of other forms of structural or context-specific violence, like xenophobia in South Africa, will give a much deeper understanding of violence in all its forms (Langa and Kiguwa 2016).

The Festive Season

Another continuity of the apartheid era is the "festive season." Linked to the pattern of migratory labor during apartheid, the festive season marks the two-week period around Christmas when black workers would leave their jobs in the cities and migrate back to their homes in the rural areas. Similarly, domestic laborers would be allowed to travel back to their homes in other areas of South Africa or another country. This tradition continues today, with much of South Africa essentially closing for a two-to-three-week holiday for December and part of January, sometimes longer, depending on the person's social class. Those with economic means (primarily white South Africans) travel for holidays to the beach or other destinations.

The stress of the festive season is a particular problem in South Africa. The economic and social pressures on reunited families in rural areas are sometimes quite pronounced. After the eleven-month absence, there is often much celebration when everyone comes home, even in the face of deep impoverishment. Regardless of geography, most black South Africans have to deal with the pressures of providing food, festivities, and Christmas presents from their meager incomes. Parties and celebrations often bring alcohol into these already-stressful situations.

Several police and service providers discussed this period as one during which violence, particularly gender-based violence, peaks each year. I spoke with a middle-aged white social worker who worked in a black township providing counseling and support services for survivors of domestic violence, child abuse, and sexual assault. When we discussed the size of her rape support group, she indicated that it ebbed and flowed around the festive season and other holidays: "It sort of goes down and up, and there are certain times of the year that the rape goes up: round about the Christmastime, the Valentine's Day, the holiday periods. After that, usually the month or so after that, it is quite high." The commercial expectations of the holidays, coupled with the lack of financial means, high levels of unemployment, and increased alcohol use, can heighten incidences of rape.

Police officers mentioned the festive season in almost every interview. They saw the holiday season as marked by increased crime in all sectors—theft, assault, battery, gender-based violence, and child abuse. Their entire caseload could increase each year during this season. Similarly, a young black South African woman who was a caseworker at a sexual assault crisis center in a black township spoke about how particular periods of the year alter people's behavior patterns and spaces: "That is where you would find most of our cases coming now in big numbers—when it is a public holiday. Most people are going out partying when it is December. December is when it is busy, it is like, it is busy almost every day." Since the festive season represents a temporal trigger for gender-based violence, it could also become a key intervention moment. One young social worker, a black South African man in a children's home in a periurban township, described how this period could be useful for addressing child abuse and family violence. He advocated for government departments and community leaders to develop awareness and intervention programs that could be implemented during the holidays: "You choose the public holidays where the parents will be around. And again, we arrange to meet everyone within the community." This social worker addressed the potential power of identifying the moments and spaces where gender-based violence is at its worst and then developing interventions specifically for those moments.

Nested Oppressions

The complexity of issues like gender-based violence bedevils policy makers who want to delineate clear paths and measurable outcomes. Rather than becoming immobilized by the complexity of gender-based violence, they could instead directly involve street-level workers in designing prevention and intervention programs, prioritize financial investment at the community level, or mobilize resources to address the full range of client needs. Given the constraints they face, service providers are calling for upstream solutions to address the range of violence their clients face, including structural and economic violence.

South Africa's legislation on gender-based violence has much to be praised. It embodies ideas that examine the entire scope of the problem, it has programs focused on prevention, and it has mechanisms in place for cross-sector collaboration. Yet, approaching the problem from the standpoint of street-level workers implementing the legislation is more complex. The layers, definitions, and accelerants of gender-based violence are often context specific. To approach gender-based violence successfully, policies and programs need to adopt a street-level view of people's lives and the multifaceted nature of gender-based violence. Attempts to approach gender-based violence outside the material realities of South African society will likely be ineffective and short-lived. Understanding the moments and spaces in which gender-based violence occurs—and the key accelerants of gender-based violence—is critical to building effective, targeted models of intervention.

Globally, there have been significant unintended consequences of focusing on gender-based violence as an isolated issue (Merry 2006), which is often the approach of carceral feminism. Carceral frameworks oversimplify intimate-partner violence into very limited scripts: women as victims / men as perpetrators beyond redemption; relationships as heterosexual; and escalations of violence as inevitable (Corvo and Johnson 2003). The emphasis on carceral approaches to gender-based violence also limits the broader social transformations necessary to address the structural violence within which gender-based violence is situated (Bernstein 2010; Bumiller 2008). To address gender-based violence from a prevention standpoint, intervention programs also need to focus on structural violence in multiple, intersectional forms.

The service providers' narratives echo the work by Abramowitz and Moran (2012) in Liberia.[5] They juxtapose conflicting understandings of gender-based violence in Liberia between international NGOs and local agents. International NGOs framed gender-based violence as a problem of power and patriarchy. When given a chance to challenge these narratives, villagers and local actors across the country opposed these programs. The NGOs in Liberia linked gender-based violence to "tradition" rather than to the current socioeconomic inequality and uncertainty and refused to allow more nuanced understandings of violence. For community members, it was impossible to separate gender-based violence from these other structural forms of violence and economic inequality. In so doing, the NGOs created more dissonance and confusion.

Given the wider context of inequality in South Africa, the patterns and legacies outlined by street-level workers and community leaders challenge the misconception that gender-based violence is an isolated act. Indeed, social context matters. The participants in this project have seen through the lives of their clients, patients, and survivors that gender-based violence cannot be targeted separately from other forces of structural violence, including racism, xenophobia, poverty, and sexism. Their narratives also speak to the misalignment between single-issue frameworks to address gender-based violence and the material realities of people's lives. Local ideas about what constitutes and accelerates gender-based violence are linked to broader, intersectional understandings of violence, justice, and social conditions. Thus, understanding the local context is just as important—perhaps even more so—than the imposition of national and international definitions of gender-based violence.

CHAPTER TWO

Place

Place and space matter enormously in the effort to combat gender-based violence. Perhaps more than in other countries, place matters in South Africa because of the legacy of apartheid. The decades-long system of racial separation continues today, with very limited social mobility and almost no transformation of living conditions and transportation systems. The majority of black, Indian, and coloured South Africans continue to live in artificially created pockets of overpopulation and poverty across de facto segregated townships or, in the case of black South Africans, shantytowns and rural areas. The majority of whites continue to live in racially homogeneous spaces with significantly better economic and political resources. Racial mobility remains limited to a sliver of upper-class black, coloured, and Indian citizens who are able to navigate their way out of the townships into often highly affluent gated communities or—even less often—into middle-class neighborhoods.

This persistent inequality is also visible throughout the country as townships and informal settlements have inched closer to rich, predominately white communities. Many of these communities are becoming gated enclaves, heavily guarded and located behind tall electrified walls (Landman 2004, 2007; Harrison and Mabin 2006; Jürgens and Gnad 2002). Retreat into securitized gated communities is an international pattern (Clement and Grant 2012; Asiedu and Arku 2009; Chase 2008; Atkinson 2006; Mycoo 2006) as those with economic means choose to wall themselves away from the disorder presented by inequality and poverty to protect their families and economic interests from threats of crime and violence. Many who develop these gated residential communities argue that they are necessary, if not warranted, in the face of state failure to provide adequate infrastructure and public goods and services, as well as to ensure the preservation of property and lifestyle

(Mycoo 2006; Jürgens and Gnad 2002). Rather than retreating behind individual barricades around their own homes, residents can extend the walls around entire carefully curated communities and move about freely with a sense of security enforced at the gates (Chase 2008). Within the South African context, these private communities serve as a contemporary demarcation of the segregation of apartheid, which was once legislatively enforced and now has become privately managed.

The economic imprint of apartheid is palpable and violent nationally. The 2012 Marikana massacre of striking miners by police highlights the very real and inhumane levels of inequality that persist decades after liberation. Similarly, the Fees Must Fall movement, which has centered on student protests over the high costs of education, reflects widespread frustration with the glacial pace of change in many sectors. The legacies of apartheid also spill over into how communities are formed and experienced. Trends such as child-headed households are very noticeable in black areas but are not prevalent in coloured or white areas. Poverty is vast, but the depth and extent of poverty are still, for the most part, racially divided. While moments of change and movements of resistance occur, the continuities of apartheid segregation and inequality remain among the most pressing concerns of contemporary South Africa.

One social worker, a young black South African woman who specialized in helping survivors of sexual assault, spoke very directly about the issues of place and race. Based in a large hospital, she had a unique vantage point because she encountered survivors, law enforcement, and service providers from several communities that represented a broad range of ethnic, racial, and economic conditions. She found that places differed in both the type of violence they witnessed and the strength of community networks they had formed. She believed that all these place-based differences were rooted in the legacies of racism cultivated and reified by apartheid:

> Bokang—it is more of the informal settlements, and most of our cases come from that side. And the Difate is like the old township. And, well, we do get some cases from there, but it is not so bad. Then you go to Roedorp, and it is a coloured community, and you get very violent cases whereby you would find a person has been stripped naked and raped, or you find that it is very bad as far as violence is concerned. And then we also get Arbeidstad. But it is a very laid-back, quiet community. It is full also of white people. And you find that they would refuse to come here because they think Difate is a township. And, I mean, after you have been raped, you would really feel like going to Difate is not safe [laughter]. . . .

> You find that you go to Arbeidstad—I have a colleague that is staying in Arbeidstad. And I go to her place, but she has never been to my place. I think it is from the apartheid regime. As much as we are now more liberated, but it is still a bit of a challenge to have a white person coming to a township visiting a friend. So we have cases whereby they refuse to come to [the crisis center] because I think maybe they do not have the information [about the services here]. Because even with Difante, you go to the township and do community outreach. . . . You can go stand with a loud speaker, and everyone will come around. And they will want to hear what you are giving, and they will even ask questions, and they will even give you cases that are happening now and say, "There is a child. My neighbour I suspect [it] is doing that and that." And then immediately you get cases. But the white community, it is more of they keep to themselves and even just an issue of talking to their neighbors. They don't even talk to their neighbors. With us you feel bad if you don't talk to your neighbors. But in the white community, it is not wrong if you don't [say hello] to a person.

The legacy of apartheid separation and violence is not subtle. It is lived, it is deep, and it is directly linked to the resources and networks available to address sexual assault, rape, and domestic violence. Gender-based violence is not caused by poverty. But the ability to address gender-based violence is often linked to poverty, which is mapped onto place, space, race, and communities. The South African policies on gender-based violence are by many standards both rigorous and progressive. However, space and place continue to affect all aspects of policy implementation.

Below I present an overview of the communities in this project, with particular emphasis on the cases where communities were attempting to address gender-based violence, rape, and sexual assault. Table 2.1 presents a summary of the community scans, and tables 2.2 and 2.3 give the corresponding explanations of the government services and community characteristics, respectively.

My goal in this chapter is to examine the impact of place, space, and geography on the contemporary context of gender-based violence in South Africa. In line with the social worker's narrative above, the next section examines how resources and proximity to services are products of apartheid's violence, neglect, and discrimination. I then examine communities that are working actively to address gender-based violence as part of larger efforts to alter patterns of inequality and violence in their communities.

Table 2.1. Summary of findings of the community scans

	Police	Victim support services	Community police forums	Gender-based violence health services	Religious engagement in gender-based violence	Community organizations engaged in gender-based violence activism	Issue leaders for gender-based violence
Mabitso Rural black community	High	High	Highly active	Distant	None	Inactive	Yes
Nokuthula Rural black community	Low	Inactive	Inactive	Distant	None	Inactive	No
Difate Urban black established township	High	High	Moderately active	On location	None	Active	Yes
Bokang Informal settlement	High	High	Moderately active	Nearby	None	Nearby	Yes
Lookodi Urban black community, newly formed	Low	Unavailable	None	Nearby	Yes	None	Yes

Table 2.1. Continued

	Police	Victim support services	Community police forums	Gender-based violence health services	Religious engagement in gender-based violence	Community organizations engaged in gender-based violence activism	Issue leaders for gender-based violence
Roedorp Urban coloured established township	High	Moderately	Highly active	Nearby	Yes	Active	Yes
Huisdorp City center	Moderate	High	Highly active	Distant	Yes	Active	Yes
Arbeidstad Predominantly white working class community, mix of residential and business	Low	Low	Moderately active	Nearby	None	None	No
Olive Vlei Suburban white community	Moderate	Inactive	Moderately active	Nearby	None	None	No

Table 2.2. Description of government services

	Police	Victim support room and services	Community police forums	Health services specializing in gender-based violence
Mabitso	High level of engagement: sexual violence team led by social worker and investigator; full support of station leadership; full engagement with offices at all levels	High functioning: well maintained and used, warm and inviting; public education available; staffed by police and not by volunteers	Highly active: street patrols; community violence prevention and intervention programs; gang violence programs; block captains in place; improved response time	Distant: victims services located more than forty-five minutes away
Nokuthula	Low level of engagement: worked on issue mainly through youth forum	Inactive: victim support room not in use for victim services; no designated or available staff to handle victims	Inactive	Distant: victim services located more than forty-five minutes away
Difate	Moderate level of engagement: full support from commander; moderate involvement of stations; strong community linkages with organizations, including counseling, medical services, traditional healers, and chief and police forums	High functioning: well maintained and used, warm and inviting; public education available; staffed by a police officer and volunteer; significant complaints of exhaustion and psychological fatigue	Moderately active: some CPF activity and decreasing crime rates overall	Present: health services for survivors located in the hospital. Nearby: community counseling services

Table 2.2. Continued

	Police	Victim support room and services	Community police forums	Health services specializing in gender-based violence
Bokang	High level of engagement: full support from commander; active involvement of station; strong community linkages with organizations, including counseling and medical services	High functioning: well maintained and used, warm and inviting; public education available; staffed by volunteers contracted by national government	Active CPF in the informal settlement	Nearby: health services for survivors located in nearby hospital Present: community counseling services
Lookodi	Low level of engagement: police station not located in township but in nearby town; difficulty in response time	Unavailable on site: victim services located in police station in nearby town	None	Nearby: services located in nearby township, less than twenty minutes away
Roedorp	High level of engagement: support of station commander; station leaders focused on integrating services across community and government agencies; strong knowledge and partnership with CPF and community	Moderately functioning: well maintained and used; public education available; staffed by police and not volunteers; underresourced (in need of clothing, toiletries, bedding)	Highly active: street patrols; community violence prevention and intervention programs; gang violence programs; block captains in place; improved response time	Nearby: services located in nearby township, less than twenty minutes away

Table 2.2. Continued

	Police	Victim support room and services	Community police forums	Health services specializing in gender-based violence
Huisdorp	Moderate level of engagement: support of station commander and officers; strong community ties; issue of priorities given the level and extent of crime in the area	High functioning: well maintained and used, warm and inviting, child friendly; public education available; staffed by volunteers contracted by national government	Highly active: active during daytime working hours; focused on visible crime and theft; community education and awareness campaigns	Distant: specialized services located in nearby township, more than thirty minutes away
Arbeidstad	Low level of engagement: station commander delegated issue to victim services and community outreach	Low functioning: victim services staffed by police employee, but person was not high ranking or trained; focus on individual intervention and not community-wide programs	Moderately active: focus on theft, home invasion, robbery, and protection of businesses	Nearby: services located in nearby township, less than thirty minutes away
Olive Vlei	Moderate level of engagement: support of station commander; engagement by officers throughout the station; few programs or outreach	Inactive: victim support room not in use for victim services; no designated or available staff to handle victims; working with detectives primarily	Moderately active: focused on theft, carjacking, and home invasions; no programs for gender-based violence	Nearby: services located in nearby township, less than thirty minutes away; victims chose to go to local hospital or doctor, feared going to township

Table 2.3. Description of community characteristics

	Religious engagement on gender-based violence	Community organizations engaged in gender-based-violence activism	Issue leaders for gender-based violence
Mabitso	None	Inactive except for police forums	Yes: located mainly within the police, CPF, and Youth Forum
Nokuthula	None	Inactive except for police-led programs	No key leaders on issues
Difate	None	Active: several women's organizations, business groups, drug and alcohol programs, children's services	Yes: located within the police, judicial systems, and hospital
Bokang	None	One: counseling services functioned as a community mobilization point	Yes: located within the police and counseling center
Lookodi	Yes: one key church involved	None	Yes: located within the church
Roedorp	Yes: Christian and Islamic communities involved	Active: HIV/AIDS groups, poverty alleviation groups, drug and alcohol groups	Yes: spread throughout the local government, police forums, religious groups, and community organizations
Huisdorp	Yes: several church leaders engaged in issue	Active: several shelters, victim support organizations, religious organizations, women's groups	Yes: strong leadership in community organizations and police
Arbeidstad	None	None	No key leaders on issues
Olive Vlei	None	None	No key leaders on issues

CHAPTER TWO

Place and Rape

Understanding how gender-based violence presents itself in communities is critical. Every community I observed had its own unique challenges of place: access to resources in rural areas, the constant movement of people and the influx of multiple nationalities in urban city centers, or the victim stigma in white areas. The communities I partnered with demonstrated that place matters, and communities continue to be nested in the layers of socioeconomic differences that apartheid imposed and violently sustained.

The police I interviewed also had a useful observation: the economic climate of an area affects the types of rapes that were reported but not necessarily the types of rapes that occur. For example, the Arbeidstad urban area is a mix of residential and industrial sectors. The residents are primarily white, with a large number of black and coloured South Africans commuting to the area daily for work. One officer in Arbeidstad stated that the rapes reported to the police station were most often "stranger" rapes: "Same problem here with sexual assault—the suspects are unknown. The people walk long distances to work, and that is when they are at risk of rape." In contrast, I spoke with a police officer who saw both "stranger rape" and "acquaintance rape" in the nearby black community of Lookodi, which was built after apartheid as part of the Reconstruction and Development Programme (RDP). Lookodi is similar to other RDP communities in that there were some improvements for residents who were coming from informal, substandard housing into government-built housing developments as part of the massive national housing program's promise of safe and sustainable housing for all (Charlton 2004; Huchzermeyer 2001). This improvement in housing was not matched by a similar investment in employment or poverty alleviation (Meth 2010; Charlton 2004). Thus, communities were formed with new houses, but often residents had no income or employment to match. This improved housing infrastructure may increase residents' safety, as the new houses are much harder to penetrate than the makeshift houses in informal settlements (Meth and Buthelezi 2017; Meth 2016). Many of the RDP communities also promised a better life with increased access to electricity, government services, and security. The "legibility" of the new developments made it easier to police and find criminals than in informal settlements because of electricity, clearly marked houses, smaller populations through "dedensification," and set roads (Meth 2016, 105).

However, Lookodi also had many of the challenges associated with RDP communities elsewhere in South Africa (Meth and Buthelezi 2017), including the changing demographics that come with an influx of people from different communities and countries who do not have established social networks of support—or income. Residents in more established formal townships had family or friendship networks that created bonds of support, survival, and security. In contrast, the Lookodi development was undergoing what feminist geographers Paula Meth and Sibongile Buthelezi call "townshipization," in which the RDP communities begin to exhibit social patterns similar to township life, especially in terms of "the daily rhythms and routines" marked by "demographic change and mixing, differentiation, and rising consumption, pleasure, and leisure activities" (2017, 82). Unlike more formal township areas, these new communities lacked social support networks to buffer these changes and social stress. These new RDP communities are often located in a peripheral position to urban areas. As such, their access to services is also peripheral, thus reproducing the discriminatory geography of apartheid era housing developments (F. Ross 2015; Charlton 2004; Huchzermeyer 2001). Access to electrification also brought with it new "leisure activities," as well as access to alcohol, gambling, and fighting. These activities are juxtaposed with "ongoing poverty and unemployment" (Meth and Buthelezi 2017, 77) and "blatant boredom," which in turn create patterns of "incivility" and crime (85). Similarly, while access to some government services is improved in these RDP communities, access to police services is often only partial (Meth and Buthelezi 2017; Charlton 2004). The police station serving the community of Lookodi was actually located some kilometers away in an adjacent community.

In contrast to the officer serving Arbeidstad who saw mainly "stranger rape," the officer I spoke with in Lookodi stated that he saw "acquaintance rape" in addition to "stranger rape" in his area: "Children are being raped. But you find they are raped by known people. Usually the people who rape, they are known. There and there you find people, especially ladies, who travel at night. They get a taxi, takes them to a wrong place. They get raped there. Those are the problems." He indicated that his police station has to respond to wide-ranging patterns of sexual violence, which will undoubtedly require a complex set of investigatory skills.

This same officer talked about how people's vulnerability and economic precarity drive them into uncertain situations. People who are desperate for food and survival may go against their better judgment and follow risky leads in hopes of gaining employment. Sometimes this might include a dicey transportation situation or it could involve taking a job with an employer who turns out to be abusive:

> You find people who are targeting ladies about work and so on. But I don't know. You see these people or poor people. They don't listen. Because

CHAPTER TWO

somebody comes and says, "I have got a work for you." And while you sensitize them, "You don't go with strangers who promise you work." You take them here in [Lookodi], go with them in town, phone, or whether he phones or pretends to be phoning.... Then they go to get a taxi.... "There is some bush there. We must take a short cut." The poor person doesn't suspect anything. Then they go in the bushes. They turn around [and] rape the person. You see, so the people are too desperate to listen to everybody, and that is also dangerous. But the abusers also go scot-free sometime. You see the act [Domestic Violence Act No. 116 of 1998] says the police must act when there is that case of domestic violence reported, failure of which we [the police] will be dealt with. We deal with it, and sometimes the members realize this situation is so serious they arrest the perpetrator. And then a victim will come and plead for the perpetrator to be released. He is a sole breadwinner and what what.

The officer is talking about a range of violence, as well as a continuum of vulnerability and abuse. What is particularly interesting about his narrative is that all these situations are linked, in his opinion, to economic vulnerability. He talks first about situations where women may go into risky or uncertain situations because they are promised a possible job—and then they are raped. The officer then shifts to the idea that a woman may withdraw a complaint of domestic violence because, again, she is economically vulnerable and is dependent on her abuser for income. In both cases, the violence is linked to economic vulnerability, which is also the vulnerability that drives someone into risk. Economic vulnerability fosters a climate of interpersonal violence.

While there is no one formula for creating a community that chooses to prioritize gender-based violence, I was able to identify some clear patterns across the communities in this study. After speaking with a number of stakeholders, I looked for a range of possible steps and programs that demonstrated if a community was engaged in anti-gender-based-violence work, including awareness programs, community outreach, school programs, 16 Days of Activism against Gender-Based Violence Campaign programs, protests and memorials to murdered women, and regular community patrols.[1] First, the communities that were the most engaged in fighting gender-based violence had three or more key allies working collaboratively on the issue. The three nodes of collaboration could be a faith community, a community-based organization (CBO), the police, government services, or antiviolence organizations. But the key seemed to be having three or more allies working on this issue. The organizations could be working on gender-based violence in isolation or as one of several issues they saw as co-occurring, including poverty, inequality, and community development. Second, one of those three partners needed to be the police—either the victim services office, the station as a whole, or the community police forums. Community organizations could foster and pressure involvement from the police, but those communities with a sustained level of engagement had the involvement of the police. If mobilized properly and with buy-in from leaders in individual stations and units, the police became a key resource for change. This is a chilling finding given the history of inaction and ineffectiveness of the police nationally on the issue of gender-based violence. Third, the strength of the community also matters. In smaller, more established townships, people know the community members involved in crime and can make the decision to drive them out or block the crime from entering their area. In these communities, service providers talked about a much higher level of community policing in their areas, as well as a more collaborative relationship with the police. Even in large townships, people know one another in their particular sector, and this community strength can limit occurrences of violence. In each of the cases below, police, community leaders, and religious organizations focused on building community networks and supporting individual leaders. What was often missing were the resources from the national government to support their efforts.

Knowing Your Neighbors: The Case of Roedorp

Roedorp is a small township with a primarily coloured population that was artificially constructed during apartheid as part of the Group Areas Act removal and relocation process. Over just a few decades, a close bond formed between community members, as they were essentially expelled from the larger society and left to survive on their own. There was a sense of "knowing your neighbors," keeping an eye on young people, and participating in community events. One community leader of a local CBO, a woman who had spent her adulthood in the township, described this closeness: "You know, the community is like one big family. Everybody knows everybody . . . [laughter]. Everybody knows everybody. I think [Roedorp] is not so big. That is why you know what is going on." Her sentiment was articulated over and over throughout the community by religious leaders, local government officials, officers, social workers, and medical professionals. People were able to connect to one another through their neighborhoods and organizations. Everyone I spoke with in Roedorp also talked about how they had survived a history of gangs and violence.

This sense of community had not always existed. For the first few decades after the township's creation, very high levels of crime dominated, much of

CHAPTER TWO

fig. 2.1 | **ROEDORP**

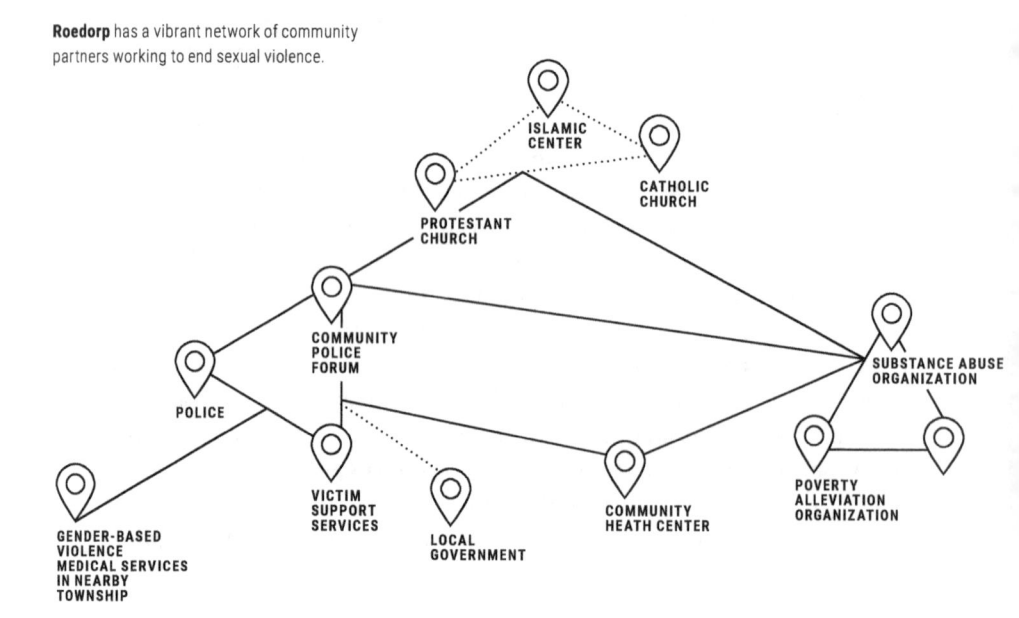

Roedorp has a vibrant network of community partners working to end sexual violence.

- ISLAMIC CENTER
- CATHOLIC CHURCH
- PROTESTANT CHURCH
- COMMUNITY POLICE FORUM
- POLICE
- VICTIM SUPPORT SERVICES
- LOCAL GOVERNMENT
- COMMUNITY HEATH CENTER
- SUBSTANCE ABUSE ORGANIZATION
- POVERTY ALLEVIATION ORGANIZATION
- GENDER-BASED VIOLENCE MEDICAL SERVICES IN NEARBY TOWNSHIP

it violent crime. Now the crime has abated significantly. Current concerns revolve around the growing influence of street drugs like nyaope that threaten to disrupt the social fabric and community ties.

One elected local official described the changes in his community and in the police services since the end of apartheid:

> I think Roedorp has grown as a community in the sense that we have matured. The things that were important then are not as important now. There are better opportunities to make legal money. In the old days, we were in Roedorp. We were left to fend for ourselves here. People in Difate [a nearby black township] experience the same thing. What happened in here was not their [the South African government's] problem. Violence was rife. It didn't matter to the SAP [the South African Police Services (SAPS)], because it affected a small community. If it was in Difate, where men were beating their wives, it didn't matter. But now the ballgame has changed. The government has to be active. They have to play a role in every community. That is why it was difficult for our police to be able to police such crimes. Their experience is what they have learnt over the last . . . twenty years,

over the last forty years. The only crime that you were not to do [during apartheid] was just not to be white. So it wasn't difficult to police. Now it is difficult. Because you can't accuse me of a crime because of my color.

This story is important because it encapsulates the challenges of police transformation and the role of the state after apartheid. During apartheid, the police were used for internal state security and for violently enforcing racial segregation. Now the police are supposed to protect the people—all people—regardless of race and gender. For decades under apartheid, gender-based violence, crime, and interpersonal violence were ignored. The only crimes that really mattered to the police were the crimes that threatened the state or that threatened the economic and political power of the white population.

The Roedorp community has struck back by making crimes public, and service providers felt that this visibility was serving as a deterrent to gender-based violence. Members of the Roedorp community have adopted intentional strategies of breaking the silence around crimes. People told me about how they now wear T-shirts at the funerals of women who have been murdered by intimate partners or during the course of sexual assaults. The T-shirts are emblazoned with a picture of the victim of gender-based violence. The funerals are attended by hundreds of people and visible to people driving by the area. Belinda Leach (2011) discusses a similar memorialization of murdered women in Canada, where communities and anti-gender-based-violence activists erect memorials to women as an act of breaking silence around these deaths and challenging state inaction, including poor funding of antiviolence work.

The community is also very tight-knit. One leader of a local CBO talked about how much of the crime in the area was decreasing, except for crime associated with drug use. She attributed this decrease in the crime rates both to the close-knit community and to the increase in police presence and the community police forums. When I asked her about rape and sexual assault, she explained how isolated the cases are. Even in those cases, they usually know everyone involved. She talked specifically about a case involving youth she had known for years, and she stated that it was drugs driving even that crime: "And even the girl that he killed, the mother was so disappointed, because they were neighbors. And the mother said, 'I am not cross with you. I am just disappointed because we don't know you like that. I just want to know why and who helped you. Because you didn't grow up that way, because of those drugs.'" She again underscored that crime within the community is akin to crime within a larger extended family—a community where people know each other.

CHAPTER TWO

The sense of closeness was also attributed to the size and space of the township. One of the interesting things about Roedorp is that it is "walkable." I heard this idea several times from police, community police forums, neighborhood patrols, service workers, and home care workers. Most people do not have cars, including the police. People can walk from one side of the township to the other in a matter of hours. Caregivers are on the street every day going to people's homes for check-ups, food parcel deliveries, terminal illness care, or shut-in visitation. The nightly patrols by community police are often on foot, and they can access the area quickly and easily. As one person told me, when the patrols are seen, criminals "go the other way."

Part of the sense of community found in Roedorp is due to the apartheid policy of separation, which created this township. As one member of Roedorp stated, "Apartheid is the only reason it is here." Families were broken up in the area, with some sent to Indian areas, some to black townships, and some to coloured townships like Roedorp. The racial segregation of apartheid ensconced this group of otherwise unconnected people onto a small portion of land. These new communities were isolated and left to fend for themselves, often without access to legitimate employment. Now, after surviving apartheid and creating a tightly woven community, Roedorp residents had positioned themselves to fight crime through the strength of their community. Over time, they had been able to create a community and were now able to use that sense of community to address crime.

This sentiment of apartheid's isolation having the unintended consequence of strengthening communities was echoed in other research sites. While working on the role of religious organizations in the efforts to address gender-based violence, I traveled to one community that was primarily Muslim and of Indian descent. A man who was a religious leader in this community voiced very similar sentiments to those heard in Roedorp:

> If we look at traditionally our society, due to apartheid, we have congregated in one place. It becomes a very closed society. This is changing now that other areas, previously white areas, are open to other people. What goes on in a flat somewhere, nobody knows. But what happens in our society very quickly becomes public knowledge—that, look, this girl is getting abused, or this man is being abused.... You know if an abused woman has to go to her parents' house, she has got a blue eye, somebody is going to see what happened here.... We meet often with extended family. So the news gets around, especially in the ladies' circles, you know.... Eventually, by evening, it will come to you. In the evening, your wife will report that "look, this is what is happening." That type of network is very strong. The type of social network, familial ties, is very strong.

These communities were violently affected by the Group Areas Act, the apartheid policy of grouping ethnic groups into separate living areas. Now they have formed close-knit networks of support. This social cohesion may be a particularly helpful tool in fighting domestic violence: while one instinct is to consider family violence a private matter, in these communities, violence is very much a public matter.

Building Community in Fluctuating Spaces: The Case of Huisdorp

Huisdorp is a major South African city, and I focused on one part of the city that included the central business district and surrounding areas. It is primarily a daytime community filled with people commuting from three different provinces and spilling into the city during the workday. The mix of people includes all ethnic groups in addition to immigrant populations from across Africa. The residents who live in or near the central business district are often impoverished and living in overcrowded urban housing situations, with very little chance of physical security.

During and just after apartheid, most city centers were inaccessible for black South Africans, except for those with government-sanctioned work passes. Twenty years ago, a common complaint I heard was that the victim support services were located in these areas near the city center. These spaces were logistically challenging because most survivors could not access them due to distance, travel costs, time constraints, or apartheid restrictions on their movement. Even when NGOs had services that were open to everyone, many of the women I spoke with twenty years ago did not feel safe or comfortable entering those spaces in town.

One social worker, a white South African woman who was living in Huisdorp, talked about those times during apartheid and the transition that has taken place in Huisdorp since the early 1990s, just as South Africa was beginning its democratic transformation. She described the vision for her organization and the racial segregation that was in place at that time: "We only had white women because the city wasn't open yet. . . . Oooh! And those white women were complex. Yoooo! Their problems were complex. They suffered depression. One woman, one night we found her. She was trying to hang herself from this tree, and we found her in time. And others were raped, and I had to sit with them." In contrast to earlier times, South African whites for the most part have relocated en masse to suburbs and gated communities. The urban core is dominated by seemingly endless, fluctuating populations of workers and business owners who commute long distances to work each

CHAPTER TWO

fig. 2.2 | **HUISDORP**

Huisdorp is the center of a major city, with strong networks and key organizations.

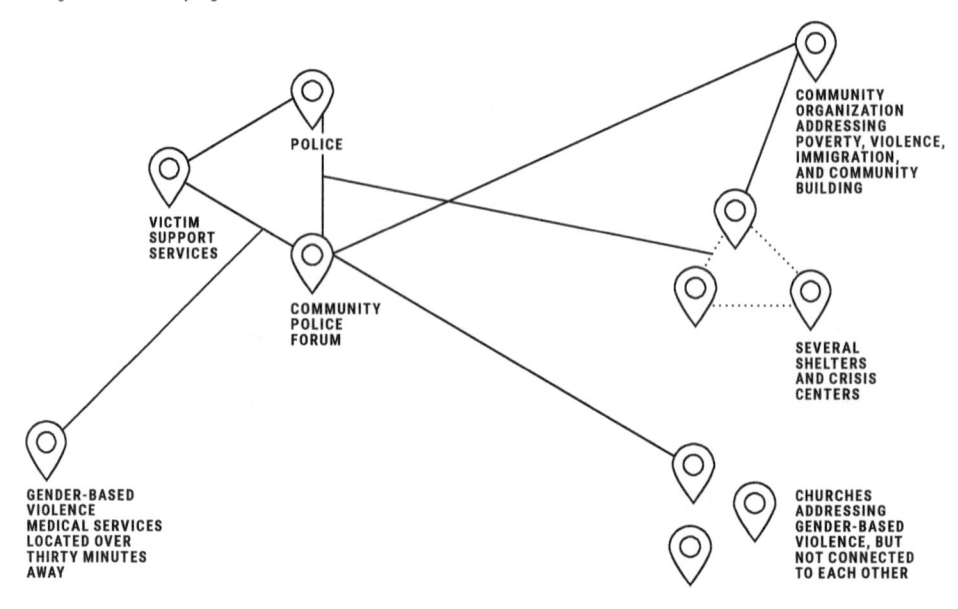

POLICE

COMMUNITY ORGANIZATION ADDRESSING POVERTY, VIOLENCE, IMMIGRATION, AND COMMUNITY BUILDING

VICTIM SUPPORT SERVICES

COMMUNITY POLICE FORUM

SEVERAL SHELTERS AND CRISIS CENTERS

GENDER-BASED VIOLENCE MEDICAL SERVICES LOCATED OVER THIRTY MINUTES AWAY

CHURCHES ADDRESSING GENDER-BASED VIOLENCE, BUT NOT CONNECTED TO EACH OTHER

day. Those who do live in the city are filling up giant tracts of apartments that are often poorly managed or unsafe. Condemned buildings are quickly populated by communities of migrants and squatters, a situation that the government rarely addresses with improvements or alternative housing. Well-publicized, regular standoffs have occurred in the last decade between apartment dwellers and the government in many urban centers. Some NGOs have adapted their services to the changing demographics of the city and its populations, some have not, and some have quietly tiptoed farther from the city and closer to the leafy suburbs.

Given the diversity and size of Huisdorp, one would expect insurmountable problems for service providers in this area. By all expectations, this area should have been the most difficult to transform into a cohesive, resilient community. As one white man who was an NGO leader stated, the city center is "a catch basin for the most vulnerable." Yet the community has found tangible, effective ways to challenge violence. Crime is taken seriously, business owners know each other, sustainable community networks are active, and religious groups and NGOs are engaged.

Many of my interview participants in the city identified a particular NGO as the principal change agent responsible for creating a viable community. The leader of this faith-based NGO, a white South African man, believes that part of the organization's success results from living in the community rather than commuting each day from the suburbs: "So it is not physical geographical communities but people communities. And we build communities of care with them.... We cannot just have communities of care when they are dying, when there are issues affecting their lives heavily.... We feel that we should be based in one place, and that is where you build your model of best practice.... You have to live there, because their issues become your issues." He illuminated several key ideas that have shaped this faith-based organization. First, it is focused on "people communities." This means that the homeless are a community, abuse survivors are a community, migrants are a community. Second, the organization also creates communities built on a shared vision of care and social justice. It looks at problems intersectionally: one cannot focus solely on housing when someone is also dying from AIDS, and one cannot focus exclusively on migration when someone is also at risk for physical violence. Finally, and perhaps most interestingly, the staff and the leadership live where they work, in the hostels and apartments next to their clients. This is unusual. Leaders of NGOs and service providers often have some slight economic advantage over those they serve. This economic privilege affords them better housing options in safer or more affluent areas, an arrangement that also provides the service workers some mental distance from work crises. Yet the staff and leadership of this faith-based NGO live where they work in a model of what they term "servant leadership": they lead with and for people as their servants and partners. Even the definition of "client" is changed in this model: service providers and clients are partners, neighbors, friends, and allies because they live and work side by side. They share the same struggles in regard to safety, public health, housing, cost of living, gender-based violence, and crime.

The leader of this NGO also stressed the importance and challenges of working with the police, a critical piece in the puzzle of addressing gender-based violence. He indicated that the police are aware and mindful of the organization's role in crime prevention, and they believe that the presence of the NGO is decreasing crime, so they value their partnership. They also know that NGO members have and will call on the media if they see a problem: "I guess they also know we can be annoying.... We can get media guys involved. So I think there is that sense of, 'We are on your side,' but we will give them that flack if they don't come. And they are very mindful. If we give them that call, they come immediately. There are one or two rotten apples." In this NGO's relationships with the police and other NGOs, the key has been to build a reputation as a partner with power—specifically, the power to use the media to mobilize action. The leaders of this NGO have created intentional partnerships with their clients so that they share the same struggles, the same living spaces, and the same community.

Police as Community Builders: The Case of Mabitso

Each of the communities that had prioritized gender-based violence in this study had a commitment from the police to work as a partner. In most places, it was a community organization that led the police to engage in addressing this violence, like in Huisdorp. In other areas, however, it was the police who were building communities. While I discuss the case of the Mabitso police station in depth later, the station deserves mention here as a contrast to the other communities, because Mabitso prioritized addressing gender-based violence through policing efforts. Mabitso is a rural area, almost exclusively black, and with woefully inadequate funding. The station was working actively to cultivate structures and networks to address gender-based violence.

What made this victim support unit so effective was the leadership of the trauma team. The station commander, a woman, had recruited a tough investigator and an experienced counselor to collaborate on every case together. These women had a reputation of being an effective team with a remarkable rapport, and their complementary approaches helped to balance what the survivors needed: a skilled and uncompromising investigator to find justice and a sympathetic counselor to focus on rehabilitation and restitution. Their effectiveness with survivors and their tenacity with the station officers demonstrated that priorities can shift when a station makes a commitment.

While this community network is a much smaller node of collaboration than in more urban or large areas, the strength, openness, and effectiveness of the police organizations (including the trauma team, victim support services, community police forums, and youth forums) were visible and tangible in the community at large. In rural towns of this size, there is often not much interaction with the national government. As a result, the police often serve as the first point of contact for most citizens with their government. When citizens are engaged with the police through programs and police forums, community ties are strengthened.

Police officials can also build community by making gender-based violence a department-wide priority, which then filters into the community. Police commanders set the agenda for their station, and they also set the

fig. 2.3 | **MABITSO**

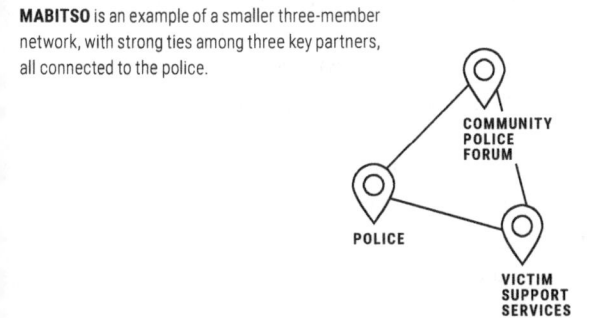

MABITSO is an example of a smaller three-member network, with strong ties among three key partners, all connected to the police.

- COMMUNITY POLICE FORUM
- POLICE
- VICTIM SUPPORT SERVICES

tone for whether or not their officers take rape cases seriously and whether or not their trauma centers are well staffed and managed. When individuals make gender-based violence a priority, they then reprioritize resources to end the violence.

The Challenges of Informal Sectors: The Case of Bokang

As an informal settlement, Bokang had its own long list of place-based challenges: fluid population, mix of domestic and international migrants, xenophobic violence and xenophobic rape, poverty and overcrowding, and lack of support structures and governance structures. While some informal sectors have established some permanent community structures or governance systems, Bokang had not. The housing and living structures in Bokang were typical of informal settlements across South Africa, and this has a direct impact on security and safety, especially for women. Feminist geographer Paula Meth (2016) describes the "hyper-permeability" of informal homes made of plastic, tin, and other substandard materials, which leave residents vulnerable to criminals entering their homes with very little effort and, in turn, leave women seemingly unprotected from perpetrators of gender-based violence. Meth also describes how "informal settlements are often criminalized spaces, and their residents often criminalized by association" (407). In South Africa, the association of criminalization and informal settlements was cultivated by the apartheid government, which deemed that these settlements were illegal and that the residents were not allowed to be in these areas without government passes to sanction their employment. Their makeshift houses were bulldozed, and the residents were relocated to rural areas.

CHAPTER TWO

Fiona Ross discusses how women were strategic in "patiently and courageously (re)settling the outskirts of the city or navigating state ideologies of the family" (2015, S99) as part of their efforts to disrupt the state-imposed division of their families between areas of urban (male) employment and rural (female) unemployment (see also F. Ross 2010). The apartheid state also criminalized these women's migration and housing in informal settlements outside of major urban settlements. Today, these informal settlements are still associated with criminality because the residents are believed to be illegal migrants from other countries or are associated with crime and violence. Throughout South Africa, the democratically elected government has intermittently continued the practice of clearing the settlements and deporting or relocating the residents.

In the informal settlement of Bokang, there were two main organizations working to address gender-based violence: one counseling center and one police station. Both appeared to be tireless and passionate in their work, but I did not find the same level of networks and structures across the informal area that I did in other communities. The Bokang police station was widely respected and known in the community for taking an active stand against gender-based violence and crime in general. Just as I found in the Mabitso police station, the station commander was a woman—still a rare accomplishment. Having a woman as a station commander is not in and of itself enough to change a station (Johnston and Houston 2018; Dick and Jankowicz 2001). However, when commanders make decisions that gender-based violence is a priority, many other things fall into place.

The best measure of a station's commitment to ending gender-based violence comes perhaps not from the statistics on arrests or prosecutions but rather from the community itself. The community knows if officers are taking a stand, actively working to change norms and practices, and choosing to end silence around gender-based violence. One of the strongest endorsements of the Bokang station came from the counseling center in the area. A long-time service provider in the community, a white South African woman who identified as a therapist and a counselor, talked about the concrete steps the station had taken on gender-based violence: "We work very closely with the police services. And we have excellent police services here in [Bokang]. Really committed people, devoted to making a difference. . . . They drag people here—abusers, as well as the victims of the abuse. So they work very hard with us to try and change the whole domestic violence story." When I asked this service provider what makes a good police station, given that the police are almost universally critiqued for their corruption and ineffectiveness, she explained that it came down to "an individual with a heart for what they are doing." In our discussion, she returned time and again to individual officers or individual commitment and passion. These are vital qualities, but they are also very hard to implement. Given the systemic problems of the police in the gender-based violence sector, it is difficult to imagine how to devise training programs that bolster commitment and passion.

One particular place-specific challenge is how to police informal settlements, specifically, how to get into the areas and ensure adequate response time and security. The Bokang station was responsible for an informal settlement, and the officers struggled with the sheer scope of the area, the problems of physically accessing the sector, and the types of issues they saw that were particular to the place and space. As Meth (2017) explains, informal settlements have a particular geography that is marked by pockets of dense overpopulation, a lack of roads and lighting, and a disorganization of the housing sites within the settlement. These real constraints of space and place are nonetheless compounded by a lack of trust in the police because of the memories of police violence during apartheid, as well as contemporary patterns of policy corruption and inaction (Meth 2017). I was able to conduct several individual interviews, as well as one group interview, with the police in the Bokang station, all of whom were black South Africans. In terms of access and reaching the entire area, police struggled to find entry points or patterns of consistent outreach, as one officer explained: "It is difficult for our people to police [the informal settlement]. . . . Cars—it is muddy during the rainy season. Cars cannot even move. Meaning that when there is a crime . . . they are suffering. There is [a] way [to get there], but it is going to cause a delay. Now we are talking of reaction time." There is a slow response time in these areas, and implementing outreach programs is equally challenging. This lack of access and slow response time create a situation that the police feel fosters crime.

Several officers also stated that there are particular types of problems caused by the dehumanizing conditions found in the informal settlements. The following quotes come from both individual interviews and a group interview with the police officers in the Bokang station. There are some striking parallel themes that emerged in each of these conversations, themes that link the behavior—even the mentality—of the residents of the informal sector to the living conditions in the sector. In these following instances, the officers seem to indicate that elements of the place itself were the factors that caused the behavior, crimes, and violence.

One Bokang officer, a black South African man, explained, "You cannot get in there—come out like that, you will be like you are coming out from a pigsty. It is sickening." Another officer, a black South African man, stated

CHAPTER TWO

that place contributed to crime and violence: "The climate—it contributes. ... There is no trust in the family.... There is overcrowdedness. It is chaos." Another officer, a black South African man, echoed this concern that the place itself facilitated the violence. When I asked him to speculate about the causes of gender-based violence, he linked it directly to place: "There is a lot that contributes to a situation, which renders people to do wrong things. It gives the opportunity for people not to be monitored and managed properly. The environment. And that thing is left out.... How do the authorities manage people who are just dumped at a place and if the influx into a place is not managed?" His response reveals many attitudes about place, environment, and the causes of violence. He believes that the environment itself is driving the "wrong things." There are too many people in the area, there is no control about who moves into the area, and these things "render people" to commit crimes and violence. While I do not believe he is dismissing the choice and agency of perpetrators of gender-based violence, I do think he is underscoring the impact that the environment itself is one of violence—structural violence created by inequality, mass poverty, and migration out of desperation. He is also revealing that the sheer scope and size of the settlement make it impossible for police to administer and patrol it—that perhaps violence could be diminished through a management infrastructure or adequate police involvement.

Another police officer in the same station went even further into the idea that the place itself was creating long-term social and psychological problems: "It [the informal settlement] is an abnormal society, and once the authorities are leaving societies like that, how do you police insane people? Because it affects the police. People are insane in terms of the environment.... They are saying the police should police that, and that must be addressed.... Domestic violence, it is contributed to by the environment because people have got needs that they cannot come across ... desires in terms of life, but people cannot [live] because of the environment they are in. You see the influences." This was one of the most direct statements by a member of the police that the informal settlement was driving violence and was creating poor mental health conditions. Again, the officer echoes the idea that the conditions in the informal sector have been caused by government failure—a failure of government to provide basic necessities for people and a functioning infrastructure. His description sounds like a wasteland or dystopian world abandoned by the government and left to deteriorate into insanity and violence.

In each of the passages above, there are several themes that continued to emerge in my interviews with officers in this station. There is outrage and indignation about the poverty and deprivation of the informal settlements. There is blame of and anger toward the government for abandoning these people and the infrastructure there. Yet, clearly, there is also a judgment that *the place* has affected the people, changed them, compromised their mental health, and perhaps made them less than human. These judgments and perceptions can only make the relationships between the police and the community even more difficult, as one officer stated: "It is something of the society themselves, the mentality." There are many problems that result from the idea that the people living in the informal settlements are now part of a deviant society with underlying mental problems. This idea creates a dichotomous perception that the police are functional/sane/human and that people living in the informal settlements are deviant/insane/less than human. This perception could also lead some to eventually ignore or normalize the violence that occurs in these spaces.

White Spaces: The Case of Olive Vlei

Place and geography affect service delivery, and often place and race are intertwined. Since the vast majority of the South African population is black, rape is seen as a black problem. Often sexual assault crisis centers, like the Thuthuzela Care Centres (TCCs), are located in black urban townships. More than two decades after the end of apartheid, the vast majority of white South Africans have never ventured near a black township. As such, the chances that these same white South Africans will then choose to go to a township after they have been raped are even less likely. A woman prosecutor who regularly worked on sexual violence cases explained that white survivors of sexual assault are more likely to visit their own doctors or private hospitals in their own neighborhoods instead of the "top of the line" TCCs:

> We still have a division in terms of where people live. So people will go to their private [doctors and hospitals] and also that [pause]—that is very strange because also this is viewed as a black problem and [pause]—but also mostly in South Africa the black people are the majority. So whatever happens, they will be highlighted as the major group, because that is the majority. So you get those misconstitutions [misrepresentations] of facts as a result. But we do see in places like Cape Town, Karl Bremer [Hospital] and Manenberg [Jooste Hospital] are more coloured areas, which you see few white people still coming. But still it will be your poor kind of white people. So there [are] still those differences. But obviously also government will concentrate on the majority.

The prosecutor's discussion again reveals the lasting legacy of apartheid and how that legacy can affect gender-based violence treatment and prosecution. Race and class are mapped onto each other very tightly. In her estimation,

CHAPTER TWO

white survivors will keep the matter private or go to see their own doctors. The government created the TCCs to be the flagship of survivor care and prosecutor-led investigations. However, it is only white survivors of lower socioeconomic classes—the "poor kind of white people"—who would go to the TCCs, specifically because the TCCs are located primarily in black or coloured townships. If the white survivors were more affluent, they would see private doctors or go to private hospitals. In some ways, the placement of the TCCs inside townships is intended to overcome the apartheid-era patterns, when crisis centers were mainly located in white urban areas. Yet that placement may also unintentionally send a message that rape and gender-based assault exist only in the black community.

A white counselor who provided counseling for sexual assault survivors had also seen this racial division in her own clinic, as well as at the gender-based-violence and rape crisis centers in the township. The clinic is located in a black urban township, and she said that many white survivors are afraid to come into the township for services: "I tell them I come here every day, and I want you to face your fears and drive in here. And I can't guarantee that anything is going to [happen]. But I had a father who I could hear that their situation was devastating, and he just refused. And he said, I had the SMS [short message service, or text message] on my phone for a long time where he said, 'I am not bringing my children to [the township] to get killed.'" My conversations with medical providers, police, social service providers, and community leaders all indicated that gender-based violence cannot be separated from the legacies of apartheid. The continued impact of poverty and inequality was deeply marked by racial differences. They also stated that the persistent racism and sexism in communities were normalizing violence.

Even in the Olive Vlei police station, the station commander and police officers were committed to investigating sexual assault and violence; however, they saw very few cases—in their estimation, almost none. They had seen so few cases that they no longer reserved space in the station for a trauma center. In my interviews with members of the station, the officers and the commander demonstrated strong training in crime prevention and investigation and a strong empathy for gender-based-violence cases. They also had strong community partners and a list of community resources available for survivors. Yet survivors simply did not come to the station to report a sexual assault or domestic violence. The officers believed, just as the prosecutor and counselors did, that the survivors in their area were either keeping the assaults private or going to private medical services for treatment and not reporting the crime.

The Geography of Gender-Based Violence

Gender-based violence often cannot be separated from the legacies of apartheid, the continued impact of poverty and segregation, and the sustained racism and sexism that normalize violence. Service providers in this study talked about the significance of place when discussing survivor services, prosecution rates, and the origins of gender-based violence. Place matters perhaps most importantly as a signifier of the segregation that persists after apartheid. Communities continue to be nested in the layers of socioeconomic differences that apartheid imposed and violently sustained.

Gender-based violence has no racial or class boundaries. Yet the responses to it, the resources available to address it, and the strategies to prevent it differ from community to community. Survivors who live in white communities like Olive Vlei and Arbeidstad often choose to see private medical providers rather than better-equipped crisis centers in black townships. They may have the resources to escape an abuser by going to a hotel rather than a shelter. They may be able to miss work for a few days until their bruises heal without fear of losing their jobs. They may also not report an assault because of the stigma and shame in their communities.

Survivors in informal communities like Bokang know there is often no separation of public and private. Their cramped living conditions mean that family, friends, and neighbors often hear or see the abuse. Residents in these communities may not have the resources to get assistance, seek private providers, or miss work. They may fear deportation and endure xenophobic rape because of their nationality. They may have to endure abusive employers in order to feed their family.

Survivors in Arbeidstad may risk rape every day as they walk great distances to their factory jobs. They may then encounter a resource-strapped police station that prioritizes property crimes rather than rape cases with unknown perpetrators. They may face a community police forum more concerned with protecting white neighborhoods and car dealerships than ensuring women's safe movement. Survivors in Roedorp may be bolstered by the decrease in crime but face a different kind of violence, like multiple-perpetrator rape, that accompanies the gang initiations in their neighborhoods.

Understanding how gender-based violence presents itself in communities is critical, as is understanding how place and space are part of the web of structural inequalities. Trying to address gender-based violence as a singular issue has been ineffective in many cases. Service providers advocate for seeing gender-based violence as part of other forms of structural violence. This structural approach requires the commitment of multiple stakeholders and the fostering of resources to assist survivors.

CHAPTER THREE

People

South African legislation presumes that survivors of gender-based violence will seek help through formal state mechanisms. Yet research shows that this is rarely the case (Rasool 2016; Rasool et al. 2002). Many survivors of gender-based violence and sexual assault in South Africa seek assistance through informal mechanisms—including religious organizations, traditional justice systems, and community organizations—because of the costly financial and geographic barriers to formal justice mechanisms. Additionally, some women are worried that the abuser, who may also be the breadwinner of the household, may be arrested if state mechanisms are engaged (Moult 2005). This hesitation to approach state services continues, despite the fact that seeking assistance after abuse often reduces or stops future violence (Rasool 2016). The obstacles survivors face point to a disjuncture between South Africa's legislative solutions and the social realities that affect survivors' access to justice and services.

Nongovernmental actors, like community organizations, have always played essential roles in the anti-gender-based-violence sector (Britton 2006). Increasingly, the South African government relies on them to provide the stopgap for poor service delivery and, in many instances, to fill the void of national leadership on gender-based violence. As I have discussed elsewhere (Britton 2006), civic leaders, leaders of NGOs, leaders of antiviolence programs, and leaders of women's and youth shelters are the key players in the anti-gender-based-violence sector. Much like the staff working in trauma centers, many civic leaders shared a few key characteristics: they are often survivors of some sort of abuse or trauma, and they are often unpaid volunteers working full time in emotionally challenging settings. While many are able to use their backgrounds to give support and compassion to other survivors, they frequently experience secondary trauma in their work. Without sufficient counseling, training, or support, they often relive their own traumas in their daily work. There is also the concern about the sustainability of these leaders to work full time with no regular salary. Given the unemployment rate in South Africa, these volunteer positions still give people a sense of purpose and skills they can use later in the job market. But much of the infrastructure for service delivery both inside and outside the government is built on a house of cards.

Here I examine two unexpected sets of nongovernmental community leaders who are taking an increasingly active role in the struggle to end gender-based violence in South Africa: (1) religious leaders and faith communities and (2) traditional leaders and healers. My decision to focus on these two understudied sectors emerged from my interviews in multiple communities across racial and economic sectors. Community leaders and activists working to end gender-based violence called my attention to the new roles these leaders were assuming.

For the government, there are some benefits for involving these new actors in the gender-based-violence sector. Working through institutions like traditional leaders can result in fast action, little to no financial costs, and fewer linguistic and cultural barriers than are found in the justice system (Wojkowska 2006; Moult 2005). By incorporating new bureaucratic players such as religious and traditional leaders into the implementation process, countries like South Africa may be able to alleviate resource scarcity through nimble bureaucratic structures that rely on community power brokers. As a result, state partnerships with religious leaders, NGOs, and traditional leaders are growing internationally, as well as in South Africa (Bernal and Grewal 2014; Brass 2012; Britton 2006).

There are also real challenges and potential problems when decentralizing services and leadership to the community level. These nongovernmental players create significant gaps in accountability, transparency, decision making, and good governance (Grindle 2004, 2011). More critically, this decentralization may be seen as part of the larger neoliberal strategy in South Africa that pushes implementation responsibility to local levels without supplying communities with the resources they need to ensure their work is effective and equitable.

The reliance on local leaders also points to a persistent dependence between (1) the framework of state feminism and its goal to build strong institutions for feminist change and (2) the need for strong policy advocates and community leaders to supplant the limitations and failures of government implementation. State feminism was a key guiding framework of the South African women's movement at the end of apartheid. These women leaders had been part of the international conferences and networks that called for the creation of government ministries, national departments, gender-based budgeting, and gender mainstreaming, all focused on improving the status and power of women in the country. The massive influx of women into national political office and leadership was celebrated globally as South Africa moved from the bottom of the list of women in national office to nearly the top of the list with the 1994 election. Indeed, South Africa's National Gender Machinery (NGM) was lauded as one of the most visible and effective achievements of the first few generations of women in the post-1994 era in South Africa.

Yet almost as soon as these institutions were created and the national elections took place, gender activists and community leaders started to question political leaders' commitment to change (Gouws 2004, 2008, 2014; Walker 2013; Seidman 1999, 2003). The institutions put in place also began to falter due to a lack of resources, unclear mandates, and overlapping responsibilities. The failures of these gendered institutions point to a disjuncture between symbols of feminist change and the very real violence faced by women in their homes, on their streets, and in their communities (P. Andrews 2007). The social change that is necessary to end gender-based violence is much more difficult than passing legislation. And, as was the case with the South African Criminal Law (Sexual Offences and Related Matters) Amendment Act No. 32 of 2007, even the processes of getting laws passed are laboriously slow.

In some ways, people may matter more than institutions in South Africa. Rather than wait on slow, corrupt, or inefficient government programs, communities have been following local leaders to advance change: religious leaders, traditional leaders, and community activists. Here, a tension arises between the desire to create national institutions of change and the need for communities to end violence now.

Leadership matters in the struggle to end gender-based violence. Leaders of NGOs can take action to address the accelerants of violence in the home and in their communities. Traditional leaders may work with government officials to sanction and punish perpetrators of gender-based violence. Evangelical charismatic churches and conservative Islamic centers can and do address these issues if religious leaders choose to make domestic peace a priority.

However, the examples in this chapter are the exceptions that prove the rule. As discussions with the leaders below indicate, most religious and customary frameworks continue to perpetuate regressive gender ideologies that lead to the subordination of women. Shanhana Rasool Bassadien and Tessa Hochfeld note that it is this "robust social discourse on domestic violence ... that is strongly patriarchal and potentially harmful to women because it deters survivors' help-seeking" (2005, 5). Finding ways to interrupt those gender scripts may be the essential key for altering patterns of gender-based violence.

Faith Traditions Addressing Gender-Based Violence

A significant force in almost every community I studied was the role of religious leaders and religious institutions in the lives of community members. I admit that I had initial concerns about approaching religious institutions on this issue. These concerns were rooted in stereotypes of many religious groups as promoting regressive ideas about gender roles and women's status. While I understood the pivotal role religious organizations played in the struggle against apartheid, I had concerns about how few groups had challenged gender subordination since that time or, frankly, ever. Yet as my work in communities progressed, I found myself listening more carefully to my participants and to the community leaders I was interviewing. Each one pointed to religious groups and/or traditional leaders who were challenging gender-based violence and gender oppression in their communities.

Their assertions are supported by the scholarship in this area. Research in South Africa shows that the role of religious leaders and organizations in addressing gender-based violence cannot be underestimated. As Kelley Moult's (2005) research in South Africa demonstrated, survivors often visit informal, nonstate actors for assistance with domestic violence and sexual assault in advance of or instead of contacting the police or state agencies. Also working in the South African context, Shahana Rasool and colleagues (2002) found that 20 percent of the women in their study went to religious leaders following abuse. To leave religious leaders out of the discussion of preventing gender-based violence and protecting its survivors would be a critical error.

While religious organizations have been part of health care systems and care work globally, they are often not at the forefront of gender empowerment programs (Karam 2014). Religious leaders have a unique, powerful, and understudied role in promoting lifestyle changes in both Christian and Islamic communities (Toh and Tan 1997; Anshel and Smith 2014; Cohen-Dar and Obeid 2017). Research has shown that some involvement with faith communities may help prevent gender-based violence through the promotion of healthier lives, both economically and physically (Gover 2004). But as the religious leaders I worked with indicated, not all faith-based efforts challenge violence. Some religious frameworks in fact dismiss or legitimize domestic violence and marital rape in favor of marital fidelity and obedience (Hermkens 2008). Thus, as Gracia Violeta Ross (2012), a Bolivian anti-AIDS and anti-gender-based-violence advocate, has stated, "Sexual violence needs prayers, but much more than prayers."

In my conversations with both Christian and Islamic community leaders, they talked about how the transformation of gender roles politically in South Africa created opportunities for women's organizations and women leaders to move into the forefront and address gender-based violence. The religious leaders also offered personal reasons to frame why they had chosen to become change agents addressing gender-based violence. Many of them had been raised in abusive households but had later witnessed positive models of family life. Others had had some transformative experience that shifted their attitudes and practices. Finally, the religious leaders described the various ideologies and frameworks they used to address gender-based violence within the confines of the scripted gender roles in their faith traditions. Often these ideologies and programs focused on separate spheres for men or women or called on men to undergo a moral regeneration. This is a risky strategy. While many of these activities could lead to a reduction in physical violence in the short run, the long-term implications of such ideologies often reinforce women's subordination and become the precursor to gender-based violence.

Political Opportunities

The end of apartheid brought about a celebrated transformation of the public sphere, most visibly along ethnic and gender lines. The transformation of the South African political landscape through constitutional protections for women and through the electoral success of women in the national parliament had ripple effects throughout the rest of society. In discussions with counselors, religious leaders, and social workers in Muslim women's organizations, I heard about the direct impact of this gender transformation in their own communities. They talked most specifically about a "mushrooming" of Muslim women's organizations since the end of apartheid, many of which had survived for well over a decade. I spoke at length with a leader of a Muslim women's organization in a major city. She had advanced educational degrees, and she considered herself a member of both the coloured and Indian apartheid racial categories. She told me about the expansion of Muslim women's groups:

About ten years ago, twelve years ago, a lot of women's groups by then ... a lot of organizations sprung up within the Muslim community doing various things, from poverty reduction to humanitarian courses to lots of other stuff in terms of financial help for destitute families, things like that, all of them from a faith-based perspective. But at the same time, and it was part of the transition and this awakening and this freedom and all that sort of stuff. All that played into a lot of Muslim women's organizations mushrooming up. Because we know that gender has been a big thing in the South African constitution and moving forward. So a lot of organizations started their own little women's sections, but a lot of women's organizations felt that they needed to come out and have their own sort of organizations, whether it is also poverty reduction or helping children or helping orphanages or stuff like that. But I think that political climate assisted in that and gave us the impetus for something like that. [Author's question: Did you see a mushrooming and then a filtering away?] No, no, no, no. I think all the mushrooms have grown and grown and grown!

The impact of democracy and the freedom of association created spaces for new groups to organize. The power of women's advancement in the public sphere also inspired the creation of women-centered organizations in her Muslim community, creating an almost contagious effect for the development of women's groups to fill these new spaces.

Given the proliferation of Muslim women's organizations, I assumed there must be some significant international funding supporting their programs. This was not the case. The same leader explained to me that most of their funding came from the provincial government or local donors. International funding in fact was decreasing: "I think part of the problem is part of the Islamophobia around the world. I think our names marginalize us to some extent. . . . But having said that, I don't want to be apologetic about that. . . . Muslim women didn't have an outlet. And it is proven that is what it has done, and that objective we have achieved." By tying the organizations directly to the Muslim community, her organization was reaching women who otherwise would not have sought or received assistance. Yet this community-specific mission limited their funding because of the growing anti-Muslim sentiment internationally.

A black South African Christian pastor who was a change agent in his community of Difate also noted that the national political transformation had had a positive effect on women's organizing and leadership to the point of what he described as "an army of women" marching forward to address key issues like gender-based violence: "I feel that women are taking their

CHAPTER THREE

places, their rightful places. . . . We need to talk about it. . . . I feel that men are talking against it now, and women are rising up. There is some sort of an army of women coming up, and I feel that we are moving into a positive direction." The national political transformation created spaces at the local level, and women were using these spaces to address gender-based violence and fill gaps in services and support.

These same political opportunities also created spaces for previously marginalized ethnic and racial groups, and many groups found themselves working productively at the intersection of race and gender. The same leader of the Muslim women's organization stated the importance of this intersectional space for the "in-betweeners": "I think working with government structures also gave us the possibilities of funding but also created the reality . . . of this rainbow nation. It is not only black. It is not only white. There are in-betweeners, minority groups like us. Unfortunately, prior to 1994—this is [the] way we Muslims feel or Indians feel or coloureds feel—we were not white enough. Right now, if you look at employment equity and all those things, then we are not black enough." Government collaboration ensured that the clients of her organization were realizing the full potential of citizenship embodied in the spirit of the new constitution—the rainbow nation. Given the in-betweener status she describes, she links this new postapartheid access to government financial and in-kind support to a sense of belonging in the new rainbow nation.

This was one of the clearest illustrations I encountered of how mutually beneficial state-society and state-NGO collaboration can be not just in terms of services but also in terms of actualizing constitutional rights and full citizenship. She talked about her ability to work with other government agencies, shelters, and programs to create Muslim-friendly services. Prior to that, her organization had difficulty finding safe housing for Muslim women, even for just one night. She collaborated with shelter staff to make modest accommodations for their clients, such as ensuring that food is either halal or vegetarian or that staff can take food to the women and children. She also worked so that shelter staff could create or find private places for clients to pray: "And the requirements are not so different or so specific that we need to be different. It is just that there are religious or cultural rituals . . . or Ramadan and the fasting. . . . I think in that way networking helped a lot." These accommodations that she facilitated through collaborations and networking had been deeply beneficial for her clients.

Yet this leader described a very different relationship between her organization and local government. She felt that there was a broad misunderstanding of her community by the local police and the local government. The local officials did not use an intersectional framework to understand how religion and gender can work to obscure violence or to normalize gender subordination. She argued that the local metropolitan police in her area often lack an understanding of violence in her Muslim community; specifically, they do not think it is a problem. She also thinks that the police are facing higher levels of gender-based violence in other racial communities, so her community is a lower priority for them: "Our stats will tell you [that] over the last twenty years the problem has grown. . . . If you look at [it] across the board, the diversity of cultures and religious groups they deal with, [we are] probably somewhere in the lower ranges [of] the incidences of gender violence in Muslim homes. So I think they don't see the need." What is interesting about this failure to connect with local government, particularly police services, is that the organization is providing an invaluable service to an overlooked community. The police, in her opinion, have other, more pressing issues, and they rely on her organization to deal with abuse and gender-based violence in her community. This is a missed window of opportunity for police, especially as her organization continues to grow in terms of the different types of populations she serves. She estimated that 10–15 percent of her clients are refugees and migrants, many from North Africa. While 85 percent of the organization's clients are Muslim, staff members also occasionally see Christians, Hindus, and other groups. These are broad constituencies that could benefit from closer collaboration with the police services.

Becoming Issue Leaders

Given that many religious institutions often have highly regressive gender attitudes (see the following section on moral regeneration), religious leaders who choose to address gender-based violence are the exception to the norm. One such change agent was the pastor of a small, predominantly black evangelical Christian church located in a major city. The church attracted middle- and working-class members from across the city center, as well as from the suburbs and neighboring townships. The pastor was from a neighboring African country. A member of the congregation invited me to attend part of a series of worship services the pastor was conducting on family violence and domestic disputes. For several weeks during the lengthy Sunday services, members of the congregation anonymously submitted questions about family issues to the pastor and a physician who was another member of the congregation. They both addressed these questions from the pulpit for several hours. The questions were remarkably forthright, honest, and intimate: How many nights a week should a couple be having sexual relations? Is a wife allowed to refuse her husband sexually? What is an appropriate spacing between children? It was unlike anything I had ever seen in a South African church previously. While many of the questions and the answers reinforced notions of normative gender roles (such as the husband protector), the pastor and physician unequivocally called for the end of all forms of violence in relationships, demanded an end to rape within a marriage, and insisted that spouses respect their partners and their partners' right to refuse sexual relations. *Power over* one another was replaced by *power with* one another with an emphasis on communication and respect.

The pastor agreed to do an interview with me later in the month. In our interview, he explained why he felt compelled to hold these question-and-answer sessions in his worship service for several weeks at a time. He often had church members tell him about marital rape and domestic abuse, and it was these repeated interactions that inspired him to create these forums to address questions from his community directly, publicly, and openly. The question-and-answer session took place during the weekly worship service in order to have as many people present as possible, to signify the importance of the topic, and to be as transparent as possible.

He understood that his role was important in the community because of the respect his position garnered: "For us in Africa, the pastor is everything. . . . When somebody is sick, he is going to call the pastor first. The pastor is the gynecologist. When somebody is in labor, they will call the pastor first. So somebody has a case, you become the lawyer. When somebody is building a house, you become the architect." This was a guiding philosophy for every aspect of his pastoral role. It did not stop on Sunday. The pastor said that he regularly invited people to stay in his home and learn from his family. He talked about a time they hosted another couple in his house. The pastor's wife accidentally caused a cooking fire in the kitchen, and the pastor responded kindly to his wife and reassured her that they would find the money to repair the damage. The visiting wife ran upstairs to get her husband. She brought her husband down and asked the pastor to repeat what he had said so calmly to his wife. Then she told the pastor: "Sir, I just want to talk. Because if it was my husband, he is going to beat me—see the marks on my body." The pastor went on to say that he believes he has to set the model for others: "They can learn from me, see what we do, although the perfect example is Christ."

The pastor then told me about how his own life was transformed while he was living with another pastor. He had grown up in a violent family, but at a formative stage he went to live with a pastor so that he could learn about religious life. In this new home, he saw that there were other ways to resolve conflict. It was through these personal experiences of violence in his own family and then subsequently seeing a different way of living that he became a change agent for his congregations. While he is resolute in his opposition to family violence, he explained to me that his efforts to end domestic violence have not always been warmly received: "They say, 'You are not an African.' But I have always told them you don't treat women that way." He pushes against the rhetoric that domestic violence is part of African tradition. He believes instead that violence is learned, and he disputes any justification that violence is cultural or is inherently African. He sees that his role as a pastor is to disrupt those patterns and demonstrate that people should live in the peaceful ways of Jesus.

Moral Regeneration

While the pastor's story above is transformative, many religious communities in contrast promote regressive gender roles that normalize women's suppression and domestic violence (Bassadien and Hochfeld 2005). Gracia Violeta Ross (2012) argues that most religious organizations are male dominated, and since most of those men were raised "in the teachings of a dominating gender system, which hardly recognises the voices and rights of women," the religious response often lacks a call for structural change. These organizations and beliefs, especially when held in the extreme, often harm women and abuse survivors through religious proscriptions of marriage and fidelity, even in the face of domestic violence (Lehrer, Lehrer, and Krauss 2009).

During my work in South African communities, I found that many religious organizations walked a difficult tightrope when discussing gender-based violence and gender roles. The religious leaders and social workers I interviewed in both Christian and Muslim organizations embraced a strong anti-gender-based-violence stance within their communities. However, many of them also invoked concepts of moral regeneration that instruct members to follow religious doctrine strictly and more intentionally. The discussions I had followed this basic script: if people led lives more in line with the Bible or the Koran, then interpersonal violence would decrease. By living more faithful lives, people would recognize that violence and abuse of any kind meant they were living outside their faith. Turning their lives toward faith and devotion would bring peaceful, conflict-free families and charitable living.

There is nuance here that becomes powerfully important, specifically in how gender roles are defined and whether they advance or suppress women. During my interviews, leaders in both religious traditions believed in separate roles for men and women, but they did challenge the idea of men's superiority over women. As feminists know, this is a precarious balancing act with potentially violent outcomes. On the one hand, the religious traditions maintain that even though men and women are different, they are both valuable and honored. If something is valued and honored, it should not be suppressed or abused; thus, gender-based violence theoretically should decrease. Yet as history demonstrates, when groups are accorded different roles and separate spaces, this is often the first step toward domination in terms of both women's suppression and racial segregation and oppression. This position becomes even more tenuous when these differences are believed to be spiritually determined. When these religious ideas of separate spheres are nested within a society with preexisting inequalities, they are just as likely to be used to justify domination as they are to challenge the status quo. Given South Africa's current state of hyperpatriarchy, as Raymond Suttner (2015b) argues, it has been easy to use the idea of gender difference to legitimize the suppression of women. This is true even within the women's branch of the ruling African National Congress, the ANC Women's League (ANCWL) (Gouws 2016). The ANCWL has long embraced regressive gender roles and essentialized women's position as maternal caregivers within nationalist frameworks, their value lying in their role as mothers of the nation (Gouws 2016). Gender advocates are leaving parliament because it does not have a place for feminist voices or dissent from the party line (Hassim 2014).

The religious leaders I interviewed were aware of these "misinterpretations" of religious teachings, as they described them. Many spoke in quite specific terms about how working within their faith traditions and following what they saw as the authentic teachings of their faith could dispel such misinterpretations and lead to less gender-based violence. One black South African pastor I spent extensive time with (through multiple interviews and regular attendance in his Sunday services in an urban township) told me about community-wide interfaith moral regeneration programs used to address gender-based violence. Moral regeneration programs can go in several directions. While unequivocally opposing gender-based violence, the rhetoric of moral regeneration is often used to reinscribe normative gender roles of male superiority, which can then lead to the vicious cycle of ideas about the subordination of women and the notion of women as property.

This pastor took a slightly different approach to the moral regeneration programs, specifically working outside of a religious framework: "These were the pillars: integrity, respect of diversity, obedience of the law, service, excellence, public approval. Morality cuts across all the boards." He continued with an example: "If a man is going to rape his own child, I don't think a Muslim is going to approve it. The traditional leaders won't approve it, I hope. The youth won't approve it. The church won't approve it, whether it is Methodist or charismatic. So the issue of morals—we felt that they cut across the book." The pastor discussed how the global movement Men for Change also held meetings locally to challenge regressive forms of masculinity and to oppose gender-based violence.[1] The organization, in his estimation, does not "push Christianity" but instead talks about abuse, anger management, and problem resolution. I was struck by how he used his position and religious community in support of these programs and initiatives that were successful, in his mind, because they were *not* religious. When I asked him about this, he stated: "Once people start seeing it as a church, they move away from it. So we try to make it issues based more than anything." Again, the framework and even perhaps the genre of messaging—in the style of preaching—came from his religious background. But he decoupled the message from any particular religion because of the pushback he had seen.

While not using the term "moral regeneration," which has particular Christian connotations, members of another Muslim women's organization explained that their approach was to use Islam and the teachings of the Koran to prevent and address gender-based violence. I met with members of this organization at their spiritual and community center, based in an urban township composed mainly of Muslim Indian, Muslim coloured, and coloured populations, all of which had been artificially grouped together under apartheid. I had a group interview with members of this organization, including two women counselors and one theologian, a man, who all lived in this community. They all said that their organization gave survivors the choice to contact the police, stressing that this decision was up to the survivor. They also believed that religious counseling often could interrupt the violence perhaps faster and more effectively. The theologian emphasized the difference between Islam and other religions and that when he reminded people of the teaching of the Koran, they had to take responsibility for their actions. There was, in his viewpoint, "no shortcut out of this":

> Abuse, in fact, not only abuse but any sort of dishonoring of a human being, is frowned upon in Islam. And so in Islam, because we still [are one of] the few religions who have retained [the] concept of sin, . . . we don't believe that anybody has been redeemed for our sake. We are personally responsible for what we do. Look, there is no shortcut out of this. So if I am going to do this, I am going to have consequences on the day of judgment. There is hell. There is real hell. There will be punishment for me when I leave this world in the grave and in the hereafter. And that conviction is there in all Muslims.

Here, the teachings stress the responsibility of every Muslim to honor the other. While Christianity believes in a Christ of redemption, this theologian stressed the personal responsibility and the threat of a real hell.

In contrast, he said there is the positive life that anyone can lead, where there is "the prophetic model for a good home. The prophetic model of a good society. The importance of women in that society. And these are the kind of cues and leads that we use, that, 'Look you don't have to live a tortured life. You can live a good life in this world, and you can enjoy a life of peace and tranquility if you mend your ways.'" This tranquility and this peace come from adopting and respecting very specific gender roles. The noise and, by extension, violence come in a relationship when people are living outside these scripted roles.

The members of this group interview believed that following Islam more closely could limit domestic abuse, both physical and psychological. These religious practices included regularly attending prayer services, serving others through community work, and engaging in global humanitarian projects in order to "move them to a point of [a] higher sense of consciousness" and rechannel their energy. They believed in the power of Islam and its emphasis on individual responsibility and accountability, the threat of a real hell, and the promise of a different life on earth through purposeful, generous living.

Much as they do in the case of Christianity, in Islam the call for moral regeneration and a return to specific gender roles still enshrine a position of men and women in separate spheres. During the group interview, some of the counselors indicated the complexity of the layers of ideas about gender roles. Some believed that women's place was separate from the male head of household, as a woman counselor stated, "No house can run with two males." The theologian then explained what he saw as more nuance in that relationship: "But really, they [wives] rule the house from behind, you know. They control the finances. They control everything." The theologian said that in his experience, much of the family abuse and male domination come from people who are following the example of their own abusive parents and not the authentic teachings of Islam.

A leader of a different Muslim women's organization in a major city articulated how different religious frameworks influence understandings of feminism and women's rights:

> Christian feminism, if you look at something like that—"We need to be equal to men," and so, "We need to be working equally with them." And I think that the difference here is God has made me a Muslim woman, and I need to be my own person, and I don't need to be equal to anybody.

And I think that alone was an impetus for us being a woman's organization. I think maybe, maybe it is like if you are working, if you are a pastor in a congregation or head of congregation where you are ministering to them, you are on par with me. Whereas here, that is not the issue for me. I am just thinking aloud now. Maybe one of the reasons why is the thing that one is equal with men. And we are saying, we are looking at it a bit differently. I don't know, I am just . . . For us working separately in a safe female environment—I am sure you know about the intermingling of the sexes and all that? And for us, this is a safe environment to work in. We don't have any men coming. If we have women in full [niqab], they don't have to be, because there are no men coming in. So it is very convenient for us to work that way. But there are added advantages to that, as I have said, because we have created our own space.

For her, the space she has created is not about a certain form of feminism that seeks equality with men. Rather, she has created a separate space where she and the women in her office have no equal. After volunteering for years in other women's organizations, she realized there were women who were not seeking help because those organizations were outside Islam. She created this Muslim women's organization through two decades of careful collaboration with the male leadership in her faith. She gained their backing—which was important for community acceptance—and recruited volunteers. Her organization now counsels 150–170 individuals or families a month, and about 40 percent of those are family violence cases. Her organization deals with family abuse, poverty reduction, hunger, jobs training, outreach, self-esteem, anger management, healthy lifestyles, and education. The organization has also taken on the role of educating theologians and imams. Her organization has also assisted victims of domestic abuse not just to be counselors but also to become advocates, "a model, a support, as well as a defense" when a woman needs to go before a religious body to seek a divorce or some sort of redress.

During apartheid, religious leaders were often the only leaders in a community. Some leaders used this position to challenge the apartheid state, others used it to further their own agendas, and some did both. Now South Africa is reaching out to these leaders to be new institutional players or to be surrogates for local governments or program implementation. This is a delicate balancing act, given the range of ideologies, beliefs, and gender norms these leaders and faith communities hold. Many of the narratives above demonstrate the power of harnessing these existing leaders as new change agents, and some religious leaders support progressive change. At the same time, many leaders are still operating within frameworks that reinforce regressive ideas about women's position in the family and society. Their ability to be transformative and to work for change within these traditions and frameworks is precarious at best.

Traditional Leaders and Traditional Healers

In many parts of the country, traditional leaders and traditional healers are often the first, perhaps only, recourse for survivors to secure justice or protection. Traditional leaders are the customary leaders whose power is based on heredity, tradition, or custom. Traditional healers, often known as sangomas in South Africa, are healers who have been trained in non-Western healing practices and/or indigenous medicines that are passed down from one healer to another, often over centuries.[2] Both traditional leaders and traditional healers are increasingly recognized and regulated by the South African state. They are often respected by their communities and occupy roles of counselors and respected advisors. Traditional leaders and healers are distinct institutions with very different norms, guiding values, and practices. I decided to discuss them together in this section because they occupy a similar space: they are institutional leaders who work within a customary framework. Historically, most traditional leaders and healers would work outside the sanction or recognition of the state. Today, both are increasingly being brought into the state as new bureaucratic actors, including on the issue of gender-based violence.

As a general rule, my interview participants voiced more distrust of traditional healers than of traditional leaders, especially among religiously affiliated service providers. Some believe that traditional healers are deeply troubled, possessed, disturbed, or anti-Christian. As one minister stated, "In actual fact, if I were in the church now, when I see a traditional healer, I would like to pray for that person and release the demons." Yet this sentiment was not shared by the traditional leaders I interviewed. One of the members of a traditional council in Difate said his group had a strong collaboration with the traditional healers in his area: "You cannot run any initiation school without having a traditional healer.[3] That is why you have to fuse them.... In any African culture, you can't build a house without inviting the traditional healers to make your house strong. Even when your child is born, he needs to be protected.... You can't have a community generally without traditional healers." Given the chief's and the council's strong devotion to Christianity, I asked about the relationship of the traditional healers to their ideas of the Bible and Christianity. The same member stated, "Yes, they pray to the ancestors through God. They pray [to] God to help them in everything that they do to give them power in everything that you do." In the minds of this traditional council, sangomas were healers inspired by God.

Traditional Systems

Both traditional leaders and healers are increasingly being recognized for their role in dealing with gender-based violence. Survivors must often overcome great financial and physical distances in order to access formal justice mechanisms (Rasool 2016; Moult 2005). Many citizens in rural areas do not have access to a phone and would not know the appropriate authorities to contact, despite government awareness campaigns. The logistical challenges also are a barrier to proper evidence collection following a sexual assault, thus creating even further obstacles to prosecutions. Traditional authorities are being brought into the struggle to end gender-based violence rather than being further marginalized. Given the resource-strapped economy and the push to have implementation and programs as close as possible to the affected populations, traditional leaders and traditional healers have the potential to become part of the strategy of combating rape and violence.

During a group interview, a chief and his council explained their role as traditional leaders within family dispute mechanisms.[4] They saw themselves as partners with the police. One council member stated that dealing with domestic violence cases was one of their most common tasks: "Sometimes a man claps his wife, and the wife came here to report, 'My husband clapped me,' whatever, you know. Then we solve them, [unless] they must go to the police station—make it a big issue, divorce." When they described their process, they said they would speak with the abused/accuser first and then send a letter to the abuser, asking them to come make their case. If the abuser did not stop, the council members all agreed that they would call the police back into the situation. They see themselves as the first attempt to stop the violence.

Another council member stated, "Yes. Work hand in hand with the police, because we can't do anything without them. These people, they are in the rural places. They are taking chances. Sometimes you call them. Sometimes they don't want to come. When you contact the police, they will go and collect them." The traditional leadership in this community asserted that they had a regular, supportive partnership with the police. It was outside the scope of my project to gain confidential access to particular domestic violence cases in order to track the strength of this statement. What I did worry about were the potential shortcomings of this partnership—such as the police telling survivors of domestic violence to go to their chiefs to resolve the issue. As Moult (2005) found, police often refer people to traditional leaders because the police do not want to handle domestic violence cases. Similarly, the police could also turn survivors away altogether, insisting these were private family matters (Alcalde 2011). Conversely, traditional leaders may not readily hand over cases to the police because leaders feel they are in a better position to adjudicate the conflict as traditional leaders, and such cases bolster their power and stature in the communities.

One of the themes that struck me the most in our conversation was the idea of swift action and real justice for cases that came before the traditional council. Several times, council members would say things like they "just solve the cases." They wished the police would send leaders *more* cases, since they can get to the bottom of the problem faster than the regular court system. This narrative is in line with Moult's (2005) research with women survivors of domestic violence in South Africa. Most women saw the courts as a last resort, and they turned to traditional mechanisms of justice because they were fast, culturally familiar, and focused on reconciliation rather than arrest of the women's partners. This is also the case across Africa, as traditional justice systems are more trusted than the formal courts, which may be seen as complicit in past atrocities or supporting former authoritarian regimes (Reddy 2014; Wojkowska 2006). Traditional courts are also seen as focusing on reconciliation and dispute resolution rather than arrest, which many survivors prioritize in order to maintain their families, their financial security, and their position in society (Wojkowska 2006; Moult 2005).

Many traditional leaders also position themselves as part of the process of education on pieces of legislation. As one council member explained, he feels leaders are much better at educating the public than the government:

> That is why you find they are involved in many initiatives, like Child Safety Promoters. They also attended the course. They understand. They know because that course, it is also maintained—the Maintenance Act, the Domestic Violence Act, women abuse. . . . When they talk, people can easily listen. . . . When we call it Imbizo [a meeting of the community called by a traditional leader or king], people they come. When they call people Lekgotla [community council or traditional court], they come. They can teach the people. But it is very difficult to go to court and ask the magistrate to tell you about the Domestic Violence Act. To explain to the community, because they don't have that kind of time.

I was surprised that the traditional council members spoke in such policy-specific terms about their role in public education and policy implementation on so many different types of legislation. This was another clear indicator of how involved the traditional leaders had become in the policy process.

Similar patterns emerged across several interviews on the topic of sangomas. The police are working to incorporate traditional healers so that they are not working at cross-purposes. By giving healers a voice, power, and a seat at the table, the police hope they can partner with traditional healers both to solve crimes and to have the sangomas "police themselves." There is a widespread belief that sangomas were able to hide a criminal or obscure a crime after it was committed. While this was not the purpose of all sangomas, who are healers, many people believed that this was a regular practice. By partnering with the sangomas, police hoped crime would fall. One male officer in an urban black township stated that police in fact met with sangomas every month: "They tell us their frustrations, and we tell them our frustrations. We try to—'You must assist us.' Because we believe that some of the criminals go to them after committing crimes, so that we mustn't catch them, blah, blah, blah. Give them muti, so that we, so that we mustn't catch them."[5] This move to collaborate with traditional healers was increasingly widespread within the police units where I was based. One station commander discussed his approach to working with traditional healers: "Well, crimes can be committed, and they use powers, things like that. And we say, 'Please prevent that. We don't want that. We want to work together.' The things they use and the methods must be within the law of the country." The police hoped that active collaboration would limit the power and influence of sangomas in obscuring crime and blocking investigations. The police were also hopeful that this move to enfranchise healers would ensure more accountability and transparency within their own ranks. Incorporating healers into government processes is one way to perhaps delineate sanctioned sangomas from unsanctioned sangomas.

One station commander, a white man who identified as a strong Christian, advocated that young people should not dismiss the traditional leaders and traditional customs: "I mean, if you talk of traditional people, the young people will laugh, and I say, 'Don't laugh.' I say, 'No, don't laugh. Culture is tradition; respect it.' You won't get their people in the cells. They will focus on their culture. . . . The children that comply with their culture are more law abiding, so I say, 'Don't laugh at them.'" From his vantage point, this station commander believes that young people who observe tradition and culture are less likely to engage in criminal activity. He may be romanticizing traditional culture because of his own personal beliefs in the importance of tradition, religion, and culture. Yet he is speaking in reaction to the rampant turn to crime, drugs, gangs, and violence in the community he serves. He believes that returning to tradition would limit this type of violence. But these traditional beliefs often reinforce the idea of women as subordinate and as property—gender attitudes that may foster gender-based violence, as described in the next section.

"Democracy Has Destroyed Everything"

There are times of clear collaboration between traditional leaders and the police. Yet if traditional leaders are pushed further, their views on domestic violence and rape become more complex. In my meeting with the chief and his council, we discussed rape and intimate-partner violence from many different angles. When I really pushed council members on these issues, they often shifted blame onto women. For example, the council members voiced strong concerns that many rape cases were not legitimate and were instead women's attempts to extort money from unsuspecting men:

> You see, the issue of democracy has more or less spoilt or destroyed everything. You find women. They will even put a trap to you. For example, if I dislike Chief [indicating his own chief in our conversation], and me and you are friends, I can send you to go and sleep with chief. And I say immediately after you have slept with chief, "You must go and open a case." Typical example is the case of that woman visit the now president, Jacob Zuma. You see, there are those kinds of tendencies. I will meet a woman, and I will propose and say, "No, I love you." I sleep with her, and she will say, "You give me five thousand or ten thousand [rand], or else I am going to open up a case." It is a two-way catch situation. . . . Women, they look for money. They are too materialistic in South Africa. You know, as long as you have got money, women will come flocking to you, and they will demand each and every thing that they want.

The linkage between then President Zuma and the council member's own chief was striking on several levels. This council member felt that rape charges were driven by an inherent flaw in women, depicting them as materialistic, cunning, and greedy. Yet this passage also suggests that he believes the rape charges are also a way to strip men of their rightful public positions and are a way of delegitimizing their leadership.

For one council member, significant problems with the South African Constitution remained: "What can I say? I can say that the constitution of South Africa is very wrong. We as traditional leaders are using the Bible as our constitution." Another council member elaborated on this point: "The traditional customary law, it also evolves. . . . It actually evolves from the Bible itself, teaching the Ten Commandments. So the law is getting lost because of these many rights. And you can see in South Africa, it has created so many wrongs because of the rights. There [are] a lot of divorce cases because of the rights." Again, in these passages, the council members are blaming democracy and the constitution for the permissive, promiscuous behavior of youth and women. One member then stated that, prior to the constitution, he was allowed to "teach" and punish children by beating them with a sjambok. But the constitution and a new rights-based culture have taken that "option" away from him. In this council member's estimation, the real "law" is the Bible.

While there are continued attempts to include traditional leaders and traditional healers in policy education and policy implementation, political leaders and gender activists should remain cautious, if not outright vigilant, about the risks this could pose. The desire for swift justice through a traditional system runs the risk of subjecting survivors to victim blaming or slander. There are also chances that cases are being pushed from the police to the traditional leaders because of resource limitations or because of the belief that interpersonal violence is a private matter. This brush-off by the police may further discourage survivors from coming forward. Gender-based violence and child abuse are complex social problems that often require multilayered solutions and ongoing care and support medically, emotionally, psychologically, and legally. Most traditional systems are ill equipped to handle such complex trauma.

The strategy of involving traditional leaders and healers in gender-based violence prevention is similar to the broader scholarship examining the changing role of traditional leaders. Thomas Koelble and Edward LiPuma found that in South Africa, "there is a connectivity between the advent of the neoliberal democratic state and the reinvigoration of chiefly authority" (2011, 6). This connectivity has been fostered by the ironic postapartheid intersection of the progressive agenda of the African National Congress for service delivery and the shrinking government services following the adoption of neoliberal political and economic policies. This is a delicate dance for a supposedly progressive government committed to electoral democracy, as "the traditional leaders have artfully reinvented themselves . . . and have discovered a variety of methods to reclaim their authority in the absence of a forceful state presence" (LiPuma and Koelble 2009, 206).

This new pattern might be acceptable for some, as these more traditional patronage systems have operated in some instances as a key network of social support accessible by rural or deeply impoverished populations (Hickey 2012). Yet there are significant risks associated with the use of traditional legal systems, especially in the sectors of gender rights (Mnisi Weeks 2015; Beall, Gelb, and Hassim 2005). As Cherryl Walker argues, "The valorization of traditional institutions that have historically excluded or marginalized women" puts customary law and traditional leaders in direct competition with the purported goals of gender equality in South Africa (2013, 78). Walker (2014) argues that the ANC has reified "culture" and "tradition" in static ways that empower key local leaders and customary rulers in order to bolster their political loyalty. Traditional systems are in many ways similar to most state and governmental organizations in their treatment of women and disadvantaged groups. Yet Walker argues that this "turn to tradition" is one of the most significant challenges to South African democracy, as it is "consolidating the powers of a petty aristocracy of hereditary chiefs and appointed headmen over the lives of rural people" (2013, 90).

Sultan Khan, Benoît Lootvoet, and Shahid Vawda (2006) remind us that such government/traditional relationships should be navigated carefully to ensure accountability and authentic democracy, as traditional leaders could follow the path of thoughtful public representatives and service providers, or they could use this space to "preserve their political hegemony" (113). These cautions are especially salient because so many informal justice systems "reinforce existing power hierarchies and social structures at the expense of disadvantaged groups" (Wojkowska 2006, 20). The inherent imbalances in this system often favor the most dominant, powerful individual in a dispute—who is often the abuser. These mechanisms often place too much emphasis on harmony, and they may force a reconciliation at the expense of individual rights, women's rights, and human rights. They lack the accountability that is often in place for state structures and may not be suited for violent crimes (Wojkowska 2006).

Some argue that the government should use the formal and informal justice systems in tandem or in some sort of hybrid model in which the guiding values are human rights and equality under the law. This hybridity extends beyond new models of traditional leadership into the adjudication of justice itself. Across the region, there is discussion of merging what leaders called "Western" judicial systems with customary judicial systems. The Western judicial system focuses on *punishment and rehabilitation*. If convicted, perpetrators serve jail time and undergo counseling and rehabilitation programs. In the customary system, emphasis is placed on *justice and compensation*. If convicted, perpetrators have to make reparations to the family of the survivor, often in the form of livestock. Many see the customary system functioning much like a restorative justice process. For example, at the 2007 National Conference on Gender-Based Violence in Namibia, traditional leaders argued for a much larger role in the adjudication of these crimes. Shocked by the low conviction rate, evidentiary problems, prohibitively long times to trial, and lack of sufficient legal resources in the Western courts, the traditional leaders argued that they could act swiftly and with the firmness of corporal punishment to protect their people.

There are significant problems with using the traditional system in isolation as the only means of recourse for a survivor. First, rape is a crime that is often repeated if perpetrators do not undergo rehabilitation, so compensation in and of itself is not a deterrent. Many rapists know they will avoid prosecution; for example, if they can afford the compensation in cattle, then they can rape without compunction. There are other problems with pursuing only the customary system. Survivors may not receive medical care or treatment, which is problematic, especially in the era of HIV/AIDS. Psychological services and ongoing counseling are not guaranteed. Finally, there are widespread reports that survivors undergo significant pressure to withdraw complaints under the traditional system, just as in the Western courts. Since there is no evidence collection or analysis, traditional leaders must make decisions based on the differing stories of the survivors and the perpetrators. Moult (2005) also found that there are problems using informal mechanisms because they are not focused on prevention and long-term solutions to gender-based violence. They often approach situations on a case-by-case basis rather than working to understand larger contexts, norms, and patterns in their communities that are driving the violence or justifying the abuse.

Bringing the two systems together in some form of hybridity may overcome some of these problems. Proponents also argue that the unity of the two systems may decrease the likelihood that a survivor will withdraw a complaint based on pressure from family or traditional leaders. Families may feel that they are being compensated swiftly for the harm to their loved one and that they are receiving some form of justice, while long-term medical and psychological services would be available for the survivor under the government system. The idea that a hybridity of processes that brings together citizens, civil society, and the state to solve pressing, acute problems is also in line with another trend in development studies called "bricolage." According to Matt Andrews, Lant Pritchett, and Michael Woolcock, bricolage describes "the process by which internal agents 'make do' with the resources at hand to foster new (or 'hybrid') structures and mechanisms" (2013, 239). In this way, actors are not constrained by one ideal model that may or may not fit their circumstances, risks, and long-term needs.

Despite this promise, similar efforts in Liberia to bridge formal and informal systems have proven inadequate and many times end in harm to the survivor of sexual and gender-based violence (Reddy 2014). While families do not trust formal legal mechanisms, the push of international donors to aid formal mechanisms has hindered the full development or incorporation of the informal systems. As families and survivors attempt to seek redress and assistance, they "pursue the system that is more beneficial to their case ... typically at the detriment of the survivor" (121). Dashakti Reddy (2014) argues that if countries do attempt to create more synthesis and hybridity in the two systems, it must be done intentionally, transparently, and with an eye toward changing social norms and harmful practices that subordinate women.

New Bureaucratic Players

Many community leaders in South Africa are navigating the key social issue of gender-based violence through innovations in bureaucratic strategies. By consciously incorporating new bureaucratic actors—religious leaders and traditional leaders—into the implementation process, South Africa is attempting to address the large scarcity of resources by using these more locally based structures. Rather than being marginalized, these community leaders have been invited to become part of a new hybrid model of bureaucratic implementation. While this raises significant issues of accountability and representativeness (Mnisi Weeks 2015; Walker 2014; Beall, Gelb, and Hassim 2005), the hope is that using these local systems will increase survivors' access to justice. There are significant gaps between the government system and a system of unelected civic leaders. Some argue that these gaps can be overcome through increased education and training of civic leaders, as well as by incorporating legal students and paralegal professionals into the process (see Wojkowska [2006] for an extensive discussion of recommendations).

The decentralization of problem solving to local levels may be a way to compensate for resource gaps (Andrews, Pritchett, and Woolcock 2013; M. Andrews 2010). Yet this type of flexibility and downsizing often works best in countries with stronger and more accountable political systems (M. Andrews 2010), something with which South Africa continues to struggle. The questions remain: Can South Africa use these local actors to develop nimble solutions to gender-based violence that are both culturally appropriate and survivor centered, or are these local mechanisms working too much on a case-by-case basis and missing larger structural inequalities that perpetuate gender-based violence? Further, is South Africa pushing the problems downward because of a lack of will and commitment nationally?

If there is to be a hybrid of the informal and formal justice systems, there also needs to be significant capacity building and rights-based education to ensure that parties in a dispute are treated equally. As is often the case, the more powerful party typically has the advantage both in the criminal justice system and in a traditional justice system. In the case of gender-based violence, the more powerful party is most often the abuser (Wojkowska 2006).

This hybridity also depends on making the two systems legible to one another. As Oyvind Eggen (2012) found in Malawi, this means that states (and international donors) want legible, ordered, tidy mechanisms to govern and evaluate informal systems. These bureaucratic aesthetics, as Eggen describes them, may be used to satisfy governments and donors while also allowing existing local practices to continue to function and perform their typical duties. While these practices may not be in line with the norms and goals of the state, they are able to respond to local realities that are "complex, dynamic, and ever-shifting, known only to those in the village" (18). This layering of bureaucratic aesthetics onto local practices may work in certain types of conflicts and programs, but there needs to be significant transparency when it comes to gender-based violence to ensure equitable decision making.

One positive aspect to this widespread engagement of community organizations is that gender-based violence advocacy has the potential to become a shared norm. While speaking of state building more broadly, Andrews, Pritchett, and Woolcock argue that "diffusion demands broad support for change which is not attained through narrow hierarchical processes" (2013, 240). Having a critical mass of organizations and leaders in a community working to end violence may result in shifting social norms.

CHAPTER FOUR

Police

The story of police failure in South Africa is one of international notoriety. There are almost continual media stories of police corruption, bribery, violence, and apathy. The failures far outweigh the successes, and the systemic problems of the police are well documented (Keehn et al. 2014; Vetten 2014; Andersson et al. 1999). This is especially the case for gender-based violence. In a study of police dockets in Gauteng, Rachel Jewkes and colleagues found that 93.5 percent of victims of multiple-perpetrator rape reported the crime. These reports did not, however, translate into arrests. Only 38.7 percent of perpetrators involved in these multiple-perpetrator rapes were arrested (Jewkes et al. 2012, 17). The rates were slightly higher for single-perpetrator rapes, but still only 54.1 percent (17). This pattern has persisted for several years. Neil Andersson and colleagues (1999) found in a study in Gauteng that of the 272 rape cases reported to the police, only seventeen files were opened. Of those, five went to court, and only one rapist was convicted. If those are the odds survivors face when reporting sexual assault—that 272 reported cases equals one conviction—why would anyone report rape?

This story is not isolated to South Africa. Police corruption and mishandling of gender-based violence cases are found the world over. Corruption and ineffectiveness of the police have been identified as a key barrier to reporting gender-based violence (see, e.g., McCleary-Sills et al. [2015] in Tanzania; Medie [2013] in Liberia; Alcalde [2011] in Peru; Walsh [2008] in Guatemala). A classic and unavoidable tension also exists between the typical reactive work of the police, who intervene after the crime has occurred, and the idea of preventing crimes that occur within personal relationships.[1] If the police truly are essential players in the effort to address gender-based violence, their widespread failures paint a bleak picture.

Communities in South Africa that seem to be moving forward against gender-based violence are doing so with the engagement and buy-in of the police. My research reveals that there are members of the police services who are using their discretion to address gender-based violence within a deeply constrained carceral environment. These officers are trying to (1) change the culture of policing within their stations, (2) transform the relationship between the police and their local communities, and (3) address gender-based violence despite their own personal histories as survivors and the complete lack of resources in their divisions.

Much of the effectiveness of the police hinges directly on this idea of discretion—specifically, the discretion the police use to engage or ignore gender-based violence. If there was a commitment by station commanders to address gender-based violence, they used their discretion to ensure that capable, effective, and qualified personnel were put in key positions to work with survivors. If detectives were committed to tracking down perpetrators and ending violence, they used their discretion to make these cases a priority. If victim services staff wanted to create warm and safe environments for survivors, they used their discretion to recruit volunteers, gather resources, and improve the physical space of trauma rooms.

One of the most salient examples from my research illustrates the idea of discretion and how decisions by the police affect the people they serve, sometimes positively and sometimes quite harmfully. In a lengthy interview and tour of a home for young girls, the organization's leader talked about the poor relationship they had with their local police station. The home took in youth who had been trafficked for labor and sex, who had survived commercial sexual exploitation, who were homeless, or who had been removed from their homes for their safety and welfare. The girls came to the home through referrals by the police, social workers, or the courts. The home had children from South Africa, the DRC (Democratic Republic of Congo), Zimbabwe, and Burundi. The house was funded mainly by donations from businesses, support from other NGOs, and some support from government departments. It was a bare-bones operation, but the organization was able to provide safe housing and meals, as well as some educational support, trauma counseling, and skills training.

What was most interesting about this interview was how the leader of the center—a migrant from a neighboring African country who had himself been homeless—described how these children were treated very differently by two separate police stations. During our conversation, I specifically asked about the relationship between the organization and the police. This turned out to be a sticking point:

> With the police, the biggest factor is they don't understand how shelters work. The police wherever they train, they are not taught how to treat

vulnerable kids. They believe that only the Child Protection Unit is the one that must take care of the children.... And for them, the rest of them, it has nothing to do with them. For example, they once picked up a girl while they were doing patrols, and they brought the girl here. Then one of the girls got up to open [the gate] for them. Apparently even the police [officer] was harsh to the girl they picked up and was now harsh to the girl who opened here. The words they used were like, "So you are also a prostitute." This is a policeman who is supposed to protect them.... You go to the police to complain. No one is prepared to listen. So it is actually frustrating that a girl has to cry because a policeman drove in here and said those things to her. It means for them they have this perception that every girl they see here is a former prostitute. The fact that they are launching the Child Protection Units and the Family Child Sexual Offences Unit, it might be helpful. But I think it must be mainstreamed as well.... These children are not criminals. They are children who are vulnerable who just need safety.

These are the most vulnerable of children—children who have been abused, who are homeless, who have been trafficked, and who need a place of safety. They should be able to look to the police to protect them. Instead, this service provider stated that they were harassed, shamed, and degraded. The leader of the group home continued with examples of several robberies, including the theft of the children's backpacks, purses, or mobile phones when they were coming and going from the shelter. Even when he could identify the criminals, the police refused to open a case. In another instance, a pedophile was watching the girls in the morning as they were getting ready for school and masturbating. The leader reported the pedophile multiple times, and the police refused to come. The leader provided numerous other examples of similar situations when the police refused to open cases.

When I asked the house leader if he thought this was a case of police failure or if it was a station-specific issue, he said he had received completely different treatment from another police station:

> But I think it all goes back to this station.... This other station, they appreciate what we do. They respect the girls. Yesterday, we were doing a function... and they gave blue cars to transport the girls. You see the difference? We have a police officer from this station who comes in and asks, "Are you a prostitute?" And then we have police from this other station that respects them enough to give them blue cars.... Because, you know, some of them have gone through a lot, only to come here to feel a little bit safe.... So the way they see the young girls on the street is the way they treat the young girls they see at the center.

He said there had been a function where the police from the problematic station had come for a public relations event to claim that they were working on the 16 Days of Activism against Gender-Based Violence Campaign. When they came to bask in the good works of the shelter, the leader called them out. He had just spent three days trying to get someone at the station to receive a letter asking the police to attend the organization's annual general meeting so they could discuss the issues directly. The police refused to take the invitation letter, but members of the same station arrived during the 16 Days of Activism against Gender-Based Violence Campaign for publicity.

The leader used that moment to force the station to take the center and the young women seriously: "I spent three days struggling to give [people at the police station] an invitation. They refused to take it. . . . So when they came here, I reminded them. . . . Their boss gave me [his] phone numbers. 'If you ever come to the police station [and] they don't help you, you call me, and I will make sure I get someone to help you. Even the police must come more often to check on you.'" While the leader was able to finally get a personal guarantee for assistance from the station, this guarantee was contingent on one officer, who may not always be at the station to provide thoughtful assistance. Rather than having a larger structural response to training and sensitizing the police, the leader had to rely on a single commander. The leader said that he wants to receive responsive, effective, and survivor-centered services from *everyone* in the South African Police Services. This is a powerful contrast between two stations—stations with similar funding, resources, and demographic profiles—located only a few kilometers apart.

Police Discretion and Gender-Based Violence

The police discretion described in the story above is precisely what anti-gender-based-violence advocates across South Africa have rallied against for decades. Many activists assert that the obstacles to gender-based violence are actually linked to the priorities and the discretion of officers, community leaders, and national politicians. Leaders choose either to make gender-based violence a priority or to brush it aside with empty rhetoric. Activists argue that the necessary resources are available, but the problem is one of priorities, discretion, and leadership.

During my research, I visited the police stations in each of the nine communities to conduct individual interviews, group interviews, and observations. When I asked members of each station what they needed in terms of dealing with gender-based violence, there were very consistent answers across all the stations, presented in table 4.1. Resources continue to top the list for

Table 4.1. Police Needs

Trauma Center Supplies	Clothing, toys, bedding, linens
Trauma Center Furniture	Beds, child-sized furniture, comforting or playful decorations
Trauma Center Physical Space	Private space for interviews, away from the busy parts of the station and where other officers would not interrupt Designated space: other officers would not use the space as a break room or sleeping quarters Private showers and bathrooms
Vehicles	Bicycles and/or horses for informal sectors Working, reliable vehicles for all sectors; too few cars for most areas; sometime an entire township has three to four cars, and they cannot leave one call until it is finished, so the response time is very long Designated vehicle for victim services
Staff	Sufficient staff Qualified staff for victim support and investigation: a few stations were assigned police who were not trained for victim support roles, were below the rank needed to assist in investigations, or were inexperienced in community outreach and prevention
Training	Training for all officers on victim support, gender-based violence, and sensitivity Retraining older police on new laws and new approaches to child abuse and gender-based violence
Volunteers	Need volunteers to assist police but not to fill role of police Training and reliable schedule for volunteers Compensation in some form, even for phone air-time, meals, transportation Converting volunteer positions into paid police positions to increase reliable, trained, and accountable service providers
Counseling	For officers working with child abuse and gender-based violence victims for secondary trauma For officers working through their own abusive relationships

many officers and stations, including material resources and appropriate training. These findings are not surprising, especially given the scholarship on the resource limitations police face in addressing gender-based violence, particularly domestic violence (Alcalde 2011; Combrink and Wakefield 2010; Walsh 2008; Vetten 2005; Mathews and Abrahams 2001; Parenzee, Artz, and Moult 2001). The police have many pressing issues, and their resources are woefully inadequate, which may become a slippery slope for corruption (Andersson et al. 1999).[2]

What follows is a reflection on three key areas that emerged in my discussions and interviews with and about the police. First, I explore how the police talked about *preventing* gender-based violence, a crime that often occurs within intimate relationships. Second, I examine the narratives about *structural issues* that continue to limit police capacity. These included racism, frequent staff turnover, and a lack of training. Third, I consider their narratives about the limitations of *human capacity*. These street-level workers are faced with remarkable secondary trauma and have very few resources to address the impact of that trauma. Other members of the police are survivors themselves who utilize their experiences as a resource to assist clients. Most police officers lack the training and preparation to do this type of work, so much of the work is outsourced to volunteers who also lack appropriate training. This lack of preparation only heightens the potential for secondary trauma. Finally, I discuss one police station that was a model of best practices because the station had made gender-based violence a priority.

"Behind Closed Doors": The Challenge of Policing

Looking for upstream approaches to prevent crime can be challenging, and this is especially true of gender-based violence (Masuku 2002). Encouraging survivors to come forward is difficult, and having communities break their silence around gender-based violence requires significant trust in the police. As one officer, a black South African man who worked in the informal community of Bokang, stated: "In terms of, what do you call it, domestic violence—it is so difficult to police something that happens behind closed doors. In your brothels . . . you don't get offended when a guy is in your bedroom. . . . 'Everything is okay, guys,' then you go. The same thing happens in close confinement." The officers say that when they arrive to many of these calls, they are often turned away. The notion that gender-based violence occurs in the "private" sphere is deeply contested (Meth 2017; Mogstad, Dryding, and Fiorotto 2016; Vetten 2014; Bassadien and Hochfeld 2005), and these narratives that domestic violence is a "private matter" embolden police to turn survivors away (Alcalde 2011; Walsh 2008). The same is true about working with communities to help their neighbors. One police officer talked about the need to build a community of trust to break the silence around gender-based violence. The police and community members know where the violence is happening, but the community does not trust the police enough to tell them about interpersonal violence.

Police in every station talked about several ways to build community, to gain the trust of the community, and to get the police closer to the people. These structures included community police forums, sector policing, visible policing, and social crime prevention, each discussed below. While these may not be the most effective ways to directly combat gender-based violence, these were the tools they had at hand and the programs they found effective for prevention broadly defined. Every police station also had various outreach and educational programs in its toolbox—public marches, radio programs, community newspapers, 16 Days of Activism against Gender-Based Violence Campaign programs, and partnerships with churches, businesses, traditional leaders, and occasionally traditional healers. In addition to these tools and strategies, I listened for the values the police expressed in their interviews, which most often included creating partnerships with the community, building trust, creating a "bond," instilling a sense of voice and ownership, increasing reporting and response time, ending stigma and silence, reaching all areas (informal settlements and rural areas) and all groups (youth, elderly, and immigrants), linking needs to resources, and creating a sense of responsibility for crime prevention in the community. These values indicate attempts to shift the perception and the mission of the police, as discussed below.

"This Is Your House": Building Trust after Apartheid

During apartheid, police were the most direct and intimate enforcers of apartheid brutality (Singh 2016; Brogden and Shearing 1993). The police were not concerned with the general welfare of the residents in townships and informal settlements, and the continued corruption of the police created a vast gap between residents and police (Meth 2017). Rape was used to control women's status and harm the resistance movement (Britton and Shook 2014; Seedat et al. 2009; Britton 2006; Scully 1995; Meintjes, Pillay, and Turshen 2001). After apartheid, the South African Police underwent massive transformation and retraining, signified also in the change of their name from the South African Police into the current South African Police Services (SAPS). This name change is an attempt to mark the shift from *surveilling* the people to *serving* them. Yet continued legacies of racism, sexism, police malfeasance, and community distrust limit their effectiveness to this day (Singh 2016; Seedat et al. 2009; Mattes 2006). The members of the SAPS with whom I worked had a very clear sense of the need to build trust, especially in terms of overcoming the continued legacy of apartheid. One black police officer located in a black township linked these apartheid legacies to the current limitations of the police in crime prevention: "Because the purpose of that is not to be reactive but to be proactive. . . . They must feel welcome, not threatened. Because in the past, the people would be fearful of the police. When you see a policeman, you run. . . . Now we want to say, 'Don't run away from us, bring your problem to us.'" This is not an easy transition to make after generations of using apartheid-era tactics that violently enforced silence and division. The values of trust and community building are central to the project of a new policing culture where the police become partners in prevention rather than predators or threats to community safety.

A common idea across officers was that the responsibility was on the police to build bridges with the community to generate trust. A black police officer working in another urban township stated that it is not his goal to have community *partnerships*; rather, he wants the community to have *ownership* of the police: "For example, not long ago we had events when we said, 'Please come to the station. This is your house.' . . . That is our success. We built trust with our community, and when there is a problem we jump in together. . . . Other stations don't want to welcome them." One particularly powerful message came from an interview with an Afrikaner man who was the station commander in the established black township of Difate. He critiqued the idea that the police should serve as a military controlling its own population, which had often been the case during apartheid:

> Sometimes they say it is the war against crime, and you can read a newspaper, and they will say that. . . . But I say, I am a police officer. Leave the war for the army. I am a police. And I say to my members, the product we must put on the table when we talk about police—it is safety, security, trust, and respect. That is the product we must put on the table. And if you want to measure us, it is safety, security, trust, and respect. If you tell me there is a murder case here, and they arrested the suspect, it is a success. I say it is a result, *because we already failed*. If one crime is committed here, we already failed. Then to tell me successful arrest is a success—I say they mustn't refer to arrest as a success. That is a result. That crime is committed. We failed. That is about my policing culture.

For this commander, police culture was focused on prevention and moving upstream to find root causes to social problems. However, prevention continues to be challenging, given the widespread failures of the police in South Africa today. When I pushed officers to move from these value statements to specific models of addressing gender-based violence, most of them presented three types of strategies: sector policing, visible policing, and community police forums, discussed below. At that stage in my research, I was still thinking of gender-based violence as a particular type of crime, perhaps even a crime that could be addressed in isolation. But the officers pushed back. They argued that gender-based violence is part and parcel of all community violence and is driven by structural violence, and such violence cannot be addressed successfully using piecemeal approaches. These interviews and observations challenged me to examine my thinking about gender-based violence and to rethink my approach to the project as a whole.

Sector Policing, Visible Policing, and Hot Spots

In every interview across all police stations, officers focused on the concept of sector policing as one of the most promising ways to build community and decrease crime and violence, including gender-based violence. Coming originally from the UK, *sector policing* refers to the program that locates officers within a particular section of a community, also known as *neighborhood policing* (Dixon 2007; Maroga 2004). The idea is that community members get to know officers personally, learn to trust them, and sometimes even have access to officers' mobile phone numbers. They should be visible, embedded, proactive, and collaborative (Maroga 2004). During interviews, when I asked for clarification about how this strategy would work, the police stressed how invaluable this type of policing was specifically for rape, sexual assault, intimate-partner violence, and child abuse. As a black middle-aged officer in the Bokang police station emphasized to me, they saw a direct link between their contact with the sector and the decrease in gender-based violence. He believed that sector policing increased trust and closeness with the community. Once the trust was established, police saw more cases coming forward.

These ideas were underscored by nearly every officer I interviewed. I was told that sector policing could increase the bonds, trust, and partnerships needed to report and prevent crime. Officers explained that working reliably with the community in these individual sectors is the key to overcoming vast structural challenges in their communities, including poverty, overcrowding, and the xenophobic violence they have seen in the past. Interpersonal violence, they consistently argued, is nested within these structural challenges.

It is not only police who see the benefits of sector policing. Citizens, community leaders, and members of the community police forums also had positive things to say about sector policing. For example, I interviewed a member of the community police forum in a rural black community I am calling Mabitso. She talked about the impact of sector policing for her community, and she echoed the same sentiments of the police. She saw that sector policing increased partnerships and a closeness with individual police members. When there was a crime, she did not call the national emergency number; instead, "I am going to the number that is written on the police vehicle." People knew the police serving their specific area, and this helped with response time and effectiveness, which in turn increased trust.

The notion of sector policing was also discussed hand in hand with the strategy of *visible policing*: having an active and visible presence through outreach programs or visibility on the streets and in the community. When officers talked about visible policing and sector policing, they commonly linked them to the identification of "hot spots" for crime. Units worked to identify areas and times during which rape and sexual assault are common: often open fields, hostels, or busy taxi ranks. While the majority of single-perpetrator rapes occur in the home of the victim or the perpetrator (58.8 percent), the majority of multiple-perpetrator rapes, also known as gang rapes, happen in these types of potential hot spots: "open spaces, roads or alleys (47.6%)" (Jewkes et al. 2012, 15). For example, members of the Difante station, the older, more established black township, identified an active taxi rank that used to be a hot spot for rape and assault at night. The police station had successfully increased its visibility during those times and claimed that rape had decreased. Another station identified hostels as hot spots and requested upgrades from the government for increased police patrols inside the hostels to search for drugs, alcohol, weapons, and stolen property. Another station identified an open field to which women were dragged and raped by multiple perpetrators. They worked with the local government to cut down trees, increase lighting, and increase police visibility.[3] Some stations in the urban core implemented increased foot patrols by their community police volunteers wearing jackets and vests to create a visible presence to deter rape. Another station in a very rural area identified rape hot spots and conducted awareness campaigns in the surrounding areas. Each of these approaches shows more active engagement than more dubious awareness-raising strategies, such as posting "rape hot spot" signs and billboards, which have been used in South Africa.[4] These signs were similar to other crime awareness tactics, like "hijack hot spot" and "high crime area" signs, all of which imply that the obligation is on the potential victim to prevent a crime rather than working to address the underlying problems in those spaces.

CHAPTER FOUR

Community Crime Forums and Community Police Forums

Another key institutional strategy mentioned by the police was the development of community police forums (CPF) or community crime forums (Maroga 2003). Each of these groups provided a way for the police to learn more about the community and to identify hot spots or new developments in crime in their areas. The participants I spoke with stressed the importance of citizen voices as a vital step in partnering with the community. This new type of partnership and role clarification takes time, and, more importantly, it can bridge a gap for the police. The police also talked about how important it can be to recruit youth who might otherwise be discouraged by a lack of employment and educational opportunities and enter into crime out of a sense of apathy, hopelessness, or desperation. A member of the police in Bokang said they specifically invite youth into the station to ensure they get involved before they "fall" into crime: "Listen, we invite you to come to our youth desk. We are situated at the police station. . . . Come to us instead of lingering and doing nothing and getting involved in crime. Come to the station." This idea of *getting involved* rather than *doing nothing* was repeated again and again in interviews with volunteers when they talked about the CPFs. Even though they were not compensated, many adult and youth volunteers participated in CPFs rather than sitting at home or being drawn into crime.

All the members of CPFs talked about the importance of social outreach events and educational programs to prevent gender-based violence. They also spoke about trying to get people involved positively with the community in hopes of challenging the boredom, desperation, and depression of the unemployed. Research now shows that there may be a correlation between unemployment and boredom and incidents of rape (Jewkes et al. 2012) or other forms of crime and violence (Meth and Buthelezi 2017). Unemployment in and of itself does not necessarily lead to crime, violence, or sexual assault. However, unemployment is part of the larger social narrative of society. In South Africa, unemployment is nested within larger patterns of racial inequality, state violence, interpersonal violence, and patriarchal norms. The partnerships and outreach programs created through visible policing, sector policing, and the community police forums / youth desks may be an ideal intervention point for working on gender-based-violence prevention.

The accomplishments of the CPF programs were again also *place* specific. In the working-class, predominantly white Arbeidstad area, there was a decrease in business crime, carjacking, electricity theft, and school crime.[5] In the rural Mabitso community, the focus was on house break-ins and interpersonal violence, along with proactive outreach activities to get youth involved in community programs and meaningful work or volunteerism before they turned to crime. The CPF also dealt with issues such as teenage pregnancy and substance abuse. In the coloured township of Roedorp, CPF accomplishments centered on reductions in gang and drug activity, which the police then linked to a decrease in gender-based violence. The wealthy white area of Olive Vlei focused on carjacking, house break-ins, and theft, with almost no focus on gender-based violence or rape.

In my discussions with a member of the police working in the central business district of a major urban city, he described the issues of creating the CPF in his area. This is an area where most of the people lived outside the city and commuted to work. I asked him how communities worked in these transient places:

> Even here, if you look at [Huisdorp Central], we actually don't have a community. We actually are a community of people coming in and out. When we talk of the community of [Huisdorp Central], the people that we police are from [surrounding townships], and all those people, they all come into town, and then they go out. But you would be shocked how our community policing is working. We have our own community policing. We have a chairperson of a community policing forum. He knows . . . these people in the flats.[6] They don't come from here. They are not very organized. Our communities are people who are climbing out of the train now, out of the taxis. Those are our people, those are the people that we police. . . . I think if you talk to the community police forum, you will find there are dynamics that are not similar to [the black township of Difante], for instance. You see the people in [Difante], they stay in [Difante]. They have addresses there. You see the people in [Huisdorp], they are people who are coming to school, who are coming to work. In the evening, there is no one here. The streets are quiet. . . . You will find that there are dynamics that are not similar to other places. But it works. But to answer your question, I find that over the years, people are learning that if you come in as a police forum and I come in as a policeman, we are not fighting for a space [moves hands together]. I am here to support you and help you.

When I asked for clarifications about what was different there from other places, the officer said that establishing the CPF and developing a trusting relationship between the CPF and the police took longer in the city center because of the transient nature of the daily population. Building community is challenging because people move in and out of the spaces daily. Residents are migrants from other areas and often do not have established communities or networks within the city. Yet community building is possible, and persistent leadership is key.

The CPFs are not without their challenges. One theme that occasionally surfaced in the interviews was confusion between the function of the CPF and the police. In some ways, this is an issue of role clarification—between what the CPF should do and what the police should do. I found this pattern in Lookodi, the newer black Reconstruction and Development Programme (RDP) housing community built after the end of apartheid. The bonds in the community were weak, and the networks and partnerships were very new. Volunteers tried to bridge the gap between the community and the police, but there was role confusion about what the CPF would do and what the police would do, as one community volunteer, a middle-aged black woman from Lookodi, explained:

> They [members of the CPF] also want to become the police, I mean the community police. . . . They don't let them [the police] do their job. You know you have to give them [the police] the case. You explain what has happened here, and then you leave them to do their job. But it is not what they are doing. With the community, most of the people believe if you are a CPF, you have to beat [here she demonstrates by beating a fist on her open hand]. You have to beat when you get a suspect. You have to beat the suspect. It is what they believe in. It is what we are trying to teach people not to do that. It is better to call the police, so that they can do their job, and then they—justice will take over.

This volunteer had a particularly challenging role. The Lookodi RDP community is located at some distance from the police station. The housing development is not large enough for its own station. Members of the community would call her first, as the community leader, before the police. Given the pattern of vigilante violence in the community, she found herself rushing into situations to calm community members and implore them to wait for the police to arrive. Given the limited number of vehicles at the station, the response time by the police was notably slow.[7] This volunteer was active in establishing neighborhood watch programs, street patrols, and outreach programs to build community, but the challenges of doing so, particularly in this newly formed RDP community, were daunting. Some members of the police also saw the CPF in Lookodi as difficult partners because of what they did and how they functioned, as one officer stated:

> They [the CPF] would assault the suspects and so on. . . . No, after training they got worse. They got worse, because now you see the problem if you

compare sector 2, 3, and 4. It is the people who are well off, I can say. They must do everything out of their pocket. Then those people [in Lookodi] after training, they were promised food parcels or whatever. For them, it is an opportunity that they must get something out of this system now. If they don't get these things, then they become frustrated, then they become problematic now. Because they don't do it out of the love of doing it. They are expecting something instead.

These are powerful tensions that reveal the very clear legacy of apartheid. Wealthier CPF programs can do this "out of love," which really means the love to protect their own livelihoods and homes by using their extensive personal means and resources. They do not expect much from the police. The officer said that the community members even bought sirens and radios for their CPF patrols. But in the impoverished Lookodi, the CPF activities revealed the structural vulnerabilities of this population, the desperation for survival, and the pattern of turning to violence to resolve crime when the police were absent or distant. In this case, the political geography of the Lookodi development as a newly formed RDP community (Meth and Buthelezi 2017) had very particular limitations for the attempts to build community. It is clear that institutional structures can only go so far to address the racial, geographical, and economic disparities that continue to mark the country.

There is also an issue of the unevenness in how CPF programs operate nationally in terms of their membership, activities, goals, and implementation strategies. In conversations with a white South African member of the national Civilian Secretariat for the Police, she discussed some of these ongoing challenges: "Before joining here, in my area, I was asked to join the CPF, and I said no. Because it was, I mean, my area is quite extensive, and it includes areas that were previously disadvantaged areas, which are predominately black areas. And yet the CPF is entirely white. And we are saying, going forward, the CPF should represent specific interests of the community. So you should have one or two people under CPF that represent women's organizations in the area and are looking at how the police handle women issues." She continued to argue that the CPF should not be addressing gender-based violence—that should be left to community organizations and the police: "And it is not the role of the CPFs anyway, because once they do that, they are no longer community. They are an extension of the police. What they should do is see that there is a *partnership* between women's organizations and the police station and how women's issues are handled, [that] there is a forum where women's organizations can address their problems at the police station. So we want to focus them on that, and the CPF must focus specifically on local needs." Given that so many police stations had mentioned the CPFs as important in the role of preventing gender-based violence, her reflections are a notable counterbalance. While the CPFs have the possibility of reducing crime more broadly and increasing trust in the police, it was still unclear how CPFs addressed gender-based violence directly.

Structural Issues

The SAPS as an institution has undertaken a much-needed process of deracialization since the end of apartheid, but many argue that it needs a much deeper transformation to overcome its past as an "instrument of white domination" (Brogden and Shearing 1993, i). Even as apartheid was ending, President De Klerk argued that the police had to accept that their role was no longer to enforce the will of a particular political party, as they had done during apartheid; instead, the police had to begin protecting all citizens from crime (Singh 2016). This was of course an ironic statement, given that the apartheid state had used the police specifically to ensure the power and political will of the white minority—not a single party but in fact a single race. The police were working primarily to legitimize and secure state power, which in turn was a protection of white minority rule and economic status.

As Anne-Marie Singh argues, at the point of the democratic transition, political leaders called on the police and communities to address crime and increase security, to work collaboratively to protect communities and private property, and to address crime at the local level: "Crime and control thus appeared as a matrix for acting to foster and increase individual and collective security, economic growth and social development *and* for specifying and activating a particular notion of citizenship—ethically reflective, active, and morally responsible" (2016, 5). This redirection was also in the interest of the National Party at the time, as the party was encouraging the police to protect *private property* and *individual rights*, the rights of the white racial minority. It was no longer acceptable to have the police fortify white power through the guise of protecting the (apartheid) state. Thus, political leaders from the white minority parties called on the police to protect rights and property, both of which rested comfortably in the hands of the white minority because of apartheid's racial distribution of resources and capital. The push for local citizens to engage in crime reduction programs was also supported by the ANC after the transition (Singh 2016), again because it was consistent with the neoliberal move of placing the burden and responsibility on local communities and individual citizens rather than the state or any type of resource redistribution.

Despite all efforts to reorient the police to be closer to the community, attitudes toward the South African police continue to fall below other African countries (Mattes 2006). Given the number of languages spoken in South Africa, there are often gaps in communication between the police and victims. Divided societies such as South Africa can have larger national challenges of legitimacy, safety, and security, and the police are often the institution tasked to maintain order and promote community building (Bradford et al. 2014).

Further, since most people still remain in the segregated areas, as they did during apartheid, police often do not live in the communities they serve. There are some reasons this distance can be beneficial. For example, one of the biggest challenges facing SAPS is corruption, and if one polices the areas in which one lives—or polices the same area for a long time—this can create prime conditions for taking and receiving bribes, working within existing criminal networks, doing favors, looking the other way, or relying on particular networks at the cost of being more objective. Yet there are some challenges when officers serve stations outside their own communities. One local government official elected in Roedorp, a long-established coloured township, discussed this at length:

> The SAPS obviously is a big problem for us. The problem comes in again with the staffing of the station. Again, our employment policy says we should employ blacks first and then coloured and Indian and then white in any government department. [The] Employment Equity Bill states that those are the references we give. As a result, if we had one hundred officers in the [Roedorp] police station, then almost ninety will be of African descent, the other ten will be—you can see the problem. There are ten people in the station, and then nine of them are black people, fluent in Zulu, Sotho, Xhosa, or whatever other name, and maybe English. But they are not always comfortable speaking English, and, worse, still many of them don't speak Afrikaans. . . . It is very difficult to explain to somebody in another language what has happened. And so the frustration goes from getting to the police station, reporting a crime, not being able to communicate with the person behind the counter. . . . Either he is not willing to listen to you or just doesn't understand you. . . . If you are a victim of crime, you are not in the best mood. And so you get to the police station, and the first person you meet doesn't treat you the way you should, and an argument ensues, and that is when sometimes I am called in. . . . Coloured people can be racists, you won't believe it, against each other and to each other. They will tell you, "These black people don't know what they are doing," and it becomes very difficult for me, because now I have to listen to what

CHAPTER FOUR

the policemen has to say, and I have to listen to what you have to say, and a lot of times the policeman might be right.

Gaps in understanding across racial gaps, language barriers, and community norms continue to plague the ability of police to become part of the communities they serve. This also may point to the continuity and power of apartheid's policies of separation and segregation. Communities have been so separated and were so bombarded with racial propaganda during apartheid that breaking through those barriers becomes quite difficult. Communities are still defined by race and language differences twenty years after apartheid ended.

"Cowboys Don't Cry": The Human Side of Policing

There were several human challenges that police faced in gender-based-violence work. Many were survivors themselves, many were volunteers with no pay or support, and many faced secondary trauma because of the cases they worked. Others feared scorn by their fellow officers about their own victimization or need for counseling, as one police colonel working in the mixed-race area of Arbeidstad stated: "But unfortunately, police officers—they are very, very stubborn. They will never come to you. It is very rarely that it happens. It is the personality that 'cowboys don't cry,' unfortunately. . . . And you will ask them, and you know you will try and get them a couple hours off to go and rest or talk about it or sort it out and so on."

As I will discuss in this section, personal histories of abuse and secondary trauma, also known as vicarious trauma, are the daily realities of the street-level bureaucrats in charge of addressing gender-based violence and domestic abuse (Mastracci, Guy, and Newman 2012; MacEachern, Jindal-Snape, and Jackson 2011; Wies and Haldane 2011; Guy, Newman, and Mastracci 2008; Perron and Hiltz 2006). As the colonel above describes, this trauma is compounded by an institutional culture that discourages vulnerability and encourages silence around personal trauma. However, in order to do their jobs well, these officers and trauma support volunteers had to be skilled at utilizing emotional labor, which means avoiding retraumatization of survivors and ensuring they are themselves using emotions in a sustainable and productive way (Mastracci, Guy, and Newman 2012). Their jobs in crisis response, victim support, and investigations required them to work with survivors at their most emotional, vulnerable times (Mastracci, Guy, and Newman 2012). In every station, there were police who said their biggest "need" was affordable, accessible, and competent counseling to help them cope with their jobs and their lives.

Some station commanders took the impact of trauma very seriously for their officers. When I asked one station commander working in an established black township about what he saw as his biggest need, he started with trauma services: "There is Employers' Assistance Service to motivate them. They must go there, because we work under abnormal circumstances. Yesterday or so, there was an accident. Twenty people died there. To go there, whether you are a police officer, is not good. But sometimes a police officer will say, 'I am a police officer. I don't care.' But to go home, maybe a baby or child died there. They go home and see their own baby. . . . So we motivate them and say, 'Don't try to be too macho. You are [a] human being. You are not from another planet.'"

Cowboys and macho men: each of these descriptions is shaped by very particular forms of masculinity within the institution of policing. Globally, scholars have examined the police as a public bureaucracy that privileges and promotes certain forms of masculinities associated with aggression, militarism, social isolation, heroism, force, power, control, unity, and discipline (Johnston and Houston 2018; Wilkins and Williams 2008; Kiely and Peek 2002; Dick and Jankowicz 2001). Research has also found evidence that the strength of the masculinist, patriarchal culture in the institution of the police has limited the effect of women's integration into the police, in part because of the strength of the institutional socialization within the organization as a whole and within the ranks (Johnston and Houston 2018; Alcalde 2011; Hautzinger 2002, 2007; Dick and Jankowicz 2001). The passive/descriptive representation of women in the police services, the "add women and stir" model, does not necessarily lead to the active/substantive representation of women's issues within the police, even on gender-based-violence cases (Johnston and Houston 2018; Dick and Jankowicz 2001). This also may include the now-global model of women's police stations, such as those found in Peru (Alcalde, Basu, and Burrill 2015; Alcalde 2011) and Brazil (Hautzinger 2002, 2007; Nelson 1996). These stations are primarily staffed by women and focus mainly on violence against women. There is some quantitative evidence that women's police stations have been effective in reducing female homicides (Perova and Reynolds [2017] in Brazil) and some qualitative evidence that survivors receive marginally better treatment in the stations (Alcalde [2011] in Peru). The women officers themselves continue to face discrimination within the police services more broadly, and the women officers may eschew associations with feminist agendas in an attempt to conform to the larger masculinist norms of the institution either consciously or unconsciously

(Alcalde 2011; Hautzinger 2002, 2007). Given that many women officers were originally assigned to these stations in Brazil, they have worried that their association with the institution could harm their long-term advancement (Nelson 1996).

The same barriers have been found in terms of racial integration—that the passive/descriptive integration of minority officers into the police may not lead to the active/substantive representation of minority issues or changes in police work (Wilkins and Williams 2008). Some studies show that officers who are from racial minority groups may, over time, shed their beliefs about race, racial stereotypes, and racial profiling in order to assimilate more directly with the culture of the police force (Wilkins and Williams 2008), while other studies argue that the passive representation of minority groups may result in active representation, especially when demographic parity is reached or approached (Lasley et al. 2011). Thus, changing institutional culture is difficult and often mirrors the larger social inequalities of society (Dick and Jankowicz 2001).

Further, in my own work with police in South Africa, I found that officers often feel the need to cultivate a stalwart persona of detachment and strength in order to face the emotional tragedy they encounter in their daily lives. What I found most interesting was that the commanders and colonels identified these attitudes and then tried to disrupt the patterns by providing assistance through leave time, counseling, and conversation. Disrupting these various narratives—cowboys and survivors, macho men and wounded healers—seems crucial in changing the institutional culture of the police.

The Wounded Healer

In many of the victim units and survivor centers, I encountered service providers—either members of the SAPS or volunteers—who were themselves survivors of domestic abuse or sexual assault. Many people working in the area of child abuse and gender-based violence talked about how they were motivated by their own backgrounds to push the work forward. Much like the work of Thea Shahrokh and Joanna Wheeler in their study in Khayelitsha, Cape Town, survivors used their personal histories of abuse to inform their work, and they found "the strength to take action against intimate-partner violence ... not wanting anyone to feel the pain that they have experienced" (2014, 20). I met a full range of survivor advocates: some had been victimized in the past, some had only recognized their own situations as abusive when they were trained for the position, and some were currently experiencing domestic violence in their relationships. One volunteer in a victim's empowerment unit in a black township explained how the police training process gave her an awareness of the abuse in her marriage:

> I was married then. I was staying with my husband. I have a daughter there. He was so abusive, but I was afraid to open the case against him because I love him so much. And I didn't know that the things that he was doing to me were an abusive thing. And I came here, and I met this captain, a lady, and she sat down with me. She explained everything: "You see in a situation of things like this, you don't have to live like this." I tried to tell her that "no, you see that I love this man. He is the one who is taking care of me." And she said to me, "No, it doesn't have to be this way." So I have started then to be interested. I joined the other ladies. We talk about our problems. . . . Then we went to the police college so that they can train us.

This volunteer stated that she only began to identify her own abuse through her work with the police; she only began to read herself into the narrative of domestic violence as a survivor because of her police training. Until that point, she felt that her abuse was both normal and a sign of love.

Another member of the police in the same unit voiced a similar realization within her police training, and she discussed how she used her own experiences to help others:

> Since I joined the SAPS, I was chosen to work here. I didn't know anything about domestic violence, so I had to learn whatever is going on in domestic violence. But unfortunately, I was a victim of that. But then maybe through the workshops and then the other people's experiences, I learned how to control [remove] myself from that. Now, recently, I am going through a divorce, and for me it was a confirmation of whatever is happening to the women. Even while I may be working here, it can happen to me. So I don't have to be harsh to everyone. I don't have to be harsh even for myself, because I didn't want the situation to be like that. But because of the things that were happening, I had to show other women that even if you are with an abusive somebody, you have to change, and you have to fight for your rights. That is why I am grateful to work here.

This officer stated that it was, in fact, the institution of the police and the training she received that allowed her to understand larger patterns of domestic violence and how her own personal experience was part of that.

Yet awareness was often the only and last step these particular survivors took—awareness was where any actions to protect themselves ended. Many women officers and volunteers felt they in particular *could not* come forward and claim protection and assistance from the police because these women were members of the institution. Their role in the police both enacted their understanding of themselves as abused but also then hindered them from coming forward. Their status as members of the SAPS proved to be one of the biggest obstacles to assistance because they feared the repercussions that could happen if they reported the abuse.

There were several layers to this fear of reporting, as one officer explained to me: "You know, sometimes you see [that] they want to blame you—that you are the one who is carrying a firearm," implying that police cannot be victims or may be inciting the abuse in some way. She said that if she brought the case to the station, her colleagues would gossip: "When you pass to the toilet, they will say, 'You see!'" The police I spoke with felt there were probably many members of the SAPS who were abused or faced domestic violence. The problem was that most of them feared gossip, shame, and discrimination on the job, as one black South African woman officer in an urban township explained: "I think it is not only us who are experiencing the domestic violence. [There are] [m]any of [us at] the police station, but they will not come and report to the police. Even [though] we do have social workers in the police service. They don't help us. You can report the case now, she will come, sit with you like this, wanting to find out what is going on with you. Thereafter, you will hear about it outside. It is not confidential." Her story encapsulates several patterns from the research. She discusses the pervasiveness of gender-based violence, specifically intimate-partner violence, throughout society and even within the police services. Similarly, she discusses the failures of her own institution to act on cases of domestic violence, and, perhaps even worse, this inaction is compounded by gossip and a lack of confidentiality. Each of these factors—pervasiveness of domestic violence, ineffectiveness of the police, inaction by their partners, and gossip and shame in the workplace—diminishes the faith and trust people have in the police and the state. Their experiences may also discourage others from reporting cases as they witness how their institution creates a climate of self-blame and hopelessness for survivors who feel they have no recourse and no exit strategy.

In a similar discussion, an officer explained that she did not think her fellow officers would take her seriously because she was a police officer with a gun and the ability to protect herself by killing her husband. Again, her double identity of being abused and being someone who could protect herself was not legible for the police:

> I couldn't open the case because I am working here, I am staying here, and my husband will be locked up here. So I rather suffer the consequences than come here and open the case. Even now, I think the police are not doing

anything about this thing of domestic [violence], because, especially for us. I report the domestic violence. I do have a firearm. I have everything I can use to kill the person or to hurt him. But because our organization doesn't take this thing serious, I will come here and report the case, and it will be pending. They will not do anything.

Rather than believing she could use the law to protect herself and reduce the violence she experienced in her home, this officer felt her colleagues would never take her seriously because she was an officer with a gun. This is a painful reality. For these survivors, police and volunteer training created an awareness of their own abuse. But because they were the ones to enforce the law, it was assumed they could not be harmed or that they should be able to protect themselves. They feared that their positions as survivors would be disbelieved and mocked. The very institution they depended on for their livelihood and their social and professional identity was the same institution that perpetuated patterns of revictimization.

Secondary Trauma

As mentioned above, another clear pattern that emerged in my interviews and observations was the impact of secondary trauma. While many victim advocates were also abuse survivors, their trauma was compounded by the abuse they witnessed in their jobs: partner violence, child abuse, rape, and sexual assault. Counseling services are slim, and the toll from their jobs is extraordinary. Yet most of the police I interviewed had been in their positions for years, some over a decade, working long hours and enduring this perpetual trauma.

In every police station I visited, the police working in some form of victim services talked about their need for counseling or coping strategies. As one officer, a black South African woman in an urban township, stated, "You have to counsel yourself. Especially when you are dealing with these rape cases, some of them are traumatizing.... Sometimes we come across these children. They are raped in the school." The police and volunteers spoke about the needs for the SAPS—as an institution—to ensure that secondary trauma is recognized and treated seriously. As with service providers in other regions, the ability to use and actually to harness emotional labor effectively is often the key to effective service provision (Mastracci, Guy, and Newman 2012). Rather than suppressing emotions or ignoring their own histories of trauma, service providers who are trained to utilize emotions in their interaction with clients and to manage their own emotional response to crises can become better at investigating cases, supporting survivors, and sustaining themselves (Mastracci, Guy, and Newman 2012).

The Costs of Contracting Out

The SAPS continue to rely on volunteers and NGOs to do much of the gender-based violence trauma counseling and advocacy. Contracting out is intended to save money and to assist in the expansion of critical services through a reliance on experts in the NGO sector or in the community (Kettl 1993, 2015; Prager 1994). NGO specialists and volunteers should bring specific expertise, thus creating more effective services for survivors and allowing police to focus on their other work. But from my time in a variety of police stations, the volunteers I encountered had vastly different levels of training and experience. Additionally, they worked long hours with little or no financial compensation. Several volunteers I met had no training in the area of gender-based violence or trauma counseling. Most volunteers were driven by either passion, a history of personal trauma, or a desire to do something useful with their time, given indefinite unemployment.

The problems of contracting out include loss of accountability, a hollowing out of government, and an overreliance on volunteers, which may lead to high turnover or poor service delivery. The volunteer in Difate I met had been working unpaid for over a decade:

> Yes, since 1999. . . . And I manage when they give us something to at least go back to school and do some subjects that I am left with. But unfortunately, I am a breadwinner at home. I have to leave something for the home. I can't just spend all the time in school. It is a calling anyway. I don't have any problem even if I don't get money, but sometimes you have people and you have children and you have to do something to take care of the children. I love this work. I don't have any problem, even if I don't get anything. I have got the captain. . . . She is always there supporting me. Even lunch. If I don't have something, she brings something for me. I am grateful because we have people like her. . . . But now I am coping. It is just that sometimes, it is very difficult when at the end of the month people are getting money, and they buy something for their children, but I am coping. I am praying one of the good days maybe manna from heaven will come, and somebody will understand that I have been here for a long time, and my experience counts.

There was deep ambivalence throughout her discussion, a tension between wanting to express how committed she was to this work and her need to support herself and her family. She works every day without any compensation, and then at the end of the week is no further along in terms of finances. She hoped that her level of dedication and service would one day be recognized and rewarded, but after a decade of volunteering matched with declining resources, such hope seems unfounded.

One station commander outlined the problems with using volunteers for their service delivery, counseling, and victim advocacy. In discussing what other stations do by relying solely on volunteers, he said:

> You see, in the police, they run that thing with volunteers. And that is not right, because, you see, the volunteers, they will be there when they've got a chance to be there, but it is not going to happen that every time there is an issue they are there. Then we are going to fail by that.... That is the way the trauma offices are run everywhere, and we don't have an alternative but to take that route. But I don't like to depend on volunteers, because I have seen here if you've depended too much on the volunteers, you tend to fail sometimes.

Because relying on volunteers to staff victim support and outreach is a growing trend, the questions of capacity and accountability will continue.[8] Having trained staff, paid or unpaid, will go a long way to improving services for survivors. Yet this arrangement cannot compensate for structural gaps within the police staff.

Best Practices: People and Priorities

All the stations I interviewed and observed had challenges, but they all had at least one particular element of success: a dedicated volunteer, a competent station commander, an exceptional police investigator, a well-appointed trauma center, or a strong partnership with the community. One station in this study had all of these things, making it the model of what is possible.

This station was located in Mabitso, a rural area serving a large population and coping with crime that spilled over from other rural areas. Due to the nature of apartheid's violent political geography, giant groups of the black population were forced into small pockets of land, creating situations of overpopulation, even in rural areas, as part of the apartheid government's Bantustans (homelands) policy.[9] Thus, a very rural area would have a significant population-to-police ratio. The Mabitso area was poor, a great distance from a hospital, and far from urban social support networks and NGOs dealing with gender-based violence. Despite these resource and geographic constraints, the station made gender-based violence a priority.

CHAPTER FOUR

The approach at the station was to first get the *right people into the right positions*. The station's victim support team had two very well trained, effective, and committed members: a woman detective experienced in investigation and trained in traumatic crime, and a woman social worker experienced in trauma support, counseling, and intervention. And these two partners clicked: they were close colleagues with a warm, visible rapport. They trusted each other, and that trust was evident to everyone. They also joked about their roles. The social worker would say, "This one is so harsh!" and then discuss how her role was to ensure that the emotional needs of the victim were met, while the officer would work on getting the facts in order to help find the perpetrator and make the case. These women also took great care in outfitting their trauma center, creating a warm, comforting, safe environment for victims through donations from their own homes. One of the biggest complaints they had was that the room was located in the station just a few steps from the station's front desk. It was noisy, and victims did not have as much privacy as they would like.

The station commander also put her full force behind these two partners. She was committed to ending violence against women and standing up for survivors. The station commander was bold in making sure that her superiors understood that the increase in reports of intimate-partner-violence and gender-based-violence crimes at her station was actually a *positive* sign. In a group interview with members of the station, the officers discussed the increase in reports as a sign of their success. The station commander said the following:

> The statistics are killing me, because they will ask me in the meeting that, "What are you going to do because your cases of domestic violence are very high?" But [I answer], "People are reporting!" The cluster commander asks me, "Why are your cases of domestic violence very high?" And I say, "People are listening to us, they are coming to report, so if you want it to be low, how will I know where I am standing?" Over time it will be going down. When I see [specific stations reporting low numbers of domestic-violence cases], it is impossible really. They are not telling the truth. That is why I am saying, in the long run, they will be reported less because they will know [that the crime is actually decreasing, not just the reporting].

The station also had a dedicated social crime officer who was deeply committed to his job and who oversaw a very active and vibrant community police forum. He helped train them, worked with them on prevention programs and patrolling plans, and sought support and donations for them. He used his own vehicle for much of his community work, since there was a drastic shortage of vehicles at the station. The station also had a youth desk at the community police forum and large numbers of volunteers for each area of community policing. The partnership with the community was central to every unit.

While these members of the police saw their share of domestic violence, rape, and child abuse, they appeared to be coping significantly better than other areas that had fewer reported cases. They were aware of the counseling available to them but at that time felt they had enough training and support to succeed in their jobs. When I asked my routine question in the group interview about what they needed to do their job better, this was the only station that answered with a list of personal qualities and not a supply list: "passion, perseverance, determination, dedication, vision, mission." I then followed up with questions about supplies, and they expanded this list to include a designated vehicle to take survivors to the hospital, to court, and to and from home; a private trauma center away from the front desk; and supplies from the government for the center, including supplies for child victims and a designated computer for filing reports so that officers would no longer have to leave victims in order to enter information in a computer in the main area. They clearly had resource needs and very specific infrastructure needs, but their first reaction was to think about the values and qualities needed to address gender-based violence.

At the microlevel, the Mabitso station commander and members of the trauma team worked in partnership with key players; gave a clear priority to breaking the silence about gender violence; prioritized staff, training, and community partnerships; and fought against pressure from superiors to have lower statistics and create a rosier picture about domestic violence. Mabitso is an example of what is possible when leaders make gender-based violence a priority and shift resources, staff, and energy to this area.

I present this closing case not as a justification for individual agency over structural change or as a naive story of individuals trumping resource gaps. Nor is it a justification for a neoliberal push to downsize the already-barebones budget of organizations and units fighting gender-based violence. Rather, I present this station as a model of positive police discretion in action. Advocates across the country underscore the reality that gender-based violence continues to be sidelined, marginalized, dismissed, and undermined. They all claimed that ample resources exist in the government and the police to address gender-based violence, but the failures are linked to political leaders—at the national and local levels—refusing to make gender-based violence a priority.

In the case of Mabitso, the station commander and her detectives made gender-based violence a priority and put the people and resources in place to address it. This is an issue of discretion—the discretion of the police to take this crime seriously and the discretion of national leaders to enforce constitutional rights and legislative promises of gender equality and freedom from violence.

The case also points to what seems to be another crucial lesson about how to institutionalize and embrace the emotional labor that is inherently part of crisis response and gender-based-violence work (Mastracci, Guy, and Newman 2012; Wies and Haldane 2011). Often in interviews, participants would talk about individuals needing a "passion" for this job, which of course can be invaluable. What was important in the Mabitso station was that there was an institutional commitment to this work and an acknowledgment of the emotional labor involved in gender-based-violence work. When the station as a whole took on the emotional challenges of survivor care, the burden was not on one individual but on the entire station. There can still be specialized units and trauma care specialists, but what was notable was that the emotional labor was named, recognized, valued, and shared. This work is difficult at its best, permanently traumatic at its worst. Stations that can shift from marginalizing, discounting, or suppressing emotional labor to instead institutionalizing it can go a long way in challenging larger institutional norms of masculinity steeped in the "cowboy" mentality.

CHAPTER FIVE

Points of Contact

Police are key actors in the effort to address all forms of community and interpersonal violence, including gender-based violence. Similarly, community activists, religious leaders, traditional leaders, and organizational actors are essential in changing norms, behaviors, and systems that dismiss or legitimize gender-based violence. In the case of South Africa, the government has institutionalized several other key mechanisms and structures as focal points to address gender-based violence. These points of contact are the trauma units, medical centers, and courts designed for survivors to engage the state in positive social change.

One of the biggest obstacles for survivors is overcoming barriers to reporting. Women often fear reporting gender-based violence, either informally to family/religious communities or formally to law enforcement, because of stigma and ineffective institutional responses (McCleary-Sills et al. [2015] in Tanzania; Medie [2013] in Liberia). Here I examine a final critical component of addressing gender-based violence: points of contact where citizens engage the state for individual protection, the prosecution of their attackers, and the long-term prevention of continued gender-based violence. These points of contact are governed by national legislation, but they are implemented and managed very differently from community to community.

First, I explore the points of contact that are located within the law enforcement and legal sectors. I begin by looking at the case of the former national commissioner of the South African Police Services (SAPS), Jackie Selebi, and the effects of his dismantling of the Family Violence, Child Protection and Sexual Offences (FCS) units. Service providers across sectors said this decision harmed years of their efforts to address gender-based violence. They also talked about the problem that one individual, Selebi, was able to take apart an entire institution. Relatedly, I examine the importance

CHAPTER FIVE

of the sexual offenses courts, which are designed to hear cases in survivor-centered settings. Yet the government has not fully implemented or utilized these courts. I then turn to an examination of the trauma units and survivor support centers I visited in each of the communities, specifically exploring the impact of the location, design, and atmosphere of the trauma units on survivor support.

Next, I turn to a point of contact located in the medical sector. The Thuthuzela Care Centres (TCCs) are designated as one-stop centers for survivors of all forms of domestic violence and sexual assault. Located in medical facilities across South Africa, the TCCs are also a point of multisector collaboration among the medical sector, the National Prosecuting Authority (NPA), the police, and NGOs. While the TCCs represent significant improvements in survivor-centered services, they are limited in number and face a continual crisis of resources, as the South African government relies on international funding for the TCCs.

Looking at these main points of contact, it is quickly apparent that most of the points of contact where survivors engage the state are nestled within a legal/prosecutorial/carceral model. Even the pinnacle of the South African anti-gender-based-violence initiatives—the TCCs—are overseen by the NPA. While the TCCs are located in medical centers and focus on treatment of survivors after an assault, they are also designed to make the process of securing arrests, trials, and prosecutions more successful and less traumatizing for survivors. The legislative framework in South Africa focuses as much on prevention as it does on prosecution, but the key spaces in which survivors engage the state are reactive and legal in nature, exemplifying carceral approaches to justice.

Points of Contact in the Law Enforcement and Legal Sectors

One of the key goals of the South African women's movement during and after the democratic transition was the creation of institutions focused on promoting gender equality and women's rights. Many activists also believe that a key element of successful institutions is effective leadership. But what happens when political leaders are wrong?

FCS Units

One of the most notorious examples of this kind of leadership failure that occurred during my project was Jackie Selebi.[1] Following his appointment as the national commissioner of the SAPS in 2000, Selebi single-handedly reorganized the entire SAPS and consolidated several specialized units, downsizing key resources and personnel. The consequences were immense and rapid. Several units lost their specialized training and networks to share best practices and information. At the level of local stations, the range of cases each station had to manage expanded exponentially. Johan Burger (2014) of the Institute for Security Studies explained the impact of the restructuring, specifically the loss of specialization: "At the station level detectives who specialised in solving rape, child abuse or corruption, for example, lost their support structures and were often allocated dockets involving other more general crimes. As a result, many experienced detectives lost their networks and their expertise went unutilised." Burger further argues that there are damaging long-term effects of the restructuring, including the inability to train new detectives in these specialized skills.

Selebi continued the reorganization and decentralization from 2000 to 2006. For the FCS units, "capacity was distributed among 176 larger sized 'accounting' police stations; stations that were meant to provide a supervisory role to four to five smaller police stations in the area" (Burger 2014). The years of capacity building the units had created in terms of training, investigations, and arrests were dispersed and dismantled within a few short months.

I saw the impact of this massive reorganization firsthand in 2008. I had the opportunity to speak with members of the Bokang police unit who had focused on rape and domestic violence. The station at that time had been recognized for its success in securing arrests and convictions for rape and domestic-violence cases. The former members of the unit I encountered were outspoken in their frustration about the massive SAPS changes. They felt their unit was being torn apart *because they were successful*. In other crimes, such as theft or carjacking, criminals often were not apprehended. In the gender-based-violence, sexual assault, domestic abuse, and child abuse cases they saw in their unit, survivors often knew the perpetrators. Their unit had an excellent record of arrest, evidence collection, and prosecutions. But they had been told their units were "too expensive," since they were able to keep cases active through the prosecution phase. One white South African woman stated that she joined the police specifically to be part of this unit because she wanted to see results and make a difference, and she felt their success was being punished. Other members felt their specializations were no longer being used, and their success rates for gender-based-violence arrests and prosecutions were falling as a result.

In 2011 I spoke with a member of the Civilian Secretariat for the Police about the dismantling of the FCS units and the decision to reinstate them:

Police initially had what was called Family Child and Sexual Violence units. During the restricting process that took place from 2000 onward, there was a move to try and look at capacitating police stations. There was a decision to close down specialized units and to reintegrate them into the police stations. . . . There was a decision to mainstream, which didn't work. I think that one of the things we have said . . . is that before any restricting of the police occurs going forward . . . before you restructure and have a major response to restricting, it has to be based on international best practice, policy approaches. . . . And I think there was a tendency in the last couple of years to keep restricting the police. . . . Now one of the things we need to do is to make sure that going forward in restricting, we have identified that there are particular areas which require specialized skills. And there is no doubt that gender and child violence is one of those.

This official described some of the obstacles that the previous FCS units faced. When I discussed what I saw in 2008 with the tension among former members of the FCS units getting reassigned to other units, this official said that similar problems existed in stations where station commanders sometimes used FCS units as dumping grounds for problematic officers.

The FCS units generally had been successful at securing arrests and prosecutions, which also meant they were costly for stations to run. By sending problem officers to these units, the stations could offload disciplinary issues to the FCS and might also decrease their effectiveness and thus their costs.

These sentiments were echoed in my conversations with local police officers, as one officer, a black South African man in the Bokang station, explained: "So you see those units were there, and then one of our commissioners came in and disbanded them and said, 'Go down to station level.' So in other words, cases of domestic violence, specialized cases were not getting the attention that they deserve because they were just 'normal' cases. They were just normal detective cases." The police recognized the specialized skills and training necessary not only to investigate these crimes but also to care for the survivors.

The official at the Civilian Secretariat for the Police said that, given the reinstatement of the FCS units in 2011–12 (discussed below), the emphasis now is on the effectiveness of the new units, as they have become "kind of a show piece." She indicated that the recruitment and training processes would make it "quite difficult" for stations to send poorly trained or problematic officers to the units.

The decisions by Commissioner Selebi also continued to haunt members of the National Gender Machinery. I spoke with one ANC member of parliament in 2011 who had taken a very public stand against the decision to dismantle the FCS units. She told me about the rapid rebuilding happening that year. She used this example to reiterate the need for strong institutions with accountability through checks and balances in order to control the actions of individual leaders so that one person could not unilaterally dismantle an entire system:

> The closure of those units was wrong. And that is why as the portfolio committee we are saying we should be strengthening systems so that we have strong systems vis-à-vis strong individuals. It should not be easy for a person to up and decide to close, if the systems are strong. [Author's question: And by systems, what do you mean?] Whether you are talking about policy or you are talking about legislation, it shouldn't be such that it doesn't take a national commissioner to close down anything. . . . It shouldn't, because what you have then is very powerful people over very powerful systems. But I think what we need is powerful systems. . . . That is my own view. We strengthen the systems. It is not easy for people to sleep, wake up the following day, "I am closing this. I am opening this." It should be such that when something is there [like the FCS units], somebody who wants to close it must find it is not that easy to do it. Particularly if it is something that we all believe it is assisting. Because now we are starting from scratch with all these units. We should not be where we are today—we should be somewhere. We should be talking [about] something else.

This ANC MP stated in strong, unqualified terms that one individual should not have the power to reorganize or dismantle entire units, especially those that had been effective. The fact that Commissioner Selebi was able to do so almost unilaterally was unacceptable to members of the public, police, and parliament who had advocated for the units' creation.

The official in the Civilian Secretariat for the Police also spoke with me about this tension between leadership and structures. When I talked about the concerns of the ANC MP that the previous police commissioner had closed the units, the official agreed: "Restructuring is a *policy* issue. So we basically want to set down very clearly priorities. For us, we want to restructure to fit with the legislation and policies. . . . It has got to be influenced by policy and approaches and scientific approach to policing." The official said the direction now is to ensure that structures and institutions are governed by policy and legislation, not by individual administrators. One person should not be able to unilaterally restructure an entire institution without seeking approval and without evidence to support the changes.

In 2012 Police Minister Nathi Mthetwa explained the reasons for relaunching the FCS units, citing the widespread condemnation of the previous decision to close them, as well as the persistent high levels of sexual crimes nationally. He stressed the importance of interdepartmental collaboration with the judiciary and the National Prosecuting Authority to investigate and prosecute these crimes: "Rape decreased by 1.9% but it is unacceptably high. More resources and better training of police mechanisms are now being put in place.... The important struggle we must continue to wage is to end violence against women, a critical part of the historic effort to change the power relations in our society" (South African Government News Agency 2012). In the call to increase resources and reprioritize gender-based violence, the minister clearly linked the patterns of gender-based violence to the larger structural issues of power inequality in the society.

During the 2011 relaunch of the units, I spoke with several members of the SAPS, as well as officials in the Secretariat, who were impressed by the actions of Brigadier Bafana Peter Linda, section head of the FCS units. While my attempts to interview him were unsuccessful, his work in this area has been widely reported in the press and in his media interviews. He considered the units and the protection of women and children to be his passion, and he hoped that his leadership would be his legacy.

Sexual Offenses Courts

In addition to reinstating the FCS units in the police, South Africa also reestablished the sexual offenses courts.[2] The first such court opened in Wynberg, Cape Town, in 1993. I first interviewed antirape activists in Cape Town about the court in 1996. They viewed the court as an important step forward that provided a more affirming atmosphere for survivors and more informed court officials and staff to deal with gender-based-violence cases and protection orders. The success of the courts then was widely celebrated: they had a conviction rate of almost 80 percent compared to regular criminal courts, which had an estimated 10–15 percent conviction rate for sexual offenses. In 2005, when seventy-four such courts existed in South Africa, the success and mandate of the courts began to fade due to problems of budget allocations, poor preparation and training of court staff, inadequate physical court spaces, and uneven monitoring and management of the courts (South African Government News Agency 2014). Following the adoption of the Criminal Law (Sexual Offences and Related Matters) Amendment Act No. 32 of 2007, government attention turned to reinvesting in and bolstering the resources, management, and function of the courts nationally (Manyathi-Jele 2013).

In August 2015 six courts had been officially upgraded to meet the status of a sexual offenses court, including specialized training for court personnel and special facilities and technology to reduce survivor retraumatization. Minister of Justice and Correctional Services Michael Masutha reported that the addition of the sexual offenses courts was responsible in part for the increase in convictions, from 59.6 percent the previous year to 63 percent (Manyathi-Jele 2015). The plan was to establish 106 sexual offenses courts over ten years.

But as attorney Alison Tilly (2016) argues, this vital point of contact within the legal systems continues to be unevenly implemented, funded, and monitored. She states that most people "have no idea that the Sexual Offences Courts exist" or how they are different from other courts. Further, the level of interagency collaboration between the NPA, the Department of Justice, the TCCs, and the magistrates needed to optimize these courts is, in her opinion, "harder than herding cats."

Court officials and judges require specific training to run these specialized courts. Without such training, it is more likely that even these specialized courts will replicate the existing judicial culture, which has been problematic in returning rape convictions. As Stacy Moreland argues, "Rape complainants require more than just the vindication of a purely legal claim; they require the validation of their interpretation and experience of harmful sexual behavior. . . . [W]hen judges let the constant noise of patriarchy . . . overwhelm them, they curtail this potential" (2014, 13). While the compartmentalization of these courts could provide a more survivor-centered space within the legal system, Moreland asserts that the larger institutional culture of the legal systems should also be addressed and that culture is a patriarchal one. Therefore, a two-pronged approach of supporting specialized courts and mainstreaming gender-sensitivity and survivor-based models may prove necessary to effect change throughout the entire system.

Trauma Units

Another key point of contact nested in the law enforcement and legal sectors is the trauma centers and survivor support facilities located in police stations. In theory, every station is supposed to have a designated space for this purpose, along with a staff dedicated specifically to its operation. The types of spaces the trauma centers and survivor support rooms occupied varied widely among the stations I visited. Some units had stand-alone buildings that were removed from the public eye of the station's holding cells or client services front desk. Others were located near the heart of the station, and officers had varying opinions about this arrangement. Those in more rural settings with more space wanted a room that was separate,

CHAPTER FIVE

private, and quiet. Others located in cramped urban stations were grateful to have any space at all.

Some spaces were designed with children and youth in mind and included colorful murals of animals and other playful images, comfortable children's seating and furniture, and ample age-appropriate toys. Some spaces had beds for survivors to rest, which were particularly helpful for sexual assault or abuse survivors who needed to recover before moving on to the next stage of interviewing or medical examinations. These beds were not supposed to be for overnight stays, I was told, because if something happened to someone staying there overnight, the station would be responsible.

Some of the rooms had their own bathrooms, but many did not, and survivors would need to be escorted either to a staff or visitor bathroom elsewhere in the station. Typically, the officers and volunteers who staffed the room were responsible for helping survivors clean themselves when recovering in the facilities, as well as then removing the blood and fluids in the room and on the sheets and towels used by survivors as they recovered. One morning, I was shown a room filled with bloody sheets and blankets from a rape and assault survivor the previous day. I spoke with the volunteer, a black middle-aged South African woman working in a station located within a primarily coloured township. This volunteer was clearly tired physically and emotionally after working that case, and now she had to clean up the physical reminders of the violence the following day:

> But they call me sometimes. They come and pick me up, but sometimes when I am so tired I say, "No, you go—I see you tomorrow morning. Take the key, but you know you mustn't do 123." When I came in here like this morning I find the lady with a child there [pointing]. She was full of blood. I don't know where the boyfriend hit her. So I tell [the officers] to take care of this lady. "When I come back, you must give me her address, and I must go and see her what's happening and what is going on." Now she just left the bleeding towels and everything there in the victim empowerment. So now I have to go and see what is going on.

She explained that the police were supposed to take a victim to the hospital first, but she found the woman at the station, bloody and in need of attention. The volunteer instructed the police to take the woman immediately to the hospital. The survivor support advocate was an unpaid volunteer with only minimal training, yet she was the intercept point for this survivor. When I asked her how many cases she saw in a month, she said she could only talk about the ones she knew about: "Some of them I don't know about them. I just hear them say, 'Somebody in the trauma room.' I say, 'Fine, but you must write in my book.' I leave two books. 'You must write it in here and there.' . . . They don't care. They don't worry. You see, that is how they are." This volunteer was working to ease the pain and trauma of survivors while trying to maintain a standard of care and services in her trauma center. Importantly, she was trying to create some system to keep track of survivors through the small effort of writing down information in two journals she purchased for this task. Even this attempt to have some way of contacting and following up with survivors was dismissed by the police.

A small number of stations I observed did not have any special space for survivor interviews or recovery. Most interestingly, this was the case in the station located in one of the wealthiest, predominately white communities I visited, Olive Vlei. Officers explained that they saw so few cases of gender-based violence and intimate-partner violence that they used the space for storage. The officers explained that many domestic-violence survivors in this area had extended families or resources to help them after abuse. They did not want to report the crime to the police and kept it as a private matter.

I observed another trauma center located in Arbeidstad, a working-class community with a mix of industrial and residential areas. This station had a designated space for survivors, but it did not have the supplies or furniture it was supposed to have. Other units and officers conducted their work, ate lunch, or made private calls in this space. They sometimes interrupted or ignored the fact that the victim support advocate was interviewing a survivor and continued to use the space. The victim support advocate was also struggling to meet the immediate needs of survivors in the space. They might need rest or food, and she didn't have any of the things most trauma units should have—a bed or a stove or a refrigerator. She also had other problems with creating a safe space. I noticed that a large, intimidating storage container labeled "firearms" in her office actually had all the toys and stuffed animals for child survivors or children of survivors. The commanding officer of this station was an older black South African man, and he was also fully aware of the failures of the center and staffing arrangements:

> That is a good question. You see, the trauma center is something very important but is not well resourced. Like you see, our trauma [center] is just not up to standard. That place must have a bed, must have other stuff that is missing there, and there must be sufficient privacy for the victims when they are there, so that they must be the victims and the people dealing with them—not the other people that will disturb the process. And we have that lady whom we placed there, and we are talking to the community about volunteers.

The commander described how he struggled against the lack of resources, staff, and supplies to run an effective center. He did not believe that this was a lack of leadership or priorities—more a lack of resources and funding for staff.

My interviews and observations preceded a national audit of stations and their implementation of the Domestic Violence Act and the trauma centers. The Civilian Secretariat for the Police conducted the first audit of the Domestic Violence Act in 2012–13. It also conducted 145 audits of police stations around the country in 2012–13 for their compliance with the Domestic Violence Act. The following year, an additional 155 stations were audited, as well as eleven thousand members of the SAPS (NCOP Security and Justice 2013; see also Civilian Secretariat for the Police 2013; Women in the Presidency 2013). The audits found consistent problems in implementation, including lack of appropriate and available documentation procedures and forms, inconsistent recording and handling of domestic-violence incidents, and poor management of the victim-friendly rooms. The audits found that only 62 percent of stations had functional and well-resourced victim-friendly rooms, 14 percent of stations used their rooms for office space or storage, and a full 24 percent did not have a room at all. Further, the victim-friendly rooms had unclear staffing and management—some were run by volunteers, some by the community police forums, some by the SAPS. Additionally, there were eighty-eight cases of domestic violence filed against members of the SAPS.

The secretariat found that across all the stations audited (145), only 4,308 officers had been trained on the Domestic Violence Act, while 7,542 officers had not been trained. The audits further found that even those officers who had been trained lacked full understanding of the Domestic Violence Act. In particular, very few if any officers knew what to do if someone did not follow a protection order (Women in the Presidency 2013). The audit found a very high percentage, 72 percent, of domestic-violence case withdrawals.

That initial audit made extensive recommendations, including several relating to other government departments, particularly Social Development. The absence of available services such as counseling and shelters falls to Social Development. The lack of these services was seen as an obstacle to full implementation of the law. Similarly, the SAPS and the National Prosecuting Authority are often unclear on the execution of protection orders, leaving survivors vulnerable after they reported a case. The member of the secretariat also voiced concerns about the reporting and handling of domestic-violence cases and survivors with disabilities. She believed there is some correlation between disability and an increased chance of domestic violence, and these cases are likely underreported and poorly handled by the police taking the report.

These abuses, failures, and inconsistencies continue today (Mkhwanazi 2016). The most recent report of the secretariat, covering 2014–15, included an audit of 187 police stations. The findings saw remarkably familiar trends (Civilian Secretariat for the Police 2016). Fifty-eight officers in the stations faced their own charges of domestic violence, which again echoes the lived experiences of the women I interviewed in the police stations. The implementation rate had increased, with 85.2 percent of all stations (the national average) in compliance with the Domestic Violence Act, though some provinces fell far short, including KwaZulu Natal at 64.9 percent, Limpopo at 63.4 percent, and the Northern Cape at 63.2 percent. These more rural provinces have the additional constraint of fewer resources for survivors, such as counseling and safe shelter. The regulatory compliance—specifically, the administrative requirements for the Domestic Violence Act—was even lower, with an average compliance per province of 74.3 percent.

Another area that continues to plague stations is the Victim Friendly Services/Rooms. Only 57.8 percent of stations had a functional and resourced room, 10.7 percent had a functional room that lacked sufficient resources, 12.8 percent had nonfunctional rooms, and 18.7 percent did not have any survivor-friendly room available. Again, this national audit of trauma centers directly aligns with the interviews and the patterns I had observed in my target communities.

A positive sign in the stations I observed was the level of care and personal sacrifice many officers and volunteers gave to the physical spaces. They frequently dipped into their own pockets to help survivors secure transportation, to provide toiletries, and to buy comforting toys for children. They brought bedding, decorations, lamps, tables, stuffed animals, toys, and pictures from their own homes to make the place welcoming for survivors. Some units seemed to have a more open policy for accepting donations from churches or local organizations—clothing, toiletries, toys and gifts for children, and blankets. Others seemed to be daunted by following a requisition process or protocol of having all donations go through the station commander.

In each case, the officers and volunteers themselves filled in the gaps through their own donations. As one black woman officer who had worked with survivors for several years in a predominately black township stated, "Just imagine. I say, 'Oh, we want the bedding for this bed.' We have to write a request, which will be approved next year. So I had to take my child's bedding, so that when people come here they say they are working in a nice environment." This station had a special trauma center space donated by a prominent South African business, but the officers then had to furnish and decorate the space. I asked about the ongoing support of the business, but one survivor advocate stated, "Yes. They just come [pause], and then they disappear. They gave the tables, but everything else we have to donate from our home." This volunteer felt that the business was investing in the trauma room merely for one-off PR purposes and not as an ongoing investment or solution.

Given the low salaries of the police and the lack of any salary for volunteers, these personal donations may take a toll on street-level service providers. One black woman volunteer who was based at the same station for years had trouble providing her own meals and taxi costs to come to her post. Yet she would work tirelessly to help secure the same things for survivors. She said a nearby police station was notorious for sending survivors to her station, even though her station had fewer resources, because the staff was better and more responsive. However, the officers then had to deal with the survivor needing to get back to their area in the township: "Some will come, and we have to take money to help them, and sometimes *you* don't have money to go back home." The volunteer continued to put her resources and time into the survivors, but she and other volunteers have worked for decades without pay and have donated what little resources and money they have to help the survivors.

The public critique of the police for their lack of response to gender-based violence is well deserved. Yet I was struck by the commitment and dedication of these street-level officers and volunteers, who are often tucked away in separate spaces and doing deeply meaningful and traumatic work in the service of survivors. They are underfunded, underresourced, overworked, and experiencing their own secondary trauma. Many are survivors themselves. These volunteers have the on-the-ground experience the SAPS needs to improve survivor-centered services, yet these volunteers and officers are often marginalized voices in the justice system.

Points of Contact in the Medical and Legal Sectors

Thuthuzela, which means "to comfort" in IsiXhosa, is the name for a network of care centers that have become the model of best practice in South Africa for assisting survivors of sexual assault and abuse. Health systems are key points of contact for survivors globally (García-Moreno et al. 2015; Lawoko et al. 2013), and medical professionals are some of the most important street-level bureaucrats in service delivery (Walker and Gilson 2004). Research indicates that in South Africa most often the "first contact women have with formal services are in health settings" (Rasool 2016, 1662). The impetus for the TCCs came from a desire to have both less traumatic treatment of survivors and more effective prosecution of perpetrators. TCCs see all forms of gender-based violence, including sexual assault, rape, intimate-partner violence, domestic violence, and child abuse. One TCC site coordinator I interviewed was a black South African woman working in a large urban black township. She said the NPA based the design of the TCCs on the model of the one-stop rape crisis centers that had existed for some time, including those I had visited in the late 1990s and early 2000: "It [the TCC] is the NPA model, but it is something that has always been there, because I was working in a center that was the same type of model that the NPA was introducing... focused on the psychosocial and group support." The TCCs were initially envisioned and developed within the NPA, but they rely on multisector collaboration among law enforcement, medical services, social services, community leaders, and NGOs for their success.

One TCC site coordinator, a young black woman, explained that the NPA was driven by a desire to improve the prosecution process. The government found that even if survivors report cases, they often decide against pursuing prosecution. She explained that many survivors face complex trauma and then are "secondarily victimized" by the police and courts. The TCCs were designed to meet the needs of survivors by providing a range of support structures within one location: "That is why we have the centers, which is to make sure that... a survivor—a victim—gets special care from the time they report to the time they go to court. They are prepared." The goal of the TCCs is not only care and support of the survivor but also about moving cases forward in the judicial process. In this way, the TCCs are part of this larger national antiviolence framework, with an emphasis on survivor-centered access to justice.

I spoke with a member of the justice system, a black South African woman who worked as a high-level administrator. She described the idea behind the TCCs and similar care centers / survivor support units, which grew after comparisons with other centers across the globe. The goal became both about medical/psychological treatment and accessing justice, both organized specifically with a survivor-friendly process through the centralization of services: "We always talk about victim-friendly services, so that it is easier for the victim... and also the issue of access to justice. So we were not accessible as a criminal justice system." The centralization of the TCCs was not simply about providing accessible support services for survivors, it was also about making it easier for the justice system to operate. This type of framework is in line with the models seen throughout the Southern African Development Community (SADC) region of having prosecutor-driven or prosecutor-led investigations (Britton and Shook 2014). Nesting the medical intervention point of contact within the larger umbrella of the NPA is supposed to build a prosecution process that is both community based and survivor centered. The same high-level administrator in the justice system described the guiding values of the TCCs:

> Also, because by nature a TCC—you wouldn't expect it to be under a prosecution service. But because of the studies that we did around the world, prosecutors must become truly people's lawyers. So you need to interact with communities; hence, we had this unit when it comes to issues of gender. And we have three objectives in the TCCs. First, reduce secondary victimization. Second, we want to reduce the case times, and which also contributes to the reduction of secondary victimization, because if the case takes longer periods, you are revictimizing the victim to relive the experience for a long period. The third is the increase in the conviction rates.

Here we can hear how the values of survivor-centered care become enmeshed with values of conviction rates, again melding the carceral approach with a survivor-centered approach. In order to provide survivor-centered access to justice, the TCCs were designed as one-stop or first-stop centers for survivors who have recently experienced an attack.

One of the key aspects of the TCC is that it brings together multiple sectors in direct collaboration to put the survivor first. This collaboration happens in different ways and at different levels, but the overall goal remains the same: making the justice system more accessible and helping survivors better prepare for prosecutions. "The victim is empowered from the word go, and she doesn't have to repeat herself over and over again to them.... And because everything is done by trained professional people, ... then we have a better chance of getting convictions, because also the victim is a better witness. She is calm, collected, so she knows exactly. She has been counseled. She doesn't fear the system anymore. The system becomes demystified." In this passage, the survivor advocate explained how the justice system is trying to improve a survivor's experience of justice not just to help the survivor but also to achieve more convictions. It is also striking how the language of empowerment is linked to the pursuit of convictions: a survivor is empowered to pursue justice, and "just" is defined here as "prosecution."

The guiding idea behind the TCCs was to end the revictimization of survivors who choose to report and come forward. Supporting someone who makes the choice to report rape or intimate-partner violence is a major accomplishment in and of itself. The legal system had vast gaps, and many survivors chose to withdraw their cases rather than move forward with prosecutions. In a large part this was due to the "runaround" survivors received at police stations and hospitals. The design of the TCCs was to streamline and humanize the reporting and recovery process for survivors. Rather than having survivors go to multiple government offices and medical facilities for care and support, the TCCs strive to bring the government to the survivor in a one-stop center. As this researcher explained, there was a recognition at the highest levels of the justice system that the process for survivors had been humiliating, ineffective, and retraumatizing.

When you walk into most TCCs, a staff member greets you immediately, twenty-four hours a day. From that initial point of contact, each TCC may have a range of staff available to assist you, and that staff varies, for example, depending on the number of cases the TCC sees each month. I interviewed one doctor in a TCC who was able to give me a few minutes before a very young survivor entered. He described what he saw as the basic structure of the TCC:

> It is a one-stop center that looks after victims and survivors of sexual assault, also domestic violence and child abuse. So it is more of a clinical, forensic medical center. The goal is to provide a holistic service to victims. So, for example, we should be having all the stakeholders in this center. So when a patient or victim or complainant walks in, we don't send them out and say, "Go to a police station. Go to [a] social worker." They will have counseling here. So the different counselors will be lay counselors, trauma counseling, and also HIV counseling. We do test for HIV, and [we do have] HIV health staff, [a] forensic nurse, or [a] forensic doctor who conduct an examination and issue medication. A social worker, some of the centers have a social worker on board also. Some have a psychologist. The center in town has got a psychologist [who] comes in three times a day, and also the police. [Author's question: Do all of the centers have all these people?] There is a slight variation. It is the ideal. But, for example, one of the centers will have police on-site. They will take statements and look after all the things on the police side. It is sort of a one-stop for all these things. So medication will be issued from here. Counseling will be issued from here. We have the stakeholders, the NGOs, nongovernmental organizations, around the community. They will liaison with shelters for placement.

From his perspective, his TCC is one of the best resourced across the nation. It was designed to serve multiple communities—urban townships, informal settlements, black and coloured areas, and white areas—but the clients were almost exclusively from the adjacent black and coloured townships, not the white suburbs.

CHAPTER FIVE

The site coordinator for this same TCC continued to explain that one of the main issues in the creation of the TCCs was to have prosecutors involved from the beginning to ensure the proper collection of evidence so that convictions were more likely. She also talked very specifically about the wait time and length of cases, believing that a delay in justice is justice denied, especially for survivors of gender-based violence. She felt that the number of case withdrawals is much smaller at the TCC than the number of case withdrawals that are reported elsewhere in the legal system (e.g., a police station). Part of that may be the quality of services and care that survivors receive in the TCC. But it may also be that the conviction rates are higher with the prosecutor-led investigations and the interagency collaboration nestled within the TCCs.

One thing that was missing from this particular TCC was a staff counselor. Some TCCs have them, but this one did not. Another staff member stated: "The hands that I think we need [are] to have people based in the center for counselling, like for psychosocial intervention. Because at the moment we are referring people to—we have interns at [a local outreach center]." Having that support located in-house would also indicate that the TCCs are not just focused on successful prosecutions. Instead, the TCCs would become the full-service center for survivors and their entire holistic recovery.

I spoke with a service provider in a TCC located in a black township who provided case management and psychosocial support services to survivors. She spoke about the need for ongoing support:

> I deal with the crisis here, so I never get to see most of the victims after. Very few of them come back after. Like we have this one. She was our very first case . . . when we started. . . . One of the guys has been convicted. The other one passed away, unfortunately. But it is one of our successes. She keeps coming back just to say hi. But having worked in my previous job, I really think that support groups and psychosocial intervention is important in terms of making a victim go out there and face the world. Because we want them to testify in court. We want them to be happy that the guy is in court. But you don't know what goes on in their lives after. Like, maybe they no longer have [a] good relationship with their husband, if they are married. Or if it is a young person, they have a difficult time moving on with their life. So it is important that, as much as we do our part, they need to go through a process of facing life again. And they will never forget their experience. But they can be able to feel that they can achieve whatever they want to achieve without them saying, "Because I was raped, I wasn't able to continue school or be able to do this or that."

This service provider saw the long-term impact of sexual assault on survivors, as well as the effects of taking the case to court. While talking about reducing retraumatization and increasing prosecutions/convictions, this service provider also addressed how much more they could do for survivor support. It is almost as if the survivors' support ends with the conviction—as if justice served will give survivors all they need in terms of peace and recovery. From her perspective, having worked in a variety of victim support agencies, these survivors need much more than support through the trial and conviction—they need support groups, couples counseling, and job and educational support. If this model is successful, then the survivors need the support to move beyond their trauma and the impact that the court case has on their lives and family. She acknowledged that no one ever forgets the assault, but she wants to know that survivors had the ongoing support and assistance to move on from the assault and live to their potential. The TCCs, while a model point of contact, are still bound by the timeline and benchmarks of a criminal trial. She is advocating for something much longer term and more sustainable.

The Citi Golf Model: "Not as Comfortable, but at Least It Is There"

Since there are only fifty-three TCCs in South Africa today, the need for survivor support far outpaces the institutions in place. Leaders are attempting to find ways to create smaller, leaner models of care that still ensure that survivors are supported. As one member of the justice system stated, "In fact, we always joke and say the TCC, they are Rolls-Royce model. And then you can come up with Citi Golf kind of model, but . . . it gets you there. Not as comfortable, but at least it's here."[3] In this way, the model of the TCC has had a positive effect for survivor services nationally, even outside of the TCC system. Given the national attention to gender-based violence, the Department of Health recognized the need to have better support for the care and identification of survivors in all its facilities, as did the police services. While the TCCs may be the ideal model—the Rolls Royce of survivor care—the diffusion of survivor-centered access to justice is just as essential. This push to mainstream identification and care of survivors throughout the health system was echoed in a study in Uganda by Stephen Lawoko and colleagues (2013). While many health-care workers in the Ugandan study had what they felt was sufficient training to identify survivors, most felt they lacked the time to do so properly or the referral options to support widespread screening. So no matter what the model, an ability to secure ongoing support is also necessary.

However, there is widespread criticism that there are not enough efforts to make accessible and effective services reach across the system. Working in Durban, Kogieleum Naidoo (2013) found that changes in health policy have not resulted in any significant changes in the quality or accessibility of survivor care outside of a handful of designated crisis centers. Naidoo asserts that the lack of services is a significant barrier to reporting. The costs associated with coming forward make it difficult both financially and emotionally. Another member of a TCC shared similar ideas—that while the other medical centers, especially those in urban areas, had many of the same components as the TCCs, they did not have all the pieces. Yet those medical centers may in fact see more cases than a TCC merely because of their location, not because of the quality and comprehensiveness of the services. A survivor's proximity to a medical location could determine where they seek assistance, or clients may have biases about going to TCCs that are located in black townships.

Fluctuating Performance: "We Are Making Sausages"

As with all the institutions discussed in this book, the TCCs are also challenged by lack of resources, uneven implementation, rapid staffing turnover, and leadership changes (Naidoo 2013). TCCs were designed as the pinnacle of one-stop crisis centers, but there are still big differences in how the TCCs perform and the quality of services survivors receive. I heard this echoed by one member of the justice system who had a system-wide knowledge of the TCCs:

> I mean, people come and go. I mean, I won't be here tomorrow, and you still expect the program to go on. We have tried in terms of developing standard policies so that whoever comes can do it. But then it also depends on your patience and a lot of that. So I always say for anyone to do this job, you must be able to have some sort of diplomacy of telling people to go to hell, and then they see themselves fit for the trip. And then they just go smiling, and then they realize, "Oh, she actually told me to [go to] hell." So you find a way of massaging people's egos here and there. Very patient, which can be very frustrating. So I say, now we have forty-five TCCs, but you might go to all of them, and you might find that they are not at the same level, all of them, even though we have tried to standardize, . . . because it depends on people, and people will come and people will leave. They find greener pastures.

This quote embodies some of the eternal problems of service delivery. While the issues of recruiting, training, and retaining staff are not limited to South

Africa (García-Moreno et al. 2015; Lawoko et al. 2011; Lawoko et al. 2013; John, Lawoko, and Svanstrom 2011), this issue may be even more pressing and destructive in resource-poor environments. Retaining skilled staff, instilling outstanding diplomacy skills, ensuring consistency of services—each demands a high level of oversight, as well as funding.

While there is pressure at all levels to increase the numbers of TCCs, there are continued problems staffing and running the existing centers. The same member of the justice system talked about the pressures they face to roll out more and more TCCs. She would rather take time to improve and strengthen the TCCs that are already in place. The pressure to create more TCCs reduces their effectiveness: "For now, I feel like we are producing sausages, which is very frustrating. . . . It becomes embarrassing when parliamentarians want to visit the TCCs, then they go there, then they are no longer the standard you had, say, when it was launched." She stated that the justice department is under pressure to have the showpieces, the Rolls-Royce model of TCC, to demonstrate the department is delivering on the government's promise to address gender-based violence. Yet turnover or shifts in funding and resources can rapidly disrupt a previously successful crisis center.

Place and location also affect the TCC system. The government is attempting to ensure access to justice in all areas, including the rural areas. TCCs are expensive and resource intensive, so finding the right combination to roll out a sufficient number of rural TCCs is slower than many would like. According to this member of the justice system, the government was starting to put more TCCs in rural areas. But the distance from urban centers was putting a strain on those TCCs with resource-allocation issues: "The TCC itself is resource intensive, . . . and also you don't have many resources in the rural areas. I mean, the roads are bad, transport is bad, and things like that. . . . So even though we prioritize rural areas, we also look at the statistics in that area because of the fact that you can't have them all in hospitals." Here again, there are constraints of place and geography—such as access to hospitals and roads—that affect the provision of TCCs throughout the country. Every area wants and deserves the Rolls-Royce of the TCC, but there are very real material constraints that limit this rollout.

The Thuthuzelas began with donor support, mostly from international sources, to address gender-based violence. Just as the process for getting the updated sexual offenses legislation through parliament was delayed over and over again, the TCCs continue to fight to get sufficient support from the government. Support and political will and leadership have proven vital globally (García-Moreno et al. 2015). One member of the justice system had advice for other programs or countries trying to begin something similar to the TCCs or the national system of survivor support centers. Her advice was to begin with the national level and to secure their support; then attracting and retaining donor support should be easier:

> Political buy-in is important. . . . I think for us what made it easy is that it was cabinet that said we need an antirape strategy. Yes, the cabinet. Because in that way, even when you look for resources, you know, it becomes much easier. It was even then they said they wanted this antirape strategy—it was an unfunded mandate for a long time, until donors came along. And then we entered into an agreement with donors that, "It is okay if you give us three years' funding, then we will sort of phase it in." . . . So my advice is always start at the political level, because then it makes it easier so that you don't depend on donors from the word go. . . . We started with donors, and then government is slowly coming in. And also, it is easier for even donors to attract other donors when the government has a buy-in.

Yet the political buy-in and sustainable government funding for the TCCs that she had hoped for have been in almost constant crisis. Seventy percent of the centers receive counselors through NGOs, and the majority of their support comes from international funding through the Global Fund to Fight Aids, Tuberculosis and Malaria. In August 2016, when the fund announced it would only support centers with high rates of HIV, combined with other cuts, it was estimated that nearly half of the TCCs would lose counseling services (Pilane 2016a, 2016b). A private donor was announced to bridge the gap later in the year, so it appears this part of the program has been given a second life. But advocates and donors insist that the South African government must begin to fully fund the centers, in large part because South Africa is now considered to be a middle-income country and therefore less eligible for international funding (Pilane 2016b).

The Precarity of Street-Level Workers

Members of the TCC stated that their biggest challenges are (1) the emotional labor they do when working with survivors and (2) the economic and employment vulnerability they face in their jobs. My conversations with the members of the TCCs echoed almost exactly the secondary trauma and financial precarity I found with the police who work in this sector. As a member of the justice system related, "One of the things we find talking to different people in this structure is that they need support structures in place, just mentally support structures in place." Many of the members of the TCC are volunteers. Several TCCs have lay counselors who work twelve-hour shifts to ensure the centers have constant coverage. There may be only one person in the TCC in the middle of the night, and they have to coordinate services, detectives, and doctors to come in to assist a victim. When I asked if the lay counselors were paid or were volunteers, a social worker in a TCC explained that most of them were volunteers: "No, they are volunteers. . . . So I think it is our biggest challenge. Because it is not fair to our staff to come to work when they are not even having money to take a taxi to come to work. And you see they can't even afford the cost of living with that money." These lay counselors are the first point of contact for survivors when they walk in the door, and they are witness to the trauma and violence their clients face. Often unpaid and overworked, they have few support structures to ensure their own well-being.

These positions face constant turnover because of the lack of pay, support, and benefits, as well as burnout. Members of the TCCs also discussed the need for institutions and counselors to help them with the secondary trauma they face each day as a part of this work. Seeing violence every day, often extraordinary violence, can affect counselors' own sense of self and their own sense of safety. A TCC member explained how this job weighed on her physically and how she tried to envision a better support model for volunteers and staff:

> I think we can also get that type of help by having our regular debriefing sessions, which is important for all of us—especially working in a situation where you get traumatic stories every day [nervous laughter]. And then, when you walk in the street, you keep looking back to see that no one is sneaking up on you. I have to travel from [nearby city] every day. So I have to wake up very early in the morning, because I am using public transport. You can just imagine having to walk to the taxi. So I am really having a difficult time with that. I am trying to get a transfer to go back to [that city]. I really love [it here], but I—Like I was telling you, I was renting here. . . . I felt that cases [here] were a bit extreme compared to what I used to see. Cases whereby someone was attacked in the veldt or somewhere because they were walking late at night. I am not saying it is OK, but it is understandable that they were walking in an unsafe area. [Here] we have cases whereby a person would break in a house with a locked door! . . . People can actually walk in your house and come in and rape you after you have locked yourself inside. Because I was renting on my own, all of my family is in [nearby city], I felt it was better to be in a house so that there was someone who heard me when I scream [nervous laughter]. Because where I was renting, I was worried about even my next-door neighbour. Because most of the time, people who rape you are guys that see you every

day. They are watching you every day. I just didn't feel safe. I moved back home. It felt better for me rather than being on your own and working with such cases.... Transport... buying my own transport... then I don't have to leave too early.

The violence she encounters every day at work in the TCC has filtered into the way she sees the world and her own sense of safety and security. She knows the reality that women are not in fact safe at home, in the street, in the community, or at their work—and this has a jarring impact on her ability to function and survive in and out of her job.

Survivors Engaging the State

Within these key points of contact, survivors engage the state during what may be the most traumatic moments of their lives. What emerged from my research was that even here, in these points of contact, the emphasis continues to be on prosecution. Even the premier medical and health-care-focused response, the TCCs, are bundled into the NPA, with the goal of increasing arrests and convictions by ensuring early collaboration between survivors and prosecutors.

The drive for prosecutions is perhaps a global norm for gender-based-violence programs, and it may be even more valorized in countries like South Africa—countries with long histories of inaction around gender-based violence. Yet these carceral approaches do not address many of the root causes of violence or understand the larger community-wide context of factors that can legitimize (or challenge) violence in all its forms: institutional violence, economic violence, and community violence. Medical professionals themselves may be reproducing a view of gender-based violence that normalizes the violence as "cultural" or that fails to recognize the discrimination that drives inequality and violence. Claudia Marcía-Moreno and colleagues assert, "Violence is often seen as solely a social or criminal-justice problem, and not as a clinical or public health issue" (2015, 1574). Addressing this intersectional discrimination is key for excavating how overlapping and compounding inequalities (race, class, gender, ethnicity) are hidden accelerants of violence or are normalized (García-Moreno et al. 2015).

Similar concerns may affect the legal systems as well. The compartmentalization of sexual assault and gender-based-violence cases into specialized courts may ensure that those accessing these spaces have survivor-centered approaches to justice. Yet even these courts continue to be underfunded and unevenly implemented. And as Stacy Moreland (2014) argues, these courts may be undermined by the larger patriarchal norms that are pervasive in the training of lawyers and judges, as well as the normal operation of the overarching legal system.

Despite these flaws, every sector of advocates I encountered working to end gender-based violence called for more resources, more staff, and more training to ensure that points of contact were functioning, widespread, and survivor centered. These points of contact represent just a handful of the spaces needed to encourage survivors to come forward and seek assistance. Much more is needed to shift toward an upstream prevention focus that can look at the sources of violence in the homes, communities, and workplaces. I next turn to the inadequacies of carceral approaches to gender-based violence that tend to focus on individual cases rather than structural factors that can normalize or hide violence in homes, relationships, and communities.

CONCLUSION

Moving beyond Carceral Feminism

While the public rights achieved by South African women have been celebrated internationally, the brutal violence they experience continues unabated. To enact the rights, values, and vision of the South African Constitution, the country will need to build on and localize those public rights, constitutionalism, and legislative framework to make violence in all forms unacceptable. Despite the legislative and electoral success of women in South Africa two decades into the new dispensation, scholars and activists from across the political spectrum question how fully democratic the country truly is. While media attention focuses on the corruption and failures of political leaders, including former president Jacob Zuma (2009–18), many also question parliament's descent into political theater, the unproductive rhetoric of opposition parties, and the very real violence that reinforces apartheid racism, sexism, and homophobia at universities, in the home, and in the workplace. Activists continue to question the viability of a democracy in which sexual violence persists almost without change. How authentic is a human rights framework when survivors cannot access legal or medical services because of continued racial segregation? How legitimate can a democracy be when the laws on paper are not part of the essential fabric of everyday lives and material experiences?

The nexus of political power and private violence, which are often positioned closely together, demonstrates the limitations of South African state feminism. The South African women's movement initially approached the transition to democracy in the 1990s through the lens of state feminism, specifically constructing institutions within government and parliament to advance women politically. The movement used these insider strategies to secure policies, programs, and budgets that would hopefully improve the social position of all women, a now well-trodden global path of moving from struggle politics to governance feminism (Halley 2006). A poignant measure of the shortcomings of state feminism and of the attempts to create institutions for feminist change is the violence individuals and communities continue to face (Walsh 2008). Legislation, programs, and policies are essential strategies to address gender-based violence, but they are clearly not sufficient to alter the social structures that normalize and perpetuate violence.

As discussed in this book, state feminism has become intermeshed with carceral approaches to feminism in South Africa. Complex social problems like gender-based violence are interpreted primarily as legal issues that may be ameliorated by arrests, prosecutions, and punishment of perpetrators. Carceral feminists concentrate on the criminalization of gender-based violence and the incarceration of offenders, often at the expense of other feminist efforts to address structural violence and economic inequality (Bernstein 2010; Bumiller 2008). These carceral frameworks create binaries between victims and perpetrators and construct the patriarchy as the monolithic cause of gender-based violence. These approaches are appealing and intelligible to governments because they are in line with what governments do best. States know how to set sentencing guidelines, monitor arrests, and track prosecutions.

Yet what the South African case reaffirms is that such reactive, carceral approaches are woefully inadequate to address the complexity of violence that individuals, families, and communities face in highly unequal societies like South Africa. Road maps that link solutions of gender-based violence to increased criminalization do not disrupt the patterns of mass incarceration of the apartheid era and do not call attention to the increases in the incarceration rates since the end of apartheid. The criminalization of poverty and mass incarceration are old strategies that are being extended into today's context across the globe. These carceral frameworks coexist with neoliberal ideologies that focus on individual perpetrators, which shifts attention away from the state and its responsibility for addressing economic and social inequalities (Gottschalk 2006, 2015). As this project demonstrates, the imposition of the carceral state in South Africa is not race neutral, which is of course true in many other contexts (Alexander 2012). For example, certain families and communities are subject to state enforcement of domestic violence arrests and prosecutions, while others can navigate or mitigate the impact of domestic abuse because of their financial means, and these economic inequalities continue to be mapped onto racial inequalities. Legacies of racism, inequality, and sexism that were the very essence of apartheid and colonization persist today (Scully 2010). Similarly, the politics of the carceral state are not new and appear to be growing in South Africa. For such a young democracy, one that was founded on decades of a powerful struggle against state-enforced racism, this is a troubling reality.

During apartheid, the state used violence against its people; violence was also used internally within the liberation struggle to ensure loyalty and compliance within the ranks. The stakes were high, the prospect of death was a daily reality, and life for many was already cut short through the structural violence of abject poverty, inhumane living and work conditions, and woefully inadequate medical care. Today's high rates of gender-based violence are nested within these legacies and the contemporary patterns of inequality and slow violence (Gouws 2016; Scully 2010).

While policy makers want linear, clear programs to address social ills, problems like gender-based violence cannot be addressed in isolation. The case studies in this book show that South Africa's quest to overcome the racial and gender inequalities of the previous era has been hampered by both financial constraints and political myopia. Funding is needed for investigation units, counseling services in police stations and hospitals, training for service providers and the communities, prosecution and legal assistance, forensic investigation, and medical treatment and testing. These resources and services often have been curtailed by South Africa's turn toward economic neoliberalism, which has limited government support for services and ironically deepened inequality in South Africa since the end of apartheid rather than lessening it. This push toward neoliberalism has also intensified the vulnerability faced by large sectors of the population, including the vast majority of black South Africans, rural populations, women, and youth (Margaretten 2015).

In this book, I have identified four key factors that shaped how communities are able to address gender-based violence in South Africa. *Place*: Apartheid was perhaps most successful in recharting the face of South Africa through its control and structure of place and space. The separation of races through the Group Areas Act divided resources and populations. It helped enforce and at times create pockets of extreme wealth adjacent to areas of overpopulation, inequality, and structural violence, including the violence of poverty, hunger, inadequate health care, abusive labor conditions, poor educational opportunities, and inadequate housing. While these laws have been repealed for decades, the lack of any substantial redistribution of wealth, land, and resources continues to affect the daily lived experiences of most South Africans. Gender-based violence is not caused by place or space, but communities' abilities to address or even understand violence are linked to these geographically based constraints. Efforts to address gender-based violence appear to be most successful when they are embedded within efforts to strengthen community networks that address the larger structures of inequality and abuse.

People: In my work across nine different communities, it was clear that individual leaders are often at the heart of significant work to end violence of all kinds in their communities. Much of the work of the South African women's movement during the transition period of the 1990s focused on putting institutions in place for women's empowerment. This project demonstrates that state feminism's efforts to enact progressive policies and create transformative institutions have not yet been enough to ensure social change. Current implementation failures are often linked to the lack of leaders who can build vibrant social networks both nationally and within local communities. In this project, I identified key leaders who were pivotal to social change: individual issue advocates, community organizers, religious leaders, and traditional leaders. The ability for a community to move forward on violence prevention was linked as much to individuals as it was to state policies. This is an unfortunate finding, because leadership can be fleeting and unpredictable. While many leaders were able to break with "traditional" ideas of male superiority, other leaders continued to deploy and justify these ideas as the basis for social harmony. Understanding how leaders become change agents may be essential for challenging social norms and implementing progressive policies.

Police: In each community, the police were either a pivotal force for social change or a problematic roadblock for progress. In communities that were actively working to address inequality, violence, and vulnerability, the service providers I interviewed pointed to the importance of the police in transforming a community. In communities that were not moving forward, service providers actively criticized and dismissed the police as ineffective.

While police involvement does not seem sufficient to address gender-based violence, it does appear to be necessary in terms of the effectiveness of community networks, based on my research. The importance of relying on the South African police to be leaders of social change is a precarious approach. The history of the police as the brutal enforcers of apartheid is still a living memory for many South Africans, and these memories are compounded by the contemporary failures and widespread corruption in the police services today. Equally problematic are my findings that the police often have an overreliance on volunteers for survivor services, and police themselves often face high levels of burnout and secondary trauma from working in this sector. Given the lack of funding available, both of these issues raise questions about how viable the police are as an institution to do this type of engaged, survivor-centered work.

Points of contact: Survivors engage with the state at critical moments in their lives, and it is essential for the state to act quickly to provide services for survivors' emotional, medical, and legal needs. These points of contact include the sexual offenses courts; trauma centers and victim support rooms in police stations; the Family Violence, Child Protection and Sexual Offences (FCS) units in the South African police services; and the multisector Thuthuzela Care Centres (TCCs). Not surprisingly, many of these points of contact replicate the strengths and weaknesses of the communities they serve. What my research finds is that these points of contact have been designed to operate within a carceral approach to gender-based violence. Even the medical units serving survivors are under the umbrella of the National Prosecuting Authority. While such legal and prosecutorial approaches are essential for the protection of survivors and the punishment of perpetrators, these approaches fail to address the larger patterns of structural violence, inequality, and vulnerability that could prevent violence before it occurs.

Beyond Neoliberalism and Carceral Feminism

The communities in this book that are challenging gender-based violence are doing so by relying on the capacity of community networks and the persistence of local leaders. In many cases, they are not turning to national leadership for vision or funding. They have essentially given up on national leadership. This is in part the result of a neoliberal strategy of pushing service delivery to local levels in order to eschew national accountability. Social responsibility is tossed onto communities and individuals rather than expecting the state to provide the direction and support necessary for social change at the broader structural levels. This creates a situation where the national government can distance itself from responsibility, accountability, and leadership. As Paula Meth argues, the state has maintained some commitments, but only in specific sectors: "The enactment of a neoliberal patriarchal democracy is not a simple story of state retreat from service provision.... Post-apartheid, the South African state actually invested quite heavily in, and improved their approaches to, the delivery of particular service such as housing provision and policing . . . , but less attention was paid to areas such as employment creation" (2010, 242).

Interestingly, the support of housing and police funding may be part of the neoliberal strategy. Housing was one of the most celebrated goals of the newly democratic state. Millions of government-built housing units sprang up across the country in the past twenty years. This was an end goal—a visible, tangible marker of what the ANC government achieved. What many are criticizing is that the housing programs were not part of a holistic development strategy. Similarly, there are perceptions of widespread corruption of the housing programs, accusations that are linked to the complexity and inefficiency of the state in delivering the houses (Rubin 2011). People were placed in new houses, but they still lack the jobs to support their lives. This became a true case of "window dressing": putting people in new houses without changing their long-term economic opportunities. Access to housing, electricity, and clean water is an important step forward to reducing structural violence, but offloading these goods and services onto individuals without ensuring people have the financial means to pay for them can actually drive people into deeper debt and make them more vulnerable than they were before they had housing, electricity, and clean water.

The investment in the police is also driven by a desire to guard and protect the current economic system as it stands. Crime has become one of the most talked about and visible markers of the new South Africa. Ironically, it is difficult to compare current crime levels against the crime rate of the apartheid era. During that time, much of the violence, murder, and sexual assault was directed by the state and at the hands of state-sanctioned security forces. Today, crime in South Africa is a real threat to the fabric of the country, and this crime is notably violent. As South Africa returns to the world stage and tries to entice businesses to invest and tourists to visit the Rainbow Nation, the country has had to contend with the very high levels of violent crime. At the point of democratic transition, the leaders of the white minority government called on the police to move away from terrorizing the population toward securing South Africa and protecting property. The previous era of police brutality existed in order to secure the white minority's political sovereignty. It is a paradoxical twist that the same leaders would call for the police to now protect private property and reduce crime—both of which would safeguard the leaders' economic sovereignty and fortify white privilege.

Thus, funding and national priorities have not yielded the much-anticipated structural transformation. Instead, communities and individual issue advocates are filling in the gap. Implementation becomes linked to the personal mission and dedication of policy actors and local leaders. In the short term, these local power brokers may be able to enact important shifts in resource budgets and program priorities. Yet this is a tenuous model, given that success is linked to people rather than positions, to individuals rather than institutions, to individual passion rather than structural change. People are not permanent.

The risks of relying on local leaders to be change agents may have significant long-term ramifications. Given the context of what Raymond Suttner

(2015b) describes as hyperpatriarchy in South Africa, it is difficult to imagine that any of the inroads made by individual leaders can shift the larger social and normative structures of their religious communities or traditional authority systems. This is true even within the ranks of the ANC broadly, which continues to view women's value as coming from their roles as mothers of the nation (Gouws 2016; Hassim 2014). Indeed, the very fact that the national government is moving back to embrace and empower religious leaders and traditional leaders may be a tacit acceptance of the patriarchal norms that have undergirded inequality for decades (Mnisi Weeks 2015; Walker 2014; Scully 2010; Merry 2006; Beall, Gelb, and Hassim 2005). While community actors are essential for changing patterns of violence and inequality, the devolution of social responsibility to individual actors and communities means that states can continue to divorce themselves from action and accountability. As my interviews revealed, most of the progress that has been made to challenge structural violence has been at the community level. Without a reprioritization by the national government, much of that progress will remain localized.

Moving Upstream

Cross-national research demonstrates the need for a multifaceted approach to addressing gender-based violence. South Africa has many of the key factors in place that could provide a solid framework for intervention, including a strong legislative framework, key points of interventions, and multisector responses (Abramsky et al. 2014). Many of these initiatives are reactive, after a crime has occurred, involving a great deal of expense and not necessarily reducing the overall rate of gender-based violence or the risk that survivors will be victimized again (Abramsky et al. 2014; Parson 2010, 2013). As is the case with many developing countries, a vital next step is focusing on prevention strategies, which are often more challenging in terms of shifting practices, norms, and beliefs but may be less costly and more effective.

It is feasible and, based on the findings of this book, probably advisable to build on the efforts of community-based interventions. But communities should do so with an investment and commitment from the national government to prioritize addressing violence in all forms. For example, the national government could support efforts to address gender-based violence with concrete investments in community networks and infrastructures, specifically those that recognize how gender-based violence is nested within larger structures of inequality. In so doing, the national government could then provide the resources and funding to local actors in order to enhance community networks and service delivery.

Internationally, there are several organizations and movements to end gender-based violence that do just that. These organizations focus on building community networks to address intersectional oppressions, challenges, and barriers to accessing services. Some key examples include the US-based Move to End Violence and Close to Home, the Ugandan-based Raising Voices, and the Tanzanian-based Jijenge! (Abramsky et al. 2014; Burrill, Roberts, and Thornberry 2010). These movements focus their work on the community and neighborhood levels to support the development and cultivation of leaders, organizations, and networks. These organizations also share the philosophy that sexism, racism, classism, colonialism, and ableism are interlocked and are often compounding forces. Accordingly, focusing on gender-based violence in isolation will not address the slow violence (Nixon 2011) these areas experience in terms of economic injustice, racial violence, and social inequality that is fueled by neoliberal economic policies. The larger, reinforcing inequalities in a community "create pernicious, deep rooted barriers to justice" (Move to End Violence 2015). Communities must address those barriers sustainably and holistically, or they will continue to reinforce them. Rather than focusing exclusively on one type of violence, these organizations recognize that the community itself needs to be supported before trying to deal with any particular issue.

The approach of building organizational capacity and leadership in a community before focusing on individual forms of violence has been shown effective at countering violence at the local and community levels (Abramsky et al. 2014; Ellsberg et al. 2014; Michau et al. 2014; Parson 2010, 2013; Michau 2007; Michau, Naker, and Swalehe 2002). When the community infrastructure itself is strong, the ability for leaders and groups to address violence in all its forms—sexual, economic, and racial—is improved.

The idea of increasing resources and service delivery in local communities is not a benign suggestion. Many governments are threatened by the strength and autonomy of local communities, as they often become critics of corruption, inefficiency, and hypocrisy at the national level (Merry 2006). This is a viable, powerful threat in South Africa as well. The national government benefits greatly when it pushes service delivery and accountability downward toward communities, thus having the ability to shift blame and social responsibility to individuals. This strategy is then reinforced by a lack of resources and funding, again ensuring that the communities, organizations, trauma units, and support centers do not have the strength and effectiveness to challenge national policies, priorities, and corruption. Blame and accountability are shifted to the local, while successes are embraced by the national leaders.

The strategy I am proposing is not an easy one, and it is complicated by the deepening corruption in the current government and in most of the opposition parties as well. It is also hard to envision today, as the ruling ANC moves further and further away from its early constitutional commitments to gender equality. Many leaders of political parties continue to embrace a rhetoric that is ostensibly about advancing women's rights when they are simultaneously hollowing out and underfunding the social infrastructure necessary to foster those rights. This is not a narrative unique to South Africa, as many developing, postconflict countries use the window dressing of women's initiatives to shore up the auspices of political legitimacy (most blatantly perhaps in Zimbabwe; see Shaw 2015).

An effective legislative framework, an understanding of place, strong leaders, shared priorities—each of these characteristics contributes to building the type of community network that can be the foundation for addressing gender-based violence. The cases in this project demonstrate that strong community networks are important in breaking silence about sexual assault and may perhaps also help to overcome resource inequalities that would otherwise deter policy implementation. No matter the size or location, community organizations and local leaders can be beneficial to the broad range of factors that contribute to gender-based violence.

Even if these networks are not specifically focused on addressing gender-based violence, the process of community building has important outcomes. Strengthening the leadership, networks, and organizations in a community builds the social infrastructure necessary to address gender-based violence as an intersectional problem. This can be done in many ways, including increasing community policing of each sector, developing stronger social networks in civil society, and finding common issues that can unite individuals in an area.

There are indeed true heroes in this book, champions and advocates who challenge policies, practices, and norms. These heroes include survivors using their own histories and recovery to assist others. Other service providers attempt to overturn old hierarchies and regressive gender attitudes to challenge gender-based violence. Each of the actors and community networks continues to work in a context of segregation, violence, and discrimination that was fostered by apartheid and that continues anew in problematic ways.

The ability of people to feel connected and have agency in local decision-making processes matters in building a sense of place in which violence of any form is not tolerated. This community building can occur in urban settings with constantly fluctuating populations just as well as it can happen in rural settings with stable populations of people who have lived there for generations. Setting priorities and building networks are both essential pieces in fostering social change on the local scale. The size, function, and shape of networks will vary based on places and spaces.

While the existence of community networks is vital for breaking silence and changing social norms, this book does not support the neoliberal belief that individuals can overcome national inaction or the continued lack of funding and resources. In fact, it makes quite the opposite argument. In order for these local networks, leaders, and support centers to be effective, they also require national funding, accountability, and prioritization.

The service providers and community leaders in this book demonstrate the need for a stronger emphasis on gender-based violence as it is nested within economic and social inequality. The inequality continues today at all levels of government, and it is a continued manifestation of the inequality that was entrenched during apartheid. Without a sea change in national resource expenditure and political action, all the progressive legislation will remain in the sphere of rhetoric. Policies must be translated from mere words on paper into lived realities that honor the intersectional experiences of the people of South Africa.

Methodological Appendix

My first interviews and observations in the gender-based-violence sector started in the 1990s. At that time, my work in South Africa spanned my efforts both as an antiapartheid activist and later as a Fulbright-Hays scholar doing research for my first book on women in the South African parliament (Britton 2005). It was during that time that I recognized the difficult position of addressing gender-based violence within the context of the antiapartheid struggle and making sense of an economic and political system that apartheid rulers enforced through sexual violence (Britton 2006; Britton and Shook 2014). I continued to conduct fieldwork for the next twenty years on the issue of gender and politics in Africa, in particular gender-based violence in the southern Africa region and women's roles as policy makers across Africa.

I was afforded the opportunity to conduct intensive fieldwork for this project through a Fulbright Faculty Research Fellowship and the Graduate Research Fund of the University of Kansas in 2011–12. My research was hosted locally in South Africa by the Institute for Democratic Alternatives in South Africa (IDASA), the former African democracy institute, and the Centre for Human Rights at University of Pretoria's Faculty of Law. I also received vital intellectual and research development support from the Institute for Policy & Social Research at the University of Kansas. My home departments, the Departments of Political Science and Women, Gender, and Sexuality Studies, provided me with the intellectual space and resources to continue my work on this project during the last several years.

This project involved semistructured in-depth interviews, group interviews, observations, document analysis, and analysis of secondary sources. I have examined media reports, government documents, speeches, government reports, and government presentations on sexual offenses, domestic violence, child protection, elder sexual abuse, and corrective rape spanning

2007 to 2018. I have also examined theses and dissertations written in South Africa on these same issues, as well as the reports and government submissions by nongovernmental organizations and community-based organizations in these fields.

Over the course of the last twenty years of fieldwork examining the issue of gender-based violence, I have conducted over ninety individual interviews, over a dozen group interviews, and an additional one hundred hours of observations, including some participant observations, in police stations, trauma units, crisis hot line centers, NGOs, counseling centers, hospitals, churches, and mosques. During the Fulbright research from 2011 to 2012, I conducted fifty-five interviews, as well as the bulk of the observations. My interviews were digitally recorded and transcribed by myself and by my research assistant from IDASA, Esther Nasikye Hephizibah, a Ugandan human rights worker who was in South Africa as an intern with IDASA. I reviewed all our transcripts against the digital recordings to check for accuracy and to correct errors. All data collection, data storage, and research member participation received Institutional Review Board approval from the University of Kansas.

My fieldwork involved interviews with and observations of women's policy agencies, members of parliament, governmental and community-based social workers, prosecutors and court advocates, community leaders, women's organizations, public health clinics, churches and mosques, NGOs dealing with gender-based violence, community-based organizations dealing with human trafficking, traditional leaders, shelters for vulnerable youth, and traditional healers. I conducted extensive participant observation work in several community churches, as well as in various community organizations that have opted to take a stand against gender-based violence, participating in services and various public outreach and small group events hosted by community and antiviolence organizations as I was invited.

I also wrote extensive fieldnotes and research memos throughout my fieldwork and subsequent transcription and analysis stage. I took fieldnotes based on my observations of the field sites and any and all activities in which I participated at these locations. In these notes, I recorded observations of each interview and focus group so that I was able to remember the key elements of the interview setting and participant information. Throughout the book, I use pseudonyms for the participants, pursuant to my human subjects' agreement and to ensure their confidentiality. I provide brief demographic descriptions for the speakers to give additional background and context. The portions of the transcripts found in this text include ellipses (. . .) to represent omitted text; otherwise, the passages are presented verbatim.

In 2011, during the relaunch of the Family Violence, Child Protection and Sexual Offences units in the South African Police Services, I also undertook observations in police stations, trauma units, crisis hot line centers, NGOs, counseling centers, hospitals, churches, and mosques. I sought and was granted research approval from the South African Police Services to conduct interviews and observations in police stations. This approval was a lengthy process, but it was necessary to be granted access to the police stations. This access proved enormously helpful in gaining a high level of collaboration with the individual police stations.

As my fieldwork progressed, I identified key characteristics of each community network in the study and mapped the networks of collaboration. I conducted interviews in each research site until I reached saturation of the key organizations and government agencies that were mentioned by participants and other community members.

It was my goal to conduct research in a sample of communities that represented each of the residential groupings of the apartheid-era racial designations, including black, coloured, Indian, and white areas. For the predominantly black townships, I also selected a representative sample across different types of communities: longer-established townships, informal settlements, newer townships created after apartheid as part of the national housing initiatives (discussed more in chapters 3 and 5). I also included rural, urban, and periurban communities. Periurban refers in this context to communities that were geographically between urban and rural settings. These communities were not what is typically considered suburban, which often refers to affluent areas near urban communities. Instead, these periurban communities were organized as townships during apartheid but located between the urban and rural townships.

By working in-depth primarily in nine different communities, I was able to look across cases to understand how organizations and leaders worked within their community context. Most of my interviews and observations occurred in nine research sites, listed below with pseudonyms:

Arbeidstad: a middle- and working-class community that is predominantly white with a combination of residential and industrial areas
Bokang: an informal settlement located next to established black township and urban areas
Difate: a long-standing and established urban black township
Huisdorp: an urban community located in the center of a major city that is dominated by commercial activities; the vast majority of daily occupants come into the city for work, while the residential population was primarily black South Africans and African immigrants living in apartment buildings
Lookodi: a newly formed urban black community created after the end of apartheid through a government Reconstruction and Development

Methodological Appendix

> Programme (RDP) initiative to improve formal housing for a mix of residents coming from many areas
>
> **Mabitso:** a rural black community
>
> **Nokuthula:** a rural black community
>
> **Olive Vlei:** a wealthy white area located on the suburban ring of a major city
>
> **Roedorp:** a long-standing and established formerly "coloured" urban township

Each of these nine sites represents the broad spectrum of communities in contemporary South Africa. (A full discussion of the characteristics of community resources and networks is presented in chapter 2, tables 2.1 through 2.3.) While the majority of the population lives in urban areas, it is still important to understand how programs are implemented in rural areas.

I did a handful of additional interviews, group interviews, and observations in communities that had only one organization working on gender-based violence or community violence broadly defined. These organizations were identified by participants in one of the other nine communities. I did not do a full network mapping in these communities, because the participants explained that their organization was the only one in each community working on these issues.

I used ATLAS.ti to code and analyze all my transcripts. I first did an open coding of the transcripts to identify the major themes across the interviews. It was through this open coding that I developed the organization of the book, specifically recognizing the importance of several key ideas to my participants. These included the ideas of the accelerants of gender-based violence and then the four groupings of place, people, police, and points of contact, what I call here the four Ps. I then did a second coding of the transcripts, looking for subcategories within the accelerants category, as well as within the four Ps categories. Within each category, I identified the key themes for each chapter and selected the most representative quotes to include in this book.

An important stage in my analysis came after I conceived of the organization of the book and selected the key themes. After identifying each theme, I went back to the scholarly literature to see how my emergent codes were in dialogue with the existing research in these areas. I finally did a review of all my codes after thinking conceptually about how my work extended or contradicted existing scholarship so that I could ensure that my work was accurately represented in this book and was engaged with the scholarship.

Notes

Introduction: "Democracy Stops at My Front Door"

1. Redi Tlhabi's book *Khwezi: The Remarkable Story of Fezekile Ntsukela Kuzwayo* was released while I was finalizing this manuscript. For a full and in-depth understanding of Kuzwayo's life, please see this powerful account.

2. South Africa does not use a jury system. It relies on judges for decisions and sentencing.

3. The Zuma case is hauntingly familiar to the political life of Daniel Ortega in Nicaragua, where it initially appeared that the high-profile political leader was insulated from the charges of the sexual assault of his stepdaughter (Cupples and Larios 2005).

4. An interesting example could be the women's police stations that are now found globally. See, for example, Alcalde (2011) on Peru and Hautzinger (2002, 2007) on Brazil, discussed more in chapter 4.

5. Please see the appendix for an explanation of the treatment of quotes from interview subjects.

6. Even though South Africa's incarceration rates have risen, they are still far below those in the United States and almost all individual US states, except for Maine and Vermont (Prison Policy Initiative 2016).

7. Jewkes et al. 2010 also found that there were some differences among groups of men in the study: coloured men were the most likely to have raped, black men were second, white men were least likely. Men with a completed university degree or high school matriculation were less likely than men with no high school matriculation. Poorer men were *less* likely to rape (monthly income of zero to R 500, or US$50) than men who made more per month (R 501–2,000, or US$50–$200).

8. The legislation also included interim language on human trafficking that remained in place until the Prevention and Combating of Trafficking in Persons Act was signed into law in 2013 (see also Parenzee, Artz, and Moult 2001).

9. Until the South African legislation was enacted, Namibia had the most far-reaching legislation on rape; it had an expansive definition of rape and clear expec-

tations for prosecution of perpetrators. It is apparent that South Africa's legislation has expanded not only what acts are covered under the term "sexual assault" but also the policies that protect victims, including a national register for sex offenders, HIV/AIDS testing and treatment, and the provisions for a national policy framework. For a full discussion of the Namibian policy, please see Britton and Shook (2014).

10. Even with the protections for the accused and with the provisions limiting the circumstances for testing, this area of compelled medical testing could eventually become the basis for additional litigation around the rights of HIV-infected persons, privacy, and the rights of survivors.

11. A full discussion of the characteristics of community resources and networks is presented in chapter 2, tables 2.1–2.3.

12. I use the term "street-level workers" to signify government employees who are often working directly with the general population to implement government policies, programs, and services. These service providers and government workers are often the most visible and accessible representatives of the government whom normal citizens encounter. In the literature, they are often referred to as "street-level bureaucrats" (Lipsky 1980), but many do not like the cold, dispassionate connotations of bureaucracy. The most contemporary scholarship calls this group "frontline workers" (Maynard-Moody and Musheno 2003). Yet this militarized language is out of step with the larger goals of this project, which are to examine the normalization of violence. The association with frontline to a war zone is problematic at best in a book on gender-based violence. Many antiviolence activists and scholars work to demilitarize their own language, as language can come to normalize and obscure violence within a society. In South Africa these workers are also sometimes said to be working "at the coalface," indicating they are at the very front of efforts to implement government policy, which is hard, difficult, and at times dangerous work—at the face of the coal surface. However, the term "coalface" in the United States has historically racist connotations, as many white miners in the rural Appalachian mines appeared black from the cold dust when they exited the mines, and the term was used in the pejorative. As such, I am avoiding that language here.

Chapter One. Genealogy of Gender-Based Violence in South Africa

1. This framework is also known as the Center for Disease Control's (2018) social-ecological model.

2. Thanks to Emily Kofron for our discussion about the relationship between substance abuse and gender-based violence.

3. Anger and punishment, alcohol, boredom, and cleansing were also motivating factors.

4. RDP stands for Reconstruction and Development Programme, which started almost immediately after the first democratic election in South Africa. The RDP was based on the most progressive and participatory approach to development at the time: massive investment in infrastructure, housing, social programs, electrification,

and access to land, health care, education, and clean water. The program stressed the importance of grassroots leadership and collaboration across governmental sectors. A massive national construction project to build new, seemingly affordable houses—often informally referred to as RDP houses—was one of the most visible outcomes of the program. Over 1.1 million affordable houses were constructed by 2001. Some criticize that the houses are not affordable and poorly made. Much of the RDP was abandoned almost as soon as it was implemented, as South Africa took a very sharp turn toward neoliberal economic and self-imposed structural adjustment policies, following the advice of Western economic advisors. Many of its major achievements have been criticized for being of poor quality or for lacking sustainability.

5. There are a few important parallels between the South African case and the Liberian case in terms of approaching gender-based violence. Following protracted civil conflicts, both of which used gender-based violence as a weapon, these countries' postconflict governments moved quickly to wrap themselves in internationally accepted ideas of human rights. But often these international ideas were not in conversation with the local political realities and structural conditions faced by citizens.

Chapter Two. Place

1. The 16 Days of Activism against Gender-Based Violence Campaign programs were established in 1991 by an international conference hosted by the Centre for Women's Global Leadership. The "16 Days" refers to the sixteen days connecting November 25, International Day for the Elimination of Violence against Women, and December 10, International Human Rights Day. The campaign is observed internationally and focuses on awareness, education, policy change, and prevention.

Chapter Three. People

1. Men for Change is an international organization focused on empowering men to challenge gender-based violence and to become community leaders. The ideologies and visions of MFC vary from country to country: some groups have progressive visions of masculinity that challenge male dominance, while others focus on reclaiming masculinity that reinforces male leadership in the household and in society.

2. While I did not include sangomas in my interview samples, which was likely an oversight on my part, I did unexpectedly meet a traditional healer. When I was interviewing members of the police and asked about their perspective on traditional healers, one officer explained that she was a traditional healer. This was particularly interesting because the station commander had said only days before that he was unaware of any healers working in his area. In fact, they were working in his own station. She spoke about how she felt that her work as a traditional healer went hand in hand with her police work—that she was a better officer because she was a healer.

3. Initiation schools are part of many ethnic groups' rites of passage into adulthood for men. While the traditions, activities, and customs of these schools differ widely, many often involve male circumcision. There is significant controversy around these schools, as some of the nonsanctioned schools abduct boys and charge their

parents high fees to have the boys released. Each year there are numerous infections and deaths from the schools' practices, in particular, the circumcision. See Nicolson 2015.

4. In my research, I was able to speak with one chief and his council. He was referred to me by officers at a local police station, and they said he was in direct cooperation with them to resolve domestic violence. This chief was not recognized by the National House of Traditional Leaders of South Africa. He believes his kingdom was taken by the apartheid regime, and all his efforts to regain official recognition since the new democracy have been unsuccessful. Yet he is widely known throughout his area as the leading chief, and he runs an initiation school each year to which many parents send their sons. He and his council were very worried about other "chiefs" coming into the area and starting ad hoc initiation schools because "then it becomes a problem. You hear some people died in the mountain" (meaning that young men died in the wilderness following complications related to the initiation rituals, which often included circumcision). Another council member criticized the Health Department for certifying the wrong people for initiation schools—people who were underage and not properly trained.

5. Muti, an alternative medicine given by traditional healers, is made primarily from plants but occasionally from animals and other materials. While sangomas are seen as healers, there are rumors and reports that they are also able to hide crimes and violence from others through muti or to apply curses. Muti murders are thought or rumored to be for the purposes of harvesting body parts. These concerns came up in my interviews with police.

Chapter Four. Police

1. As discussed in the introductory chapter, the idea of a public/private divide persists, even though this is often not the reality. The violence may be quite public, given the tight living conditions in many households and communities, and it also may be socially sanctioned or legitimized and therefore not at all private (Mogstad, Dryding, and Fiorotto 2016; Vetten 2014; Bassadien and Hochfeld 2005).

2. Corruption as a means of individual enrichment is seen both globally and across the continent, perhaps most clearly documented in Liberia by Peace Medie (2013, 2015, 2016).

3. The notion of cutting down trees to prevent gender-based violence seems problematic at best. While the short-term goal of reducing gender-based violence may have been helped, there are long-term considerations. Natural spaces can also increase a sense of community and a sense of pride in a community. Given the lack of natural spaces within most townships, destroying the natural environment could in the long-term perpetuate a sense of despair that in turn could fuel other forms of violence or despair.

4. Reportedly, community members and not the government put up these signs.

5. The cost of electricity at the time of the research was unsustainable. At the time of the fieldwork, there had been a giant increase in electricity costs. One of my long-

time host families started receiving electricity bills three times her monthly pension, and this was typical throughout the country. Throughout townships and even in the semiresidential/semi-industrial area of Arbeidstad, individuals run illegal lines to tap into someone else's electricity.

6. "The flats" refer to the extensive number of apartment buildings in the city center mainly inhabited by renters. They are often associated with migrants from other parts of South Africa and Africa.

7. This is exacerbated by the rule many officers told me about, that they cannot leave one complaint for another complaint before the first one is resolved.

8. Many stations partnered with LifeLine (http://lifelinesa.co.za/) to provide counseling, support, and advocacy for victims. LifeLine initially began in order to extend pastoral care to those in crisis, but it has since evolved into a national telephonic counseling hotline for survivors of gender-based violence, and Lifeline members now work within some police stations to provide rape counseling, trauma counseling, and outreach programs. Some of these members were paid a small stipend, but many were not. All counselors receive training for trauma intervention and support.

9. The apartheid government established homelands for the black majority based on ethnic identities and often-fictive scholarship about where each group was "from" and what areas were supposed to be their original homes—all as part of the policy of separation of races. The government forcibly relocated the black population onto these homelands. Then the government began a process of declaring them independent or self-governing in order to separate them from the South African state. Separating the races and declaring them independent was also part of the strategy of creating a white South Africa.

Chapter Five. Points of Contact

1. Selebi was widely criticized at the time of his appointment because he lacked any experience with law enforcement, and his career ended in a massive corruption scandal. He was convicted in 2012 of receiving bribes from a known drug trafficker, receiving a fifteen-year prison sentence. He was released within the year following a terminal medical diagnosis, and he died in 2015. See Fox 2015.

2. For a full discussion of the courts, see Department of Justice and Constitutional Development 2013.

3. The Citi Golf was a popular entry-level compact car made by Volkswagen and sold in South Africa from 1984 to 2009.

References

Abrahams, Naeemah, Rachel Jewkes, Ria Laubscher, and Margaret Hoffman. 2006. "Intimate Partner Violence: Prevalence and Risk Factors for Men in Cape Town, South Africa." *Violence and Victims* 21 (2): 247–64.

Abrahams, Naeemah, Rachel Jewkes, Lorna Martin, Shanaaz Mathews, Carl Lombard, and Lisa Vetten. 2009. "Mortality of Women from Intimate Partner Violence in South Africa: A National Epidemiological Study." *Journal of Violence and Victims* 24 (4): 546–55.

Abramowitz, Sharon, and Mary H. Moran. 2012. "International Human Rights, Gender-Based Violence, and Local Discourses of Abuse in Postconflict Liberia: A Problem of 'Culture'?" *African Studies Review* 55 (2): 119–46.

Abramsky, Tanya, Karen Devries, Ligia Kiss, Janet Nakuti, Nambusi Kyegombe, Elizabeth Starmann, Bonnie Cundill, Leilani Franciso, Dan Kaye, Tina Musuya, Lori Michau, and Charlotte Watts. 2014. "Findings from the SASA! Study: A Cluster Randomized Controlled Trial to Assess the Impact of a Community Mobilization Intervention to Prevent Violence against Women and Reduce HIV Risk in Kampala, Uganda." *BMC Medicine* 12 (122): 1–17. http://www.biomedcentral.com/1741-7015/12/122.

Adelman, Madelaine. 2017. *Battering States: The Politics of Domestic Violence in Israel*. Nashville: Vanderbilt University Press.

Aizenman, Nurith. 2015. "Alarming Number of Women Think Spousal Abuse Is Sometimes OK." *National Public Radio*, March 18, 2015. http://www.npr.org/sections/goatsandsoda/2015/03/18/392860281/alarming-number-of-women-think-spousal-abuse-is-sometimes-ok. Accessed June 6, 2016.

Alcalde, M. Cristina. 2010. *The Woman in the Violence: Gender, Poverty, and Resistance in Peru*. Nashville: Vanderbilt University Press.

———. 2011. "Institutional Resources (Un)Available: The Effects of Police Attitudes and Actions on Battered Women in Peru." In *Anthropology at the Front Lines of Gender-Based Violence*, edited by Jennifer R. Wies and Hillary J. Haldane, 91–106. Nashville: Vanderbilt University Press.

References

Alcalde, M. Cristina, Srimati Basu, and Emily Burrill. 2015. "Feminist Organizing around Violence against Women in Mali, Peru, and India." In *Provocations: A Transnational Reader in the History of Feminist Thought*, edited by Susan Bordo, M. Cristina Alcalde, and Ellen Rosenman, 402–12. Berkeley: University of California Press.

Alexander, Michelle. 2012. *The New Jim Crow: Mass Incarceration in the Age of Colorblindness*. New York: New Press.

Amisi, Baruti, Patrick Bond, Nokuthula Cele, and Trevor Ngwane. 2011. "Xenophobia and Civil Society." *Politikon* 38 (1): 59–83.

Andersson, Neil, Ari Ho Foster, Steve Mitchell, Esca Scheepers, and Sue Goldstein. 2007. "Risk Factors for Domestic Physical Violence: National Cross-Sectional Household Surveys in Eight Southern African Countries." *BMC Women's Health* 7:1–13.

Andersson, Neil, Sharmila Mhatre, Nzwakie Mootsi, and Marina Penderis. 1999. "How to Police Sexual Violence." *CIETAfrica*, no. 15:18–22.

Andrews, Matt. "Good Government Means Different Things in Different Countries." 2010. *Governance: An International Journal of Policy, Administration, and Institutions* 23 (1): 7–35.

Andrews, Matt, Lant Pritchett, and Michael Woolcock. 2013. "Escaping Capability Traps through Problem Driven Iterative Adaptation (PDIA)." *World Development* 51:234–44.

Andrews, Penelope. 1999. "Violence against Women in South Africa: The Role of Culture and the Limitations of the Law." *Temple Political and Civil Rights Law Review* 8 (Spring): 425–57.

———. 2001. "From Gender Apartheid to Non-sexism: The Pursuit of Women's Rights in South Africa." *North Carolina Journal of International Law and Commercial Regulation* 26 (3): 693–722.

———. 2002. "Evaluating the Progress of Women's Rights on the Fifth Anniversary of the South African Constitution." *Vermont Law Review* 26 (4): 829–36.

———. 2007. "'Democracy Stops at My Front Door': Obstacles to Gender Equality in South Africa." *Loyola University Chicago International Law Review* 5 (1): 15–28.

Anshel, Mark H., and Mitchell Smith. 2014. "The Role of Religious Leaders in Promoting Healthy Habits in Religious Institutions." *Journal of Religion and Health* 53 (4): 1046–59.

Asiedu, Alex Boakye, and Godwin Arku. 2009. "The Rise of Gated Housing Estates in Ghana: Empirical Insights from Three Communities in Metropolitan Accra." *Journal of Housing and the Built Environment* 24 (3): 227–47.

Atkinson, Rowland. 2006. "Padding the Bunker: Strategies of Middle-Class Disaffiliation and Colonisation in the City." *Urban Studies* 43 (4): 819–32.

Baldez, Lisa. 2001. "Coalition Politics and the Limits of State Feminism in Chile." *Women and Politics* 22 (4): 1–28.

Banaszak, Lee Ann, Karen Beckwith, and Dieter Rucht. 2003. *Women's Movements Facing the Reconfigured State*. New York: Cambridge University Press.

Barker, G., J. M. Contreras, B. Heilman, A. K. Singh, R. K. Verma, and M. Nascimento. 2011. *Evolving Men: Initial Results from the International Men and Gender Equality Survey (IMAGES)*. Washington, DC: International Center for Research on Women (ICRW) and Instituto Promundo.

Bass, Jennifer. 2012. "Blurring Boundaries: The Integration of NGOs into Governance in Kenya." *Governance: An International Journal of Policy, Administration, and Institutions* 25 (2): 209–35.

Bassadien, Shahana Rasool, and Tessa Hochfeld. 2005. "Across the Public/Private Boundary: Contextualizing Domestic Violence in South Africa." *Agenda: Empowering Women for Gender Equity* 19 (66): 4–15.

Bauer, Gretchen. 2008. "Fifty/Fifty by 2020: Electoral Gender Quotas for Parliament in East and Southern Africa." *International Feminist Journal of Politics* 10 (3): 348–68.

Bauer, Gretchen, and Hannah Britton, eds. 2006. *Women in African Parliaments*. Boulder, CO: Lynne Rienner.

BBC News. 2015. "Why Is South Africa Still So Unequal?" May 13, 2015. http://www.bbc.com/news/world-africa-32623496. Accessed July 27, 2016.

Beall, Jo, Stephen Gelb, and Shireen Hassim. 2005. "Fragile Stability: State and Society in Democratic South Africa." *Journal of Southern African Studies* 31 (4): 681–700.

Beckwith, Karen. 2000. "Beyond Compare? Women's Movements in Comparative Perspective." *European Journal of Political Research* 37 (4): 431–68.

Bensley, L., J. Van Eenwyk, and K. W. Simmons. 2003. "Childhood Family Violence History and Women's Risk for Intimate Partner Violence and Poor Health." *American Journal of Preventive Medicine* 25 (1): 38–44.

Bernal, Victoria, and Indepal Grewal, eds. 2014. *Theorizing NGOs: States, Feminisms, and Neoliberalism*. Durham, NC: Duke University Press.

Bernstein, Elizabeth. 2010. "Militarized Humanitarianism Meets Carceral Feminism: The Politics of Sex, Rights, and Freedom in Contemporary Antitrafficking Campaigns." *Signs: Journal of Women in Culture and Society* 36 (1): 45–71.

Bhana, Deevia, Naydene de Lange, and Claudia Mitchell. 2009. "Male Teachers Talk about Gender Violence: 'Zulu Men Demand Respect.'" *Educational Review* 61 (1): 49–62.

Bradford, Ben, Aziz Huq, Jonathan Jackson, and Benjamin Roberts. 2014. "What Price Fairness When Security Is at Stake? Police Legitimacy in South Africa." *Regulation and Governance* 8 (2): 246–68.

Brass, Jennifer. 2012. "Blurring Boundaries: The Integration of NGOs into Governance in Kenya." *Governance: An International Journal of Policy, Administration, and Institutions* 25 (2): 209–35.

Britton, Hannah. 2005. *Women in the South African Parliament: From Resistance to Governance*. Champaign: University of Illinois Press.

———. 2006. "Organizing against Gender Violence in South Africa." *Journal of South African Studies* 32 (1): 145–63.

Britton, Hannah, and Jennifer Fish. 2009. "Engendering Civil Society in the Democratic South Africa." In *Women's Activism in South Africa: Working across Divides*, edited by Hannah Britton, Shelia Meintjes, and Jennifer Fish, 1–43. Scottsville: University of KwaZulu Natal Press.

Britton, Hannah, and Lindsey Shook. 2014. "'I Need to Hurt You More': Namibia's Fight to End Gender-Based Violence." *Signs: Journal of Women in Culture and Society* 40 (1): 153–74.

Brogden, Mike, and Clifford Shearing. 1993. *Policing for a New South Africa*. New York: Routledge.

Brown, Ryan Lenora. 2015. "The Student Protests Rocking South Africa Are about More Than Tuition." *Foreign Policy*, October 30, 2015. http://foreignpolicy.com/2015/10/30/the-student-protests-rocking-south-africa-are-about-more-than-tuition/. Accessed June 6, 2016.

Bueno-Hansen, Pascha. 2015. *Feminist and Human Rights Struggles in Peru: Decolonizing Transitional Justice*. Champaign: University of Illinois Press.

Bumiller, Kristen. 2008. *In an Abusive State: How Neoliberalism Appropriated the Feminist Movement against Sexual Violence*. Durham, NC: Duke University Press.

Burger, Johan. 2014. "The South African Police Service Must Renew Its Focus on Specialised Units." *Institute for Security Studies Today*. https://www.issafrica.org/iss-today/the-south-african-police-service-must-renew-its-focus-on-specialised-units.

Burman, Erica, Sophie Smailes, and Khatidja Chantler. 2004. "'Culture' as a Barrier to Service Provision and Delivery: Domestic Violence Services for Minoritized Women." *Critical Social Policy* 24 (3): 332–57.

Burrill, Emily S., Richard L. Roberts, and Elizabeth Thornberry. 2010. "Introduction: Domestic Violence and the Law in Africa." In *Domestic Violence and the Law in Colonial and Postcolonial Africa*, edited by Emily S. Burrill, Richard L. Roberts, and Elizabeth Thornberry, 1–31. Athens: Ohio University Press.

Cabezas, Amalia L., Ellen Reese, and Marguerite Waller. 2007. *The Wages of Empire: Neoliberal Policies, Repression, and Women's Poverty*. New York: Routledge.

Campbell, Catherine. 1992. "Learning to Kill? Masculinity, the Family and Violence in Natal." *Journal of Southern African Studies* 18 (3): 614–28.

Center for Disease Control. 2018. "The Social-Ecological Model: A Framework for Prevention." http://www.cdc.gov/violenceprevention/overview/social-ecological model.html.

Chappell, Louise. 2002. *Gendering Government: Feminist Engagement with the State in Australia and Canada*. Vancouver: UBC Press.

Charlton, Sarah. 2004. *An Overview of the Housing Policy and Debates, Particularly in Relation to Women (or Vulnerable Groupings)*. Johannesburg: Centre for the Study of Violence and Reconciliation.

Chase, Jacquelyn. 2008. "Their Space: Security and Service Workers in a Brazilian Gated Community." *Geographical Review* 98 (4): 476–95.

Civilian Secretariat for the Police. 2013. "Domestic Violence Act Implementation Challenges." http://pmg-assets.s3-website-eu-west-1.amazonaws.com/131106dva.ppt. Accessed June 22, 2016.

———. 2016. "DVA Monitoring Report." http://www.policesecretariat.gov.za /downloads/reports/DVA_IMPLEMENTATION_AND_COMPLIANCE _MARCH_2015.pdf. Accessed June 23, 2016.
Clark, Janine A., and Wacheke M. Michuki. 2009. "Women and NGO Professionalisation: A Case Study of Jordan." *Development in Practice* 19 (3): 329–39.
Clement, Raquel, and Jill L. Grant. 2012. "Enclosing Paradise: The Design of Gated Communities in Barbados." *Journal of Urban Design* 17 (1): 43–60.
Cohen-Dar, Michal, and Samira Obeid. 2017. "Islamic Religious Leaders in Israel as Social Agents for Change on Health-Related Issues." *Journal of Religion and Health* 56 (6): 2285–96.
Combating Rape Act. No. 8 of 2000. Namibia. http://www.ilo.org/dyn/natlex/docs /ELECTRONIC/82559/90506/F1283246486/NAM82559.pdf.
Combrinck, Helene, and Lorenzo Wakefield. 2010. "Going the Extra Mile: Police Training on Domestic Violence." *South Africa Crime Quarterly* 31:27–34.
Connor, Jennie L., Kypros Kypri, Melanie L. Bell, and Kimberly Cousins. 2011. "Alcohol Involvement in Aggression between Intimate Partners in New Zealand: A National Cross-Sectional Study." *BMJ Open* 1:e000065. https://doi.org/10.1136 /bmjopen-2011-000065.
Constitution of the Republic of South Africa. 1996. https://www.gov.za/documents /constitution-republic-south-africa-1996.
Cooper, Diane, Chelsea Morroni, Phyllis Orner, Jennifer Moodley, Jane Harries, Lee Cullingworth, and Margaret Hoffman. 2004. "The Years of Democracy in South Africa: Documenting Transformation in Reproductive Health Policy and Status." *Reproductive Health Matters* 12 (24): 70–85.
Corvo, Ken, and Pamela Johnson. 2003. "Vilification of the 'Batterer': How Blame Shapes Domestic Violence Policy." *Aggression and Violent Behavior* 8 (3): 259–81.
Crenshaw, Kimberlé. 1997. "Intersectionality and Identity Politics." In *Reconstructing Political Theory*, edited by Mary L. Shanley and Uma Narayan, 1198–1213. Boston: Policy Press.
———. 2012. "From Private Violence to Mass Incarceration: Thinking Intersectionally about Women, Race, and Social Control." *UCLA Law Review* 59 (6): 1418–73.
Crowley, Úna. 2009. "Genealogy Method." In *International Encyclopedia of Human Geography*, edited by Rob Kitchin and Nigel Thrift, 341–44. Amsterdam: Elsevier Science.
Cullingworth, Margaret Hoffman. 2004. "The Years of Democracy in South Africa: Documenting Transformation in Reproductive Health Policy and Status." *Reproductive Health Matters* 12 (24): 70–85.
Cupples, Julie, and Irving Larios. 2005. "Gender, Elections, Terrorism: The Geopolitical Enframing of the 2001 Nicaraguan Elections." *Political Geography* 24 (3): 317–39.
Currier, Ashley. 2012. *Out in Africa: LGBT Organizing in Namibia and South Africa*. Minneapolis: University of Minnesota Press.
Debusscher, Petra, and Maria Martin de Almagro. 2016. "Post-conflict Women's Movements in Turmoil: The Challenges of Success in Liberia in the 2005-Aftermath." *Journal of Modern African Studies* 54 (2): 293–316.

References

Department of Justice and Constitutional Development. 2013. *Report on the Re-establishment of Sexual Offences Courts*. Ministerial Advisory Task Team on the Adjudication of Sexual Offence Matters.

Desivilya, Helena Syna, and Dalit Yassour-Borochowitz. 2008. "The Case of Checkpoint Watch: A Study of Organizational Practices in a Women's Human Rights Organization." *Organization Studies* 29 (6): 887–908.

Devries, Karen M., Jennifer C. Child, Loraine J. Bacchus, Joelle Mak, Gail Falder, Kathryn Graham, Charlotte Watts, and Lori Heise. 2014. "Intimate Partner Violence Victimization and Alcohol Consumption in Women: A Systematic Review and Meta-analysis." *Addiction* 109 (3): 379–91.

Devries, Karen M., Joelle Y. T. Mak, Claudia García-Moreno, Max Petzold, Jennifer C. Child, Gail Falder, S. Lim, Loraine J. Bacchus, Rebecca E. Engell, Lisa C. Rosenfeld, Christina Pallitto, Theo Vos, Naeemah Abrahams, and Charlotte H. Watts. 2013. "The Global Prevalence of Intimate Partner Violence against Women." *Science* 340 (6,140): 1527–28.

Dick, Penny, and Devi Jankowicz. 2001. "A Social Constructionist Account of Police Culture and Its Influence on the Representation and Progression of Female Officers." *Policing: An International Journal of Police Strategies and Management* 24 (2): 181–99.

Dixon, Bill. 2007. "Globalising the Local: A Genealogy of Sector Policing in South Africa." *International Relations* 21 (2): 163–82.

Dunkle, K. L., R. K. Jewkes, M. Nduna, J. Levin, N. Jama, N. Khuzwayo, M. P. Koss, and N. Duvvury. 2006. "Perpetration of Partner Violence and HIV Risk Behaviour among Young Men in the Rural Eastern Cape, South Africa." *AIDS* 20 (16): 2107–14.

Dworkin, S. L., C. Colvin, A. Hatcher, and D. Peacock. 2012. "Men's Perceptions of Women's Rights and Changing Gender Relations in South Africa: Lessons for Working with Men and Boys in HIV and Antiviolence Programs." *Gender and Society* 26 (1): 97–120.

Eggen, Oyvind. 2012. "Performing Good Governance: The Aesthetics of Bureaucratic Practice in Malawi." *Ethnos* 77 (1): 1–23.

Ellsberg, Mary, Diana J. Arango, Matthew Morton, Floriza Gennari, Sveinung Kiplesund, Manuel Contreras, and Charlotte Watts. 2014. "Prevention of Violence against Women and Girls: What Does the Evidence Say?" *Lancet* 385 (9,977): 1555–66.

Evans, Jenni, and Riaan Wolmarans. 2006. "Timeline of the Jacob Zuma Rape Trial." *Mail and Guardian*, March 21, 2006. http://mg.co.za/article/2006-03-21-timeline-of-the-jacob-zuma-rape-trial.

Fallon, Kathleen. 2008. *Democracy and the Rise of Women's Movements in Sub-Saharan Africa*. Baltimore, MD: Johns Hopkins University Press.

Faul, Michelle. 2013. "South Africa Violence against Women Rate Highest in the World." *Star*, March 8, 2013. http://www.thestar.com/news/world/2013/03/08/3_women_killed_each_day_in_south_africa_worlds_worst_gender_violence.html. Accessed August 8, 2013.

Fihlani, Pumza. 2016. "Has Oscar Pistorius Got Off Lightly with Six-Year Sentence?" *BBC*, July 6, 2016. http://www.bbc.com/news/world-africa-36727551. Accessed July 7, 2016.

Finnemore, Martha, and Kathryn Sikkink. 1998. "International Norm Dynamics and Political Change." *International Organization* 52 (Autumn): 887–917.

Foucault, Michel. 1977. "Nietzsche, Genealogy, History." In *Language, Counter-Memory, Practice: Selected Essays and Interviews*, edited by D. F. Bouchard, 139–64. Ithaca, NY: Cornell University Press.

Fox, Margalit. 2015. "Jackie Selebi, South Africa Police Head Convicted in Bribery Case, Dies at 64." *New York Times*, January 24, 2015. http://www.nytimes.com/2015/01/24/world/africa/jackie-selebi-south-african-police-head-convicted-in-corruption-case-dies-at-64.html?_r=0. Accessed June 23, 2016.

Freeman, Hadley. 2014. "Oscar Pistorius and Reeva Steenkamp's Relationship Was Far from 'Normal.'" *Guardian*, September 12, 2014. https://www.theguardian.com/commentisfree/2014/sep/12/oscar-pistorius-reeva-steenkamp-murder-normal-relationship. Accessed February 21, 2017.

Friedman, Elisabeth. 2000. "State-Based Advocacy for Gender Equality in the Developing World: Assessing the Venezuelan National Women's Agency." *Women and Politics* 21 (2): 601–13.

Fulu, E., X. Warner, S. Miedema, R. Jewkes, T. Roselli, and J. Lang. 2013. *Why Do Some Men Use Violence against Women and How Can We Prevent It? Findings from the UN Multi-country Study on Men and Violence in Asia and the Pacific.* Bangkok: UNDP, UNFPA, and UN Women.

Galtung, Johan. 1969. "Violence, Peace, and Peace Research." *Journal of Peace Research* 6 (3): 167–91.

García-Moreno, Claudia, Kelsey Hegarty, Ana Flavia Lucas d'Oliveira, Jane Koziol-McLain, Manuela Colombini, and Gene Feder. 2015. "The Health-Systems Response to Violence against Women." *Lancet* 385 (9,977): 1567–79.

Gass, Jesse, Dan Stein, David Williams, and Soraya Seedat. 2011. "Gender Differences in Risk for Intimate Partner Violence among South African Adults." *Journal of Interpersonal Violence* 26 (14): 2764–89.

Gelles, R. J., and M. M. Cavanaugh. 1993. "Alcohol and Other Drugs Are Not the Cause of Violence." In *Current Controversies on Family Violence*, edited by Donileen R. Loseke, Richard J. Gelles, and Mary M. Cavanaugh, 182–96. Thousand Oaks, CA: Sage.

Gil-Gonzalez, D., C. Vives-Cases, C. Alvarez-Dardet, and J. Latour-Perez. 2006. "Alcohol and Intimate Partner Violence: Do We Have Enough Information to Act?" *European Journal of Public Health* 16 (3): 278–84.

Goetz, Anne Marie. 1998. "Women in Politics and Gender Equity in Policy: South Africa and Uganda." *Review of African Political Economy* 25 (76): 241–62.

Goetz, Anne Marie, and Shireen Hassim. 2003. *No Shortcuts to Power: African Women in Politics and Policy Making.* New York: Zed Books.

Goldscheid, Julie. 2011. "Gender Violence and Work in the United States and South

References

Africa: The Parallel Processes of Legal and Cultural Change." *Journal of Gender, Social Policy and the Law* 19 (3): 921–58.

Gottschalk, Marie. 2006. *The Prison and the Gallows: The Politics of Mass Incarceration in America*. Cambridge: Cambridge University Press.

———. 2015. *Caught: The Prison State and the Lockdown of American Politics*. Princeton, NJ: Princeton University Press.

Gould, Chandré. 2013. "On the Record . . . Professor Rachel Jewkes." *South African Crime Quarterly* 43:43–47.

Gouws, Amanda. 2004. "The Politics of State Structures: Citizenship and the National Machinery for Women in South Africa." *Feminist Africa* 3:27–47.

———. 2008. "Obstacles for Women in Leadership Positions: The Case of South Africa." *Signs: Journal of Women in Culture and Society* 34 (1): 21–27.

———. 2014. "Recognition and Redistribution: State of the Women's Movement in South Africa 20 Years after Democratic Transition." *Agenda: Empowering Women for Gender Equity* 28 (2): 19–32.

———. 2016. "Women's Activism around Gender-Based Violence in South Africa: Recognition, Redistribution and Representation." *Review of African Political Economy* 43 (149): 400–415.

Govender, Pregs, Debbie Budlender, and N. Madlalal. 2004. *Beijing Conference Report: 1994. Country Report on the Status of South African Women*. Pretoria: Office of the President.

Gover, Angela R. 2004. "Risky Lifestyles and Dating Violence: A Theoretical Test of Violent Victimization." *Journal of Criminal Justice* 32:171–80.

Gqola, Pumla Dineo. 2007. "How the 'Cult of Femininity' and Violent Masculinities Support Endemic Gender-Based Violence in Contemporary South Africa." *African Identities* 5 (1): 111–24.

Graham, Kathryn, Sharon Bernards, Sharon Wilsnack, and Gerhard Gmel. 2011. "Alcohol May Not Cause Partner Violence, but It Seems to Make It Worse: A Cross-National Comparison of the Relationship between Alcohol and Severity of Partner Violence." *Journal of Interpersonal Violence* 26 (8): 1503–23.

Green, December. 1999. *Gender Violence in Africa: African Women's Responses*. New York: St. Martin's.

Grindle, Merilee. 2004. "Good Enough Governance: Poverty Reduction and Reform in Developing Countries." *Governance: An International Journal of Policy, Administration, and Institutions* 17 (4): 525–48.

———. 2011. "Good Enough Governance Revisited." *Development Policy Review* 29 (S1): 199–221.

Guy, Mary, Meredith Newman, and Sharon Mastracci. 2008. *Emotional Labor: Putting the Service in Public Service*. New York: M. E. Sharpe.

Halley, Janet. 2006. *Split Decisions: How and Why to Take a Break from Feminism*. Princeton, NJ: Princeton University Press.

Harrison, Philip, and Alan Mabin. 2006. "Security and Space: Managing the Contradictions of Access Restriction in Johannesburg." *Environment and Planning B: Planning and Design* 33 (1): 3–20.

Hassim, Shireen. 2003. "Representation, Participation, and Democratic Effectiveness: Feminist Challenges to Representative Democracy in South Africa." In *No Shortcuts to Power: African Women in Politics and Policy Making*, edited by Anne Marie Goetz and Shireen Hassim, 81–109. New York: Zed Books.

———. 2005. "Terms of Engagement: South African Challenges." *Feminist Africa* 4. http://www.agi.ac.za/sites/default/files/image_tool/images/429/feminist_africa_journals/archive/04/fa_4_feature_article.pdf.

———. 2006. *Women's Organizations and Democracy in South Africa: Contesting Authority*. Madison: University of Wisconsin Press.

———. 2009. "Democracy's Shadows: Sexual Rights and Gender Politics in the Rape Trial of Jacob Zuma." *African Studies* 68 (1): 57–77.

———. 2014. *The ANC Women's League*. Johannesburg: Jacana Press.

Hassim, Shireen, Tawana Kupe, and Eric Worby, eds. 2008. *Go Home or Die Here: Violence, Xenophobia, and the Reinvention of Difference in South Africa*. Johannesburg: Wits University Press.

Hatcher, A. M., P. Romito, M. Odero, E. A. Bukusi, M. Onono, and J. M. Turan. 2013. "Social Context and Drivers of Intimate Partner Violence in Rural Kenya: Implications for the Health of Pregnant Women." *Culture, Health and Sexuality* 15 (4): 404–19.

Hatcher, Abigail M., Christopher J. Colvin, Nkuli Ndlovu, and Shari L. Dworkin. 2014. "Intimate Partner Violence among Rural South African Men: Alcohol Use, Sexual Decision Making, and Partner Communication." *Culture, Health and Sexuality* 16 (9): 1023–39.

Hautzinger, Sarah J. 2002. "Criminalising Male Violence in Brazil's Women's Police Stations: From Flawed Essentialism to Imagined Communities." *Journal of Gender Studies* 11 (3): 243–51.

———. 2007. *Violence in the City of Women: Police and Batterers in Bahia, Brazil*. Berkeley: University of California Press.

Heise, Lori. 2011. "What Works to Prevent Partner Violence? An Evidence Overview." STRIVE Research Consortium. http://r4d.dfid.gov.uk/PDF/Outputs/Gender/60887-PartnerViolenceEvidenceOverview.pdf.

Heise, Lori, Mary Ellsberg, and Megan Gottemoeller. 1999. "Ending Violence against Women." In *Population Reports, Series L, No. 11*. Baltimore, MD: Johns Hopkins University School of Public Health Population Information Program.

———. 2002. "A Global Overview of Gender-Based Violence." *International Journal of Gynecology and Obstetrics* 78:S5–S14.

Hermkens, Anna-Karina. 2008. "Josephine's Journey: Gender-Based Violence and Marian Devotion in Urban Papua New Guinea." *Oceania* 78:151–67.

Hickel, Jason. 2014. "'Xenophobia' in South Africa: Order, Chaos, and the Moral Economy of Witchcraft." *Cultural Anthropology* 29 (1): 103–27.

References

Hickey, Sam. 2012. "Turning Governance Thinking Upside-Down? Insights from 'The Politics of What Works.'" *Third World Quarterly* 33 (7): 1231–47.

Holodny, Elena. 2016. "South Africa's Unemployment Rate Just Surged to a 12-Year High." *Business Insider*, May 9, 2016. http://www.businessinsider.com/south-africa-unemployment-rate-rises-2016-5. Accessed June 6, 2016.

Hornak, Leo. 2015. "South Africa's New Drug Cocktail of Choice Is Devastating Its Townships." *Public Radio International*, March 18, 2015. http://www.pri.org/stories/2015-03-18/south-africas-new-drug-cocktail-choice-devastating-its-townships. Accessed June 6, 2016.

Htun, Mala, and S. Laurel Weldon. 2012. "The Civic Origins of Progressive Policy Change: Combating Violence against Women in Global Perspective—2005." *American Political Science Review* 106 (3): 548–69.

Huchzermeyer, Marie. 2001. "Housing for the Poor? Negotiated Housing Policy in South Africa." *Habitat International* 25:303–31.

Hunter, Chris. 2006. "The Master's Tools Revisited: Can Law Contribute to Ending Violence against Women?" *IDS (Institute of Development Studies) Bulletin* 37 (6): 57–68.

Hunter, Mark. 2010. *Love in the Time of AIDS: Inequality, Gender, and Rights in South Africa*. Bloomington: Indiana University Press.

Institute for Criminal Policy Research. 2016. "South Africa." http://www.prisonstudies.org/country/south-africa. Accessed July 27, 2016.

International Business Times. 2015. "Oscar Pistorius Appeal: Justice Eric Leach's Judgement in Full." December 4, 2015. https://www.ibtimes.co.uk/oscar-pistorius-appeal-justice-eric-leachs-judgement-full-1531812. Accessed July 7, 2016.

Jewkes, Rachel. 2002. "Intimate Partner Violence: Causes and Prevention." *Lancet* 359 (9,315): 1423–29.

Jewkes, Rachel, and Naeemah Abrahams. 2002. "The Epidemiology of Rape and Sexual Coercion in South Africa: An Overview." *Social Science and Medicine* 55:153–66.

Jewkes, Rachel, Michael Flood, and James Lang. 2015. "From Work with Men and Boys to Changes of Social Norms and Reduction of Inequities in Gender Relations: A Conceptual Shift in Prevention of Violence against Women and Girls." *Lancet* 385:1580–89.

Jewkes, Rachel, Jonathan Levin, and Loveday Penn-Kekana. 2002. "Risk Factors for Domestic Violence: Findings from a South African Cross-Sectional Study." *Social Science and Medicine* 55:1603–17.

Jewkes, Rachel, and Robert Morrell. 2010. "Gender and Sexuality: Emerging Perspectives from the Heterosexual Epidemic in South Africa and Implications for HIV Risk and Prevention." *Journal of the International AIDS Society* 13 (6): 1–11.

Jewkes, Rachel, Loveday Penn-Kekana, Jonathan Levin, M. Ratsaka, and M. Schrieber. 2001. "Prevalence of Emotional, Physical, and Sexual Abuse of Women in Three South African Provinces." *South African Medical Journal* 91:421–28.

Jewkes, Rachel, Yandisa Sikweyiya, Robert Morrell, and Kristin Dunkle. 2009. *Un-

derstanding Men's Health and Use of Violence: Interface of Rape and HIV in South Africa. Pretoria, South Africa: Medical Research Council.

———. 2010. "Why, When and How Men Rape: Understanding Rape Perpetration in South Africa." *South African Crime Quarterly* 34 (December): 23–31.

———. 2011. "Gender Inequitable Masculinity and Sexual Entitlement in Rape Perpetration South Africa: Findings of a Cross-Sectional Study." *PLoS ONE* 6 (12): e29590.

Jewkes, Rachel, Lisa Vetten, Ruxana Jina, Christofides Nicola, Romi Sigsworth, and Lizle Loots. 2012. "Single and Multiple Perpetrator Rape in South Africa." *South African Crime Quarterly* 41:11–19.

John, Ime Akpan, Stephen Lawoko, and Leif Svanstrom. 2011. "Screening for Intimate Partner Violence in Healthcare in Kano, Nigeria: Extent and Determinants." *Journal of Family Violence* 26:109–16.

Johnston, Karen, and John Houston. 2018. "Representative Bureaucracy: Does Female Police Leadership Affect Gender-Based Violence Arrests?" *International Review of Administrative Science* 84 (1): 3–20.

Jürgens, Ulrich, and Martin Gnad. 2002. "Gated Communities in South Africa—Experiences from Johannesburg." *Environment and Planning B: Planning and Design* 29 (3): 337–53.

Karam, Azza. 2014. "On Faith, Health, and Tensions: An Overview from an Intergovernmental Perspective." *Heythrop Journal* 55 (6): 1069–79.

Keehn, Emily, Lara Stemple, Cherith Sanger, and Dean Peacock. 2014. "Uneven and Still Insufficient: South African Police Services' Station-Level Compliance with Sexual Offences Laws." *Feminist Criminology* 9 (2): 87–112.

Kettl, Donald. 1993. *Sharing Power: Public Governance and Private Markets.* Washington, DC: Brookings Institution.

———. 2015. "The Job of Government: Interweaving Public Functions and Private Hands." *Public Administration Review* 75 (2): 219–29.

Khan, Sultan, Benoît Lootvoet, and Shahid Vawda. 2006. "Transcending Traditional Forms of Governance: Prospects for Co-operative Governance and Service Delivery in Durban's Tribal Authority Areas." *Transformation: Critical Perspectives on Southern Africa* 62 (1): 84–117.

Kiely, Julia A., and Grahame S. Peek. 2002. "The Culture of the British Police: Views of Police Officers." *Service Industries Journal* 22 (1): 167–83.

Kilgore, James. 2016. "Opposing Mass Incarceration Is 'Trendy,' but Can We Stop the Train of Piecemeal Reform?" *Truthout,* June 3, 2016. http://www.truth-out.org/opinion/item/36277-opposing-mass-incarceration-is-trendy-but-can-we-stop-the-train-of-piecemeal-reform. Accessed July 27, 2016.

Klandermans, Bert, Marlene Roefs, and Johan Olivier. 1997. "A Movement Takes Offices." In *The Social Movement Society: Contentious Politics for a New Century,* edited by David S. Meyer and Sidney Tarrow, 173–94. New York: Rowman and Littlefield.

References

Koelble, Thomas, and Edward LiPuma. 2011. "Traditional Leaders and the Culture of Governance in South Africa." *Governance: An International Journal of Policy, Administration, and Institutions* 24 (1): 5–29.

Krog, Antjie. 2001. "Locked into Loss and Silence: Testimonies of Gender and Violence at the South African Truth Commission." In *Victims, Perpetrators or Actors? Gender, Armed Conflict and Political Violence*, edited by Caroline O. N. Moser and Fiona C. Clark, 203–17. New York: Zed.

Kulawik, Teresa. 2009. "Staking the Frame of a Feminist Discursive Institutionalism." *Politics and Gender* 5 (2): 262–71.

Landau, Loren B., Kaajal Ramjathan-Keogh, and Gayatri Singh. 2005. "Xenophobia in South Africa and Problems Related to It." In *Forced Migration Working Series* 13. Johannesburg: Forced Migration Studies Programme, University of the Witwatersrand.

Landman, Karina. 2004. "Gated Communities in South Africa: The Challenges for Spatial Planning and Land Use Management." *Town Planning Review* 75 (2): 151–72.

———. 2007. "Exploring the Impact of Gated Communities on Social and Special Justice and Its Relation to Restorative Justice and Peacebuilding in South Africa." *Acta Juridica* 2007 (1): 134–55.

Langa, Malose, and Peace Kiguwa. 2016. "Race-ing Xenophobic Violence: Engaging Social Representations of the Black African Body in Post-apartheid South Africa." *Agenda: Empowering Women for Gender Equity* 30 (2): 75–85. http://dx.doi.org/10.1080/10130950.2016.1222086.

Lasley, James R., James Larson, Chandrika Kelso, and Gregory Chris Brown. 2011. "Assessing the Long-Term Effects of Officer Race on Police Attitudes towards the Community: A Case for Representative Bureaucracy Theory." *Police Practice and Research: An International Journal* 12 (6): 474–91.

Latour, Bruno. 2005. *Reassembling the Social*. Oxford: Oxford University Press.

Lawoko, Stephen, Sören Sanz, Lotti Helström, and Maaret Castren. 2011. "Screening for Intimate Partner Violence against Women in Healthcare Sweden: Prevalence and Determinants." *International Scholarly Research Notices: Nursing* 2011:1–7.

Lawoko, Stephen, Gloria K. Seruwagi, Iryna Marunga, Milton Mutto, Emmanuel Ochola, Geoffrey Oloya, Joyce Piloya, and Muhamadi Lubega. 2013. "Healthcare Providers' Perceptions on Screening for Intimate Partner Violence in Healthcare: A Qualitative Study of Four Health Centres in Uganda." *Open Journal of Preventative Medicine* 3:1–11.

Leach, Belinda. 2011. "Memorializing Murder, Speaking Back to the State." In *Anthropology at the Front Lines of Gender-Based Violence*, edited by Jennifer R. Wies and Hillary J. Haldane, 191–209. Nashville: Vanderbilt University Press.

Legal Assistance Centre. 2006. *Rape in Namibia: Full Report*. Windhoek, Namibia: Legal Assistance Centre.

Lehrer, Evelyn, Vivian Lehrer, and Ramona Krauss. 2009. "Religion and Intimate Partner Violence in Chile: Macro- and Micro-level Influences." *Social Science Research* 38:635–43.

Leibbrandt, Murray, Ingrid Woolard, Arden Finn, and Jonathan Argent. 2010. "Trends in South African Income Distribution and Poverty Since the Fall of Apartheid." *OECD Social, Employment and Migration Working Papers, No. 101.* OECD Publishing.

Leonard, K. E. 1999. "Alcohol Use and Husband Marital Aggression among Newlywed Couples." In *Violence in Intimate Relationships*, edited by X. B. Arriaga and S. Oskamp, 113–38. Thousand Oaks, CA: Sage.

Leonard, K. E., and M. Senchak. 1996. "Prospective Prediction of Husband Marital Aggression within Newlywed Couples." *Journal of Abnormal Psychology* 105:369–80.

Lipsky, Michael. 1980. *Street-Level Bureaucracy: Dilemmas of the Individual in Public Services.* New York: Russell Sage Foundation.

LiPuma, Edward, and Thomas Koelble. 2009. "Deliberative Democracy and the Politics of Traditional Leadership in South Africa: A Case of Despotic Domination or Democratic Deliberation?" *Journal of Contemporary African Studies* 27 (2): 201–33.

Lundgren, Rebecka, and Melissa K. Adams. 2014. "Safe Passages: Building on Cultural Traditions to Prevent Gender-Based Violence throughout the Life Course." *Working Paper #304*, 53–77. Gender, Development, and Globalization Program, Center for Gender in Global Context, Michigan State University.

Luyt, Russell, and Don Foster. 2001. "Hegemonic Masculine Conceptualisation in Gang Culture." *South African Journal of Psychology* 31 (3): 1–11.

MacEachern, Alison D., Divya Jindal-Snape, and Sharon Jackson. 2011. "Child Abuse Investigation: Police Officers and Secondary Traumatic Stress." *International Journal of Occupational Safety and Ergonomics* 17 (4): 329–39.

MacKay, Fiona, Surya Monro, and Georgina Waylen. 2009. "The Feminist Potential of Sociological Institutionalism." *Politics and Gender* 5 (2): 245–52.

Mama, Amina. 2005. "Editorial." *Feminist Africa* 4. http://www.agi.ac.za/sites/default/files/image_tool/images/429/feminist_africa_journals/archive/04/fa_4_editorial.pdf.

Manyathi-Jele, Nomfundo. 2013. "Sexual Offences Courts to Be Re-established." http://www.saflii.org/za/journals/DEREBUS/2013/163.html. Accessed June 22, 2016.

———. 2015. "Justice Department on Target with Establishment of Sexual Offences Courts." *De Rebus*, August 25, 2015. http://www.derebus.org.za/justice-department-target-establishment-sexual-offences-courts/.

Margaretten, Emily. 2015. *Street Life under a Roof: Youth Homelessness in South Africa.* Urbana: University of Illinois Press.

Maroga, Millicent. 2003. "Two Sides of the Same Coin? Sector Policing and Community Policing Forums." *South African Crime Quarterly* 6 (December): 13–16.

———. 2004. "Sector Policing: What Are the Challenges?" Center for the Study of Violence and Reconciliation. http://www.csvr.org.za/docs/policing/sectorpolicing.pdf. Accessed September 13, 2016.

Mastracci, Sharon H., Mary E. Guy, and Meredith A. Newman. 2012. *Emotional Labor and Crisis Response: Working in the Razor's Edge.* New York: M. E. Sharpe.

Masuku, Sibusiso. 2002. "Prevention Is Better Than Cure: Addressing Violent Crime in South Africa." *South African Crime Quarterly* 2 (November): 5–12.

Mathews, Shanaaz, and Naeemah Abrahams. 2001. *Combining Stories and Numbers: An Analysis of the Impact of the Domestic Violence Act (No. 116 of 1998) on Women.* Gender Advocacy Programme, Cape Town, South Africa, and Medical Research Council, Tygerberg, South Africa.

Mattes, Robert. 2006. "How Does SA Compare: Experiences of Crime and Policing in an African Context." *South African Crime Quarterly* 18 (December): 17–24.

Maynard-Moody, Steven, and Michael Musheno. 2003. *Cops, Teachers, Counselors: Stories from the Front Lines of Public Service.* Ann Arbor: University of Michigan Press.

McCleary-Sills, Jennifer, Sophie Namy, Joyce Nyoni, Datius Rweyemamu, Adrophina Salvatory, and Ester Steven. 2015. "Stigma, Shame, and Women's Limited Agency in Help-Seeking for Intimate Partner Violence." *Global Public Health* 11 (1–2): 224–35.

Medie, Peace. 2013. "Fighting Gender-Based Violence: The Women's Movement and the Enforcement of Rape Law in Liberia." *African Affairs* 112 (448): 377–97.

———. 2015. "Women and Postconflict Security: A Study of Police Response to Domestic Violence in Liberia." *Politics and Gender* 11 (3): 478–98.

———. 2016. "Sexual Violence and Justice in Liberia." *Project Syndicate*, July 26, 2016. https://www.project-syndicate.org/commentary/liberia-justice-for-rape-victims-by-peace-a-medie-2016-07. Accessed July 27, 2016.

Meintjes, Sheila. 2003. "The Politics of Engagement: Women Transforming the Policy Process—Domestic Violence Legislation in South Africa." In *No Shortcuts to Power: African Women in Politics and Policy Making*, edited by Anne Marie Goetz and Shireen Hassim, 140–59. New York: Zed Books.

Meintjes, Sheila, Anu Pillay, and Meredeth Turshen. 2001. *The Aftermath: Women in Post-conflict Transformation.* London: Zed.

Menjívar, Cecilia. 2011. *Enduring Violence: Ladina Women's Lives in Guatemala.* Berkeley: University of California Press.

Menjívar, Cecilia, and Shannon Drysdale Walsh. 2016. "Subverting Justice: Sociolegal Determinants of Impunity for Violence against Women in Guatemala." *Laws* 5 (31): 1–20.

Merry, Sally Engle. 2006. *Human Rights and Gender Violence: Translating International Law into Local Justice.* Chicago: University of Chicago Press.

Meth, Paula. 2003. "Rethinking the 'Domus' in Domestic Violence: Homelessness, Space and Domestic Violence in South Africa." *Geoforum* 34 (3) : 317–327.

———. 2010. "Unsettling Insurgency: Reflections on Women's Insurgent Practices in South Africa." *Planning Theory and Practice* 11 (2): 241–63.

———. 2016. "The Gendered Contradictions in South Africa's State Housing: Accumulation alongside an Undermining of Assets through Housing." In *Gender, Asset Accumulation and Just Cities: Pathways to Transformations*, edited by Caroline O. N. Moser, 100–116. New York: Routledge.

———. 2017. "Informal Housing, Gender, Crime and Violence: The Role of Design in Urban South Africa." *British Journal of Criminology* 57 (2): 402–21.

Meth, Paula, and Sibongile Buthelezi. 2017. "New Housing / New Crime? Changes in Safety, Governance and Everyday Incivilities for Residents Relocated from Informal to Formal Housing at Hammond's Farm, eThekwini." *Geoforum* 82: 77–86.

Michau, Lori. 2007. "Approaching Old Problems in New Ways: Community Mobilization as a Primary Prevention Strategy to Combat Violence against Women." *Gender and Development* 15 (1): 95–109.

Michau, Lori, Jessica Horn, Amy Bank, Mallika Dutt, and Cathy Zimmerman. 2014. "Prevention of Violence against Women and Girls: Lessons from Practice." *Lancet* 385 (9,978): 1672–84.

Michau, Lori S., Dipak Naker, and Zahara Swalehe. 2002. "Mobilizing Communities to End Violence against Women in Tanzania." In *Responding to Cairo: Case Studies of Changing Practice in Reproductive Health and Family Planning*, edited by Nicole Haberlan and Diana Measham. New York: Population Council. http://raisingvoices.org/wp-content/uploads/2013/03/downloads/resources/Mobilizing_Communities_to_end_violence.pdf.

Misri, Deepti. 2014. *Beyond Partition: Gender, Violence, and Representation in Postcolonial India*. Urbana: University of Illinois Press.

Mkhwanazi, Siyabonga. 2016. "Report Lifts Lid on Abusive Cops." *IOL News*, March 24, 2016. http://www.iol.co.za/news/crime-courts/report-lifts-lid-on-abusive-cops-2001403. Accessed June 23, 2016.

Mngxitama, Andile. 2008. "We Are Not All Like That: Race, Class and Nation after Apartheid." In *Go Home or Die Here: Violence, Xenophobia and the Reinvention of Difference in South Africa*, edited by Eric Worby, Shireen Hassim, and Tawana Kupe, 189–205. Johannesburg: University of Witwatersrand Press.

Mnisi Weeks, Sindiso. 2015. "South Africans Braced for New Confrontation with Government over Controversial Law." *Conversation*, June 8, 2015. https://theconversation.com/south-africans-braced-for-new-confrontation-with-government-over-controversial-law-42829. Accessed July 8, 2015.

———. 2015–16. "Access to Justice? Dispute Management Process in Msinga, KwaZulu-Natal, South Africa." *New York Law School Law Review* 60 (1): 227–50.

Moffett, Helen. 2009. "Sexual Violence, Civil Society and the New Constitution." In *Women's Activism in South Africa: Working across Divides*, edited by Hannah Britton, Jennifer Fish, and Sheila Meintjes, 157–86. Durban: University of KwaZulu Natal Press.

Mogale, Ramadimetja, Kathy Kovacs Burns, and Solina Richter. 2012. "Violence against Women in South Africa: Policy Positions and Recommendations." *Violence against Women* 18 (5): 580–94.

Mogstad, Heidi, Dominique Dryding, and Olivia Fiorotto. 2016. "Policing the Private: Social Barriers to the Effective Policing of Domestic Violence." *South African Crime Quarterly* 56 (June): 5–17.

Montoya, Celeste, and Lise Rolandsen Agustín. 2013. "The Othering of Domestic Violence: The EU and Cultural Framings of Violence against Women." *Social Politics* 20 (4): 534–57.

References

Moreland, Stacy. 2014. "Talking about Rape—and Why It Matters: Adjudicating Rape in the Western Cape High Court." *South African Crime Quarterly* 47 (March): 5–15.

Moser, Caroline O. N., and Fiona C. Clark, eds. 2001. *Victims, Perpetrators or Actors: Gender, Armed Conflict and Political Violence*. New York: Zed.

Moult, Kelley. 2005. "Informal Mechanisms for Dealing with Domestic Violence." *South African Crime Quarterly* 12 (June): 19–24.

Move to End Violence. 2015. "Using an Intersectional Approach." http://www.movetoendviolence.org/resources/using-an-intersectional-approach/.

Mycoo, Michelle. 2006. "The Retreat of the Upper and Middle Classes to Gated Communities in the Post-structural Adjustment Era: The Case of Trinidad." *Environment and Planning A: Economy and Space* 38 (1): 131–48.

Naidoo, Kogieleum. 2013. "Rape in South Africa—a Call to Action." *South African Medical Journal* 103 (4): 210–11.

Narayan, Uma. 1997. *Dislocating Cultures: Identities, Traditions, and Third World Feminism*. New York: Routledge.

NCOP Security and Justice. 2013. "Report by the Select Committee on Security and Constitutional Development on the Domestic Violence Reports." https://pmg.org.za/tabled-committee-report/316/. Accessed June 22, 2016.

Nelson, Sara. 1996. "Constructing and Negotiating Gender in Women's Police Stations in Brazil." *Latin American Perspectives* 23 (1): 131–48.

Nicholson, Zara, and Michelle Jones. 2013. "Up to 3,600 Rapes in South Africa Every Day." *Cape Times*, February 8, 2013. http://www.iol.co.za/news/crime-courts/up-to-3-600-rapes-in-sa-every-day-1.1466429#.UgEeiGTXgTg. Accessed August 8, 2013.

Nicolson, Greg. 2015. "South Africa Initiation Schools: Botched Circumcisions, Kidnap and Death Threats." *Guardian*, September 25, 2015. https://www.theguardian.com/global-development-professionals-network/2015/sep/25/south-africa-initiation-schools-botched-circumcisions-kidnap-death-threats.

———. 2016. "How South African Anti-rape Protesters Disrupted Zuma's Speech." *Guardian*, August 9, 2016. https://www.theguardian.com/world/2016/aug/09/south-africa-zuma-rape-protesters-disrupt.

Nixon, Rob. 2011. *Slow Violence and the Environmentalism of the Poor*. Cambridge, MA: Harvard University Press.

No Ceilings. 2016. "No Ceilings: The Full Participation Report." http://noceilings.org/report/report.pdf. Accessed June 6, 2016.

Orthofer, Anna. 2016a. "Figures Suggest SA Has the Highest Concentration of Wealth in the Hands of a Few." *Mail and Guardian Online*, August 4, 2016. http://mg.co.za/article/2016-08-04-00-figures-suggest-sa-has-the-highest-concentration-of-wealth-in-the-hands-of-a-few.

———. 2016b. "Wealth Inequality in South Africa: Evidence from Survey and Tax Data." *REDI3x3 Working Paper 15*. Cape Town: Research Project on Employment, Income Distribution, and Inclusive Growth.

Parenzee, Penny, Lillian Artz, and Kelley Moult. 2001. *Monitoring the Implementation of the Domestic Violence Act*. Cape Town: Institute of Criminology, University of Cape Town.

Parson, Nia. 2010. "Transformative Ties: Gender Violence, Forms of Recovery, and Shifting Subjectivities in Chile." *Medical Anthropology Quarterly* 24 (1): 64–84.

———. 2013. *Traumatic States: Gendered Violence, Suffering, and Care in Chile*. Nashville: Vanderbilt University Press.

Perron, Brian E., and Barbara S. Hiltz. 2006. "Burnout and Secondary Trauma among Forensic Interviewers of Abused Children." *Child and Adolescent Social Work Journal* 23 (2): 216–34.

Perova, Elizaveta, and Sarah Anne Reynolds. 2017. "Women's Police Stations and Intimate Partner Violence: Evidence from Brazil." *Social Science and Medicine* 174 (February): 188–96.

Pilane, Pontsho. 2016a. "Almost Half of Centres for Rape Survivors May Lose Funding for Counselling Services." *BHEKISISA*, August 29, 2016. http://bhekisisa.org/article/2016-08-29-00-almost-half-of-centres-for-rape-survivors-may-lose-funding-for-counselling-services.

———. 2016b. "Government Rape Counselling Services Saved Just Weeks from Slated Closure." *BHEKISISA*, September 19, 2016. http://bhekisisa.org/article/2016-09-19-00-government-rape-counselling-services-saved-just-weeks-from-slated-closure/.

Polgreen, Lydia. 2013. "Dropped Charges in Deadly Rape Provoke Fury in South Africa, and Pessimism." *New York Times*, June 8, 2013. http://www.nytimes.com/2013/06/09/world/africa/rape-and-murder-stirs-fury-in-south-africa.html?pagewanted=all&_r=0. Accessed August 8, 2013.

Prager, Jonas. 1994. "Contracting Out Government Services: Lessons from the Private Sector." *Public Administration Review* 54 (2): 176–84.

Prison Policy Initiative. 2016. "States of Incarceration: The Global Context." http://www.prisonpolicy.org/global/. Accessed July 27, 2016.

Rasool, Shahana. 2016. "Help-Seeking after Domestic Violence: The Critical Role of Children." *Journal of Interpersonal Violence* 31 (9): 1661–86.

Rasool, Shahana, Kerry Vermaak, Robyn Pharoah, Antoinette Louw, and Aki Stavrou. 2002. *Violence against Women: A National Survey*. Pretoria: Institute for Security Studies.

Reddy, Dashakti. 2014. "Managing Sexual and Gender-Based Violence (SGBV) in Liberia: Exploring the Syncretisation of Western and Traditional Approaches." MA thesis, University of Bergen, Department of Geography.

Rees, Kate, Virginia Zweigenthal, and Kate Joyner. 2014. "Implementing Intimate Partner Violence Care in a Rural Sub-district of South Africa: A Qualitative Evaluation." *Global Health Action* 7 (1): 1–12.

Revillard, Anne, and Laure Bereni. 2016. "From Grassroots to Institutions: Women's Movements Studies in Europe." In *Social Movement Studies in Europe: The State of the Art*, edited by Olivier Fillieule and Guya Accornero, 156–72. New York: Berghahn Books.

Ross, Fiona. 2010. *Raw Life, New Hope: Decency, Housing, and Everyday Life in a Post-apartheid Community*. Cape Town: University of Cape Town Press.

———. 2015. "Raw Life and Respectability: Poverty and Everyday Life in a Post-apartheid Community." *Current Anthropology* 56 (S11): S97–S107.

References

Ross, Gracia Violeta, quoted in Rowan Williams and Michel Sidibe. 2012. "More Than a Prayer: Faith Communities' Response to Sexual Violence." November 30, 2012. https://www.newstatesman.com/lifestyle/2012/11/more-prayer-faith-communities-response-sexual-violence. Accessed July 14, 2016.

Rubin, Margot. 2011. "Perceptions of Corruption in the South African Housing Allocation and Delivery Programme: What It May Mean for Accessing the State." *Journal of Asian and African Studies* 46 (5): 479–90.

Saleh, Ibrahim. 2015. "Is It Really Xenophobia in South Africa or an Intentional Act of Prejudice?" *Global Media Journal: Africa Edition* 9 (2): 293–313.

Salo, Elaine. 2005. "Multiple Targets, Mixing Strategies: Complicating Feminist Analysis of Contemporary South African Women's Movements." *Feminist Africa* 4. http://www.agi.ac.za/sites/default/files/image_tool/images/429/feminist_africa_journals/archive/04/fa_4_standpoint_1.pdf.

Samuelson, Meg. 2007. "The Disfigured Body of the Female Guerrilla: (De)Militarization, Sexual Violence, and Redomestication in Zoë Wicomb's *David's Story*." *Signs* 32 (4): 833–56.

Saniei-Pour, Alireza. 2015. "Inequality in South Africa: A Post-apartheid Analysis." *World Policy Institute*, July 7, 2015. http://www.worldpolicy.org/blog/2015/07/07/inequality-south-africa-post-apartheid-analysis. Accessed July 27, 2016.

Scanlon, Helen. 2008. "Militarization, Gender, and Transitional Justice in Africa." *Feminist Africa* 10:31–48.

Scully, Pamela. 1995. "Rape, Race, and Colonial Culture: The Sexual Politics of Identity in Nineteenth-Century Cape Colony, South Africa." *American Historical Review* 100 (2): 335–59.

———. 2010. "Afterword: Finding Gendered Justice in the Age of Human Rights." In *Domestic Violence and the Law in Colonial and Postcolonial Africa*, edited by Emily S. Burrill, Richard L. Roberts, and Elizabeth Thornberry. Athens: Ohio University Press.

Seedat, Mohamed, Ashley VanNiekerk, Rachel Jewkes, Shahnaaz Suffla, and Kopano Ratele. 2009. "Violence and Injuries in South Africa: Prioritising an Agenda for Preventions." *Lancet* 374 (9,694): 1011–22.

Seidman, Gay W. 1999. "Gendered Citizenship: South Africa's Democratic Transition and the Construction of a Gendered State." *Gender and Society* 13 (3): 287–307.

———. 2003. "Institutional Dilemmas: Representation versus Mobilization in the South African Gender Commission." *Feminist Studies* 29 (3): 541–63.

Shahrokh, Thea, and Joanna Wheeler. 2014. *Agency and Citizenship in a Context of Gender-Based Violence*. Institute of Developmental Studies, University of Sussex, Brighton, UK.

Shaw, Carolyn Martin. 2015. *Women and Power in Zimbabwe: Promises of Feminism*. Champaign: University of Illinois Press.

Sherrill, Andrew M., Kathryn M. Bell, and Nicole Wyngarden. 2016. "A Qualitative Examination of Situational Risk Recognition among Female Victims of Physical Intimate Partner Violence." *Violence against Women* 22 (8): 966–85.

Shikola, Teckla. 1998. "We Left Our Shoes Behind." In *What Women Do in Wartime: Gender and Conflict in Africa*, edited by Meredeth Turshen and Clotilde Twagiramariya, 138–49. New York: Zed.

Singh, Anne-Marie. 2016. *Policing and Crime Control in Post-apartheid South Africa*. New York: Routledge.

Smit, Jeanette, and Fransisca Nel. 2002. "An Evaluation of the Implementation of the Domestic Violence Act: What Is Happening in Practice?" *Acta Criminologica* 15 (3): 45–55.

Smythe, Dee, and Lillian Artz. 2005. "Structural Problems with Implementing the DVA." *Agenda: Empowering Women for Gender Equity* 1 (1): 24–33.

Sokoloff, Natalie, and Ida Dupont. 2005. "Domestic Violence at the Intersections of Race, Class, and Gender: Challenges and Contribution to Understanding Violence against Marginalized Women in Diverse Communities." *Violence against Women* 11 (1): 38–64.

South African Government News Agency. 2012. "Fighting for SA's Women and Children." December 7, 2012. http://www.sanews.gov.za/features/fighting-sas-women-and-children. Accessed June 23, 2016.

———. 2014. "SA to Set Up More Sexual Offences Courts." July 16, 2014. http://www.southafrica.info/services/rights/justice-160714. Accessed June 22, 2016.

Statistics South Africa. 2012. "Quarterly Labour Force Survey." http://www.statssa.gov.za/publications/P0211/P02114thQuarter2011.pdf. Accessed June 6, 2016.

———. 2016. "Quarterly Labour Force Survey." http://www.statssa.gov.za/publications/P0211/P02111stQuarter2016.pdf. Accessed June 6, 2016.

Staudt, Kathleen. 1998. "Women in Politics: Mexico in Global Perspective." In *Women's Participation in Mexican Political Life*, edited by Victoria E. Rodriguez, 23–40. Boulder, CO: Westview Press.

Stetson, Dorothy McBride, and Amy G. Mazur, eds. 1995. *Comparative State Feminisms*. Thousand Oaks, CA: Sage.

Suttner, Raymond. 2014. "The Abahlali/DA Pact: Difficult Situations Require Difficult Decisions." *Daily Maverick*, May 6, 2014. http://www.dailymaverick.co.za/article/2014-05-05-op-ed-the-abahlalida-pact-difficult-situations-require-difficult-decisions/#.VaWErXgTHFI. Accessed July 14, 2015.

———. 2015a. *Recovering Democracy in South Africa*. Johannesburg: Jacana Media.

———. 2015b. "Zuma Period: Depoliticised but Distinct Character." http://raymondsuttner.com/2015/02/20/raymond-suttner-zuma-period-depoliticised-but-distinct-character/.

Tamale, Sylvia. 1999. *When Hens Begin to Crow: Gender and Parliamentary Politics in Uganda*. Boulder, CO: Westview Press.

Teghtsoonian, Katherine, and Louise Chappell. 2008. "The Rise and Decline of Women's Policy Machinery in British Columbia and New South Wales: A Cautionary Tale." *International Political Science Review* 29 (1): 29–51.

Testa, M., B. M. Quigley, and K. E. Leonard. 2003. "Does Alcohol Make a Difference? Within-Participants Comparison of Incidents of Partner Violence." *Journal of Interpersonal Violence* 18 (7): 735–43.

References

Thaler, Kai. 2012. "Norms about Intimate Partner Violence among Urban South Africans: A Quantitative and Qualitative Vignette Analysis." Working Paper 59. Cape Town: Centre for Social Science Research.

Tilly, Alison. 2016. "One Way to #rememberkhwezi: Re-establish Sexual Offences Courts." *Daily Maverick*, August 7, 2016. https://www.dailymaverick.co.za/opinionista/2016-08-07-one-way-to-rememberkhwezi-re-establish-sexual-offences-courts/#.WxBwxVMvxPN.

Tlhabi, Redi. 2017. *Khwezi: The Remarkable Story of Fezekile Ntsukela Kuzwayo*. Johannesburg: Jonathan Ball Publishers.

Toh, Yiu-Meng, and Siang-Yan Tan. 1997. "The Effectiveness of Church-Based Lay Counselors: A Controlled Outcome Study." *Journal of Psychology and Christianity* 16 (3): 260–67.

Tremblay, Manon. 2008. *Women and Legislative Representation: Electoral Systems, Political Parties, and Sex Quotas*. New York: Palgrave Macmillan.

Tripp, Aili Mari. "Uganda: Agents of Change for Women's Advancement?" In *Women in African Parliaments*, edited by Gretchen Bauer and Hannah Britton, 158–89. Boulder, CO: Lynne Rienner.

Tripp, Aili Mari, and Alice Kang. 2008. "The Global Impact of Quotas: On the Fast Track to Female Legislative Representation." *Comparative Political Studies* 41 (3): 338–61.

Turshen, Meredeth. 2000. "The Political Economy of Violence against Women during Armed Conflict in Uganda." *Social Research* 67 (3): 803–24.

Turshen, Meredeth, and Clotilde Twagiramariya, eds. 1998. *What Women Do in Wartime: Gender and Conflict in Africa*. New York: Zed Books.

Utas, Mats. 2005. "West-African Warscapes: Victimcy, Girlfriending, Soldiering: Tactic Agency in a Young Woman's Social Navigation of the Liberian War Zone." *Anthropological Quarterly* 78 (2): 403–30.

Uthman, Olalekan A., Stephen Lawoko, and Tahereh Moradi. 2009. "Factors Associated with Attitudes towards Intimate Partner Violence against Women: A Comparative Analysis of 17 Sub-Saharan Countries." *BCM International Health and Human Rights* 9 (14): n.p.

Vanwesenbeeck, Ine. 2008. "Sexual Violence and the MDGs." *International Journal of Sexual Health* 20 (1–2): 25–49.

Vetten, Lisa. 2005. "Show Me the Money: A Review of Budgets Allocated towards the Implementation of South Africa's Domestic Violence Act." *Politikon: South African Journal of Political Studies* 32 (2): 277–95.

———. 2014. "Deserving and Undeserving Women: A Case Study of South African Policy and Legislation Addressing Domestic Violence." MA thesis, University of Witwatersrand, Johannesburg. http://www.genderlinks.org.za/article/deserving-and-undeserving-women-a-case-study-of-south-african-policy-and-legislation-addressing-domestic-violence-2014-08-04. Accessed October 6, 2014.

Vetten, Lisa, Rachel Jewkes, Romi Sigsworth, Nicola Christofides, Lizle Loots, and Olivia Dunseith. 2010. "Worth Their While? Pursuing a Rape Complaint through the Criminal Justice System." *South African Crime Quarterly* 32 (June): 19–25.

Vetten, Lisa, and Joy Watson. 2009. "Engendering the Parliamentary Agenda: Strategic Opportunity or Waste of Feminist Energy?" GAP Policy Brief 3, Gender Advocacy Programme and Tshwaranang Legal Advocacy Centre. http://shukumisa.org.za/wp-content/uploads/2017/09/Engendering-the-parliamentary-agenda.pdf.

Walker, Cherryl. 2013. "Uneasy Relations: Women, Gender Equality, and Tradition." *Thesis Eleven* 115 (1): 77–94.

———. 2014. "Critical Reflections on South Africa's 1913 Natives Land Act and Its Legacies: Introduction." *Journal of Southern African Studies* 40 (4): 655–65.

Walker, Liz, and Lucy Gilson. 2004. "'We Are Bitter but We Are Satisfied': Nurses as Street-Level Bureaucrats in South Africa." *Social Science and Medicine* 59 (6): 1251–61.

Walsh, Shannon Drysdale. 2008. "Engendering Justice: Constructing Institutions to Address Violence against Women." *Studies in Social Justice* 2 (1): 48–66.

Watt, Melissa, Kathleen Sikkema, Laurie Abler, Jennifer Velloza, Lisa Eaton, Seth Kalichman, Donald Skinner, and Desiree Pieterse. 2015. "Experiences of Forced Sex among Female Patrons of Alcohol-Serving Venues in a South African Township." *Journal of Interpersonal Violence* 30 (9): 1533–52.

Watts, Charlotte, and Cathy Zimmerman. 2002. "Violence against Women: Global Scope and Magnitude." *Lancet* 359 (9,313): 1232–37.

Waylen, Georgina. 2009. "What Can Historical Institutionalism Offer Feminist Institutionalists?" *Politics and Gender* 5 (2): 245–52.

Weldon, S. Laurel. 2002. *Protest, Policy, and the Problem of Violence against Women: A Cross-National Comparison*. Pittsburg, PA: University of Pittsburgh Press.

Weldon, S. Laurel, and Mala Htun. 2013. "Feminist Mobilisation and Progressive Policy Change: Why Governments Take Action to Combat Violence against Women." *Gender and Development* 21 (2): 231–47.

Wells, Julia C. 1993. *We Now Demand! The History of Women's Resistance to Pass Laws in South Africa*. Johannesburg: Witwatersrand University Press.

Wies, Jennifer R., and Hillary J. Haldane. 2011. "Ethnographic Notes from the Front Lines of Gender-Based Violence." In *Anthropology at the Front Lines of Gender-Based Violence*, edited by Jennifer R. Wies and Hillary J. Haldane, 1–17. Nashville: Vanderbilt University Press.

Wilkins, Vicky M., and Brian N. Williams. 2008. "Black or Blue: Racial Profiling and Representative Bureaucracy." *Public Administration Review* 68 (4): 654–64.

Wojkowska, Ewa. 2006. *Doing Justice: How Informal Justice Systems Can Contribute*. United Nations Development Programme, Oslo Governance Centre.

Women in the Presidency. 2013. "Domestic Violence Report: Civilian Secretariat for Police, Minister and Department on Second Quarter 2013 Performance." https://pmg.org.za/committee-meeting/16714/. Accessed June 23, 2016.

Wood, Alan. 2006. "Correlating Violence and Socio-Economic Inequality: An Empirical Analysis." In *Attacking the Root Causes of Torture, Poverty, Inequality and Violence*, edited by Thomas E. McCarty, 23–94. Geneva: World Organisation Against Torture.

Worden, Alissa Pollitz. 2000. "The Changing Boundaries of the Criminal Justice System: Redefining the Problem and the Response in Domestic Violence." In *Boundary Changes in Criminal Justice Organizations: Volume 2, Criminal Justice,* edited by Charles Friel, 215–66. Rockville, MD: National Institute of Justice.

World Bank. 2016. "GINI Index (World Bank Estimate)." http://data.worldbank.org/indicator/SI.POV.GINI. Accessed June 6, 2016.

World Health Organization. 2010. *Preventing Intimate Partner and Sexual Violence Against Women: Taking Action and Generating Evidence.* Geneva: World Health Organization.

———. 2013. "Global and Regional Estimates of Violence against Women: Prevalence and Health Effects of Intimate Partner Violence and Non-partner Sexual Violence." Geneva: WHO, Department of Reproductive Health and Research.

———. 2016. "The Ecological Framework." http://www.who.int/violenceprevention/approach/ecology/en/ Accessed August 3, 2016.

Index

Abramowitz, Sharon, 38, 41
accelerants of gender-based violence, 30–31; environmental factors, 34–35; "festive season," 44–45; nested oppressions, 45–46; poverty and inequality, 16, 35–38; sexual entitlement and "gender jealousy," 38–41; substance abuse, 30, 31–34; xenophobia, 41–44
African National Congress (ANC), 1–2, 19, 84, 128–129, 155
alcohol use, 33–34
ANC Women's League (ANCWL), 2, 84
Andrews, Matt, 95, 97
Andrews, Penelope, 17
apartheid: police trust-building after, 104–106, 167n9; politics of, 7–8; racial segregation codified under, 6–7, 49; religious leaders under, 87–88; South African exceptionalism and, 5–10; state violence during, 151; structural violence as imprint of, 5, 15; transition away from, 8–9
Arbeidstad, 73
Artz, Lillian, 38

Bassadien, Shanhana Rasool, 76–77
Bokang, challenges of informal sectors in, 67–71
bricolage, 95
Bueno-Hansen, Pascha, 15, 23
Burger, Johan, 127
Buthelezi, Sibongile, 57

carceral feminism, 10–13, 29, 146–147, 150; beyond neoliberalism and, 153–155

Chile, 9–10
Christianity, moral regeneration and, 85–87
Citi Gold Model, 141–142
Close to Home, 156
coloured, definition of, 6
community-based approach to understanding gender-based violence, 22–23
community builders, police as, 66–67, 103–104
community-building, 63–66; change to, 51–66
community crime forums, 49, 50–55, 106–112
community organizations, 49, 50–55, 58–59, 97
community police forums, 49, 50–55, 106–112
context of gender-based violence, 14–15
contracting out, costs of, 120–121
Corvo, Ken, 11
criminal justice system, South African: conflicts between traditional leaders and, 92–96; new bureaucratic players in, 96–97; sexual offences courts, 130–131; Western judicial systems and, 94–95
Criminal Law (Sexual Offences and Related Matters) Amendment Act No. 32 of 2007, 18–19, 20, 76
culture, 14

Ddlakvu, Simamkele, 2
Domestic Violence Act No. 116 of 1998, 18, 134–135
Dunkle, K. L., 17

Index

Eggen, Oyvind, 97
emotional labor, 24–25, 27, 114–116, 119, 124
environmental factors, 34–35

faith traditions addressing gender-based violence, 49, 50–55, 77–88
Family Violence, Child Protection and Sexual Offences (FCS) units, 125, 126–130, 153
family violence, history of, 30, 34
Fees Must Fall, 37, 48
feminism: black feminist protest strategy of silence and, 2; carceral, 10–13, 29, 146–147, 150, 153–155; Christian, 86; Islam and, 86–87; state, 8–9, 10–13, 150
"festive season," 44–45

gangs, 35
gated communities, 47–48, 63
gender-based violence in South Africa: accelerants of, 30–31; analyzed in terms of postconflict society, 12; community-based approach to understanding, 22–23; community organizations and, 49, 50–55, 58–59; context of, 14–15; culture and, 14; defining, 13; dismissed and normalized, 11–12, 15; geography of, 73; high-profile cases of, 1–4; issue leaders for, 49, 50–55; legislation against, 18–22, 28, 45–46, 74; methodological appendix on research on, 159–162; as part of larger structural inequalities, 4–5, 155–158; people and (*see* people); place and (*see* place and space); points of contact and (*see* points of contact); police and (*see* South African Police Services [SAPS]); policy approaches to, 17–22, 28; politics and, 14; power and, 13–14; prevention of, 12; religious organizations and, 49, 50–55, 77–88; service providers and (*see* service providers); South African exceptionalism and, 5–10; statistics on, 16–17; worldwide ideas of democracy and, 9–10
"gender jealousy," 38–41
geography of gender-based violence, 73
Gouws, Amanda, 19
Govender, Pregs, 9, 18
governance feminism, 150
Group Areas Act, 59, 63, 151

healers: traditional, 88–92, 166n5; wounded, 116–119
health services, 49, 50–55

Hephizibah, Esther Nasikye, 160
HIV/AIDS testing and treatment, 21, 32
Hochfeld, Tessa, 76–77
hot spots, crime, 106–107
Huisdorp, community-building in, 63–66
human side of policing, 114–121
hyperpatriarchy, 84, 155

income inequality, 16, 35–38
Independent Electoral Commission, 1
informal justice, 74–77, 94–97
informal sectors/settlements, 7, 67–71
issue leaders/issue advocates/gender advocates/policy advocates, 4, 8, 10, 21, 24–26, 49, 50–55, 75, 101, 152, 154

Jewkes, Rachel, 17, 33, 35
Jijenge!, 156
Johnson, Pamela, 11
Joint Monitoring Committee on the Improvement of the Quality of Life and Status of Women, 9, 18

Khan, Sultan, 94
Khanga, 1
Khwezi, 1, 2, 164n
knowing your neighbors, 59–63
Kuzwayo, Fezekile Ntsukela, 1–2, 163n1

Lawoko, Stephen, 141–142
Leach, Eric, 3
leaders, traditional, 88–92, 165–166n3–4; conflicts with the South African Constitution, 92–96
legal sector, points of contact in, 125–126, 136–141; FCS units, 126–130; sexual offenses courts, 130–131; trauma units, 131–136
legislation, anti-gender-based-violence, 18–22, 28, 45–46, 74
LGBT (lesbian, gay, bisexual, and transgender) communities, 13, 30–31
Liberia, 38, 41, 46, 95–96, 126, 165n5
LifeLine, 167n8
Linda, Bafana Peter, 130
Lootvoet, Benoit, 94

Mabitso, police as community builders in, 66–67, 121–124
Marcia-Moreno, Claudia, 146
Masipa, Thokozile, 3
Masutha, Michael, 131

Index

Medical Research Council, 17
medical sector, points of contact in: Citi Golf Model, 141–142; fluctuating performance in, 142–144; precarity of street-level workers and, 144–146; Thuthuzela Care Centers (TCCs), 71–72, 126, 136–146; trauma units, 131–136
Men for Change, 85, 165n1
Meth, Paula, 57, 67, 69, 153
Misri, Deepti, 14–15
Moffett, Helen, 9
moral regeneration, 83–88
Moran, Mary, 38, 41
Moreland, Stacy, 131, 146–147
Moult, Kelley, 35–36, 77, 90, 95
Move to End Violence, 156
Mthetwa, Nathi, 129–130
Muslim's women's groups, 78–81, 86–87

Namibia, 20, 163–164n9
Namibian Combating Rape Act No. 8 of 2000, 20
National Gender Machinery (NGM), 76, 128–129
National Prosecuting Authority, 21, 126, 131, 137, 138, 146
neighborhood policing, 106–107
neoliberalism, 5, 10, 11, 26, 42, 75, 93, 112, 123, 150, 151; beyond carceral feminism and, 153–155
nested oppressions, 45–46
new bureaucratic players, 96–97
nongovernmental actors, 74–75, 120–121
Nyaope, 32–33

Olive Vlei, 71–72, 73
Ortega, Daniel, 163n3

patriarchy/patriarchal culture/norms, 46, 76–77, 108, 115, 131, 147, 150–153; heteropatriachy 23; hyperpatriarchy 84, 154–155
people, 74–77, 152; new bureaucratic players, 96–97; of religious organizations, 77–88; traditional leaders and traditional healers, 88–92
people communities, 65–66
Pistorius, Oscar, 2–3, 20
place and space, 47–49, 151–152; building community in fluctuating spaces, 63–66; challenges of informal sectors in, 67–71; community scans of, 49, 50–55; geography of gender-based violence and, 73; knowing your neighbors and, 59–63; police as community builders in, 66–67; rape and, 56–72; white spaces in, 71–72
points of contact, 125–126, 153; in law enforcement and legal sectors, 125, 126–136; in medical and legal sectors, 136–146; survivors engaging the state in, 146–147
police. See South African Police Services (SAPS)
policy approaches to gender-based violence, 17–22, 28
politics: of apartheid, 7–8; of gender-based violence, 14; religious organizations and, 78–81; women's movement and, 39–40, 149–150
poverty and inequality, 16, 35–38
power, 13–14
prevention of gender-based violence, 12
Pritchett, Lant, 95, 97
private sphere, public/private, 6, 8–10, 18, 19, 22, 23, 36, 63, 90, 93, 103, 133, 149, 166n1

Raising Voices, 156
rape: "acquaintance rape," 56–57; carceral feminism and, 10–13; place and, 56–72; "stranger rape," 56–57; trials for, 1–4
Reconstruction and Development Programme (RDP), 56, 110, 164–165n4
Reddy, Dashakti, 96
religious organizations, 49, 50–55, 77–88; issue leaders in, 81–83; moral regeneration and, 83–88; political opportunities and, 78–81
Roedorp, 113–114; knowing your neighbors in, 59–63
Ross, Fiona, 68
Ross, Gracia Violeta, 78, 83
Rwanda, 9

Safe Space NGO, 9–10
secondary trauma, 21, 25, 27, 75, 102, 103, 114, 119–120, 136, 138, 144, 145, 152
sector policing, 106–107
Seedat, Mohamed, 33–34
Selebi, Jackie, 125, 126–127, 128–129, 167n1
service providers, 23–28, 29, 164n12; community police forums, 49, 50–55; on environmental factors, 34–35; on the "festive season," 44–45; gender-based violence understandings of, 31–38; health, 49, 50–55; on nested oppressions, 45–46; on poverty and inequality, 35–38; religious, 49,

193

Index

50–55; on sexual entitlement and "gender jealousy," 38–41; on substance abuse, 30, 31–34; victim support room and services, 49, 50–55; as wounded healers, 116–119; on xenophobia, 41–44
sexual entitlement, 38–41
sexual offences courts, 130–131
Shahrokh, Thea, 116
Shukumisa Campaign, 19
silence/breaking silence, 2, 61, 68, 103–105, 114, 123, 157–158
Singh, Anne-Marie, 112
16 Days of Activism against Gender-Based Violence Campaign, 58, 101, 104, 165n1
slow violence, 151, 176
Smythe, Dee, 38
social-ecological model/ecological model, 31
South Africa: attention on crime in, 154–155; exceptionalism of, 5–10; hyperpatriarchy in, 84, 155; sexual entitlement and "gender jealousy" in, 38–41; Western judicial system and, 94–95; women's movement in, 39–40, 149–150; xenophobia in, 41–44
South African Constitution/constitutional, xii, xiii, 1, 8, 17–19, 21, 41, 78–80, 92–93, 124, 149, 157
South African Development Community (SADC), 137
South African Police Services (SAPS), 20, 32, 33, 98–101, 152; best practices for, 121–124; challenges for, 103–104; as community builders, 66–67, 103–104; community crime forums/police forums and, 49, 50–55, 106–112; corruption and failures of, 98–101, 166n2; costs of contracting out for, 120–121; differing levels of engagement of, 49, 50–55; discretion used by, in gender-based violence cases, 101–112; on "festive season," 44–45; human side of policing and, 114–121; materials needs of, 102; on place and rape, 56–58; as point of contact, 125, 126–136; post-apartheid trust building by, 104–106; on poverty and inequality contributions to gender-based violence, 36, 37; racial integration of, 116; secondary trauma and, 114, 119–120; sector policing, visible policing, and hot spots used by, 106–107; structural issues with, 112–114; traditional leaders and, 91–92; trauma units and, 134–135; women officers of, 115–116; wounded healers of, 116–119; on xenophobia, 42–43

state feminism, 8–9, 75–76, 150; complicity with carceral feminism, 10–13
Steenkamp, Reeva, 2–3
street-level workers. *See* service providers
structural issues with the police, 112–114
structural violence, 5
substance abuse, 30, 31–34, 61
Suttner, Raymond, 84, 154–155
S v. Zuma, 1–2

Thuthuzela Care Centers (TCCs), 27, 71–72, 126, 136–140, 153; fluctuating performance in, 142–144; precarity of street-level workers and, 144–146
Tilly, Alison, 131
townshipization, 57
townships, creations of, 7
traditional healers, 88–92, 166n5
traditional justice, 74–75, 88–97
traditional leaders, 88–92, 165–166n3–4; conflicts with the South African Constitution, 92–96
trauma, secondary, 114, 119–120
trauma units, 131–136. *See also* victim support rooms and services

Vawda, Shahid, 94
Vetten, Lisa, 18
victim support room and services, 5, 27, 49, 50–55, 110, 116, 124–130, 127–137, 153, 156
visible policing, 106–107
volunteers, 52–54, 75, 87, 99, 102–103, 108–110, 114–119, 120–121, 123, 132–136, 144–145, 152

Walker, Cherryl, 93–94
wealth inequality, 16
Western judicial systems, 94–95
Wheeler, Joanna, 116
white spaces, 71–72
women officers, 115–116
women's policy agencies, 9
women's rights, 39–40, 149
Wood, Alan, 35
Woolcock, Michael, 95, 97
World Health Organization (WHO), 31
wounded healers, 116–119

xenophobia, 41–44

Zuma, Jacob, 3, 20, 149; rape trial of, 1–2, 163n3; silent protest against, 1, 2

HANNAH E. BRITTON is a professor of political science and women, gender, and sexuality studies at the University of Kansas. She is the author of *Women in the South African Parliament: From Resistance to Governance* and coeditor of *Women's Activism in South Africa: Working across Divides*.

The University of Illinois Press
is a founding member of the
Association of University Presses.

University of Illinois Press
1325 South Oak Street
Champaign, IL 61820-6903
www.press.uillinois.edu